CATERPILLAR GAS TRACTOR
Restoration & Interchange Manual

Bob LaVoie

Motorbooks International
Publishers & Wholesalers ®

Dedication

This book is dedicated to the memory of my nephew, Jesse Haskins, and to the memory of Alan "AJ" Johnson. AJ spoke the language of these tractors better than any of us.

First published in 1996 by Motorbooks International Publishers & Wholesalers, 729 Prospect Avenue, PO Box 1, Osceola, WI 54020-0001 USA

© Robert La Voie, 1996

Motorbooks International books are also available at discounts in bulk quantity for industrial or sales-promotional use. For details write to Special Sales Manager at the Publisher's address

Library of Congress Cataloging-in-Publication Data Available

ISBN 0-7603-0105-0

On the front cover: The mighty Caterpillar 60 was one of the most powerful tractors in the line, and brought tracked power to the world.

On the back cover: Top: These high-clearance models—a 10 and a 15—are some of the rarest Caterpillar tractors. Bottom: A wide-gauge spacer for the Model 40.

Printed in the United States of America

CONTENTS

FOREWORD

This book is a detailed reference of the history and development of early gasoline-powered Caterpillar track-type tractors. The charts and information contained here will be valuable to collectors worldwide, including members of the Antique Caterpillar Machinery Owners Club (ACMOC), which was formed in July 1991. The rising interest in collecting and restoring Caterpillar tractors has boosted the membership of ACMOC to more than 1,000 members in less than five years. Caterpillar, Inc., has been the leader in track type-tractor design, manufacturing technology, service, and customer satisfaction from the start, and this history needs to be recorded.

Dave Smith
Secretary and Treasurer
Antique Caterpillar Machinery
Owners Club

ACKNOWLEDGMENTS

This book would not have been possible without the help and research of some wonderful people. First, I thank Dave Smith, secretary and treasurer of the Antique Caterpillar Machinery Owners Club, for his never-ending support and assistance with this project. I also thank Steve Christensen and Russ Kruse of Midland Press Corporation for the use of the Caterpillar Legendary Literature library and the wonderful reproduction literature they produce.

Special thanks go to Dick Ryan of Gresham, Oregon, for his photographs of machines at the Brooks, Oregon, annual club meeting and show. I also thank Ted Halton of Halton Caterpillar for supplying some of the information on the more rare large tractors.

The following people were instrumental in the creation of this book: Ron Meeder, Ripley, New York; Jeff Moyle, Fairmont, Nebraska; Willard Lyons, Marne, Nebraska; Bob Hill, Miami, Manitoba, Canada; Webers Printing, Park Falls, Wisconsin; Kay Sue Belan, Phillips, Wisconsin; CarQuest Auto Parts, Park Falls, Wisconsin; Keith Clark, Spokane, Washington; Rich Danielson, Park Falls, Wisconsin; Bob Pripps, Springstead, Wisconsin; Larry Maasdam, Clarion, Iowa; George Shinners, Anitgo, Wisconsin; and my parents, Bob and Kathleen LaVoie, Park Falls, Wisconsin. I sincerely thank you all.

Most of all, I thank my lovely wife, Heather, for her time and patience with my crazy hobby (and her excellent computer skills).

Bob LaVoie
Park Falls, Wisconsin

INTRODUCTION

The Caterpillar Tractor Company was formed in 1925 when Holt and Best tractor companies of California merged. Initially, the new company went through a period of experimenting and testing, eventually producing a line of tractors that varied almost yearly in appearance, horsepower, and design.

Many of these tractors were produced in limited numbers. Today these are some of the most desirable tractors to collect. But because of their rarity, they can be sources of confusion when one attempts to preserve them. Often little or no information can be obtained on the machines, so much is left to speculation or opinion.

This book should aid the new tractor collector. We cover only the gasoline-powered tractors due to the vast model range from the Model 10 to the 70.

Understand this is only one of many guides on the market to assist you in your endeavor. There are many other fine books that should be used in conjunction with this one. Much of this book is based on conversations between collectors and theories drawn from manuals, advertisements, drawings, photos, yes, even speculations, and mistakes that I and others have made in our collecting pursuits. I have tried to include as much concrete information as possible, but most of the information comes from owning and working on the machines.

I hope you enjoy this book as much as I have enjoyed writing it. Remember, you are restoring the finest piece of machinery ever made. Restore and display it proudly as a tribute to the longevity and pride built into every Caterpillar product.

CHAPTER ONE

MODEL OVERVIEW

At the turn of the century, in the San Joaquin Valley of California, agricultural pioneers were growing larger by the year, and the Holt and Best tractor companies were becoming the pioneers of track-type power.

The crawler tractor was designed for use in the rolling hills of the western United States. The principle of using an endless belt for traction was experimented on by many other tractor manufacturers, but Benjamin Holt and C. L. Best were the first to develop a usable and practical track-type arrangement.

In 1925, the two industrial giants merged to form the Caterpillar Tractor Company. The early product line of the company contained the Models 2-Ton, 5-Ton, and 10-Ton from the Holt tractor line. The 30 and 60 were from the Best company. The 5-Ton and 10-Ton tractors were dropped virtually right away, while the 2-Ton, 30, and 60 stayed in the line-up for many years. Though Holt had perfected the crawler tractor principle, the Best machine far outperformed it. The Best design was used in other models introduced years after the merger. During this period, much experimentation was done to perfect the design of the crawler tractor into the machine style that became standard in the mid-1940s. The various models are represented in this book.

In 1931, Caterpillar pioneered the use of diesel engines in track-type tractors. This was a breakthrough that changed the entire path of heavy equipment engineering and design forever. The use of gasoline engines in these tractors was coming to an end. Even though production of gasoline tractors continued well into the 1940s, the diesel engine was now the most accepted power source for agricultural and construction tractors.

The engineering used in the manufacturing and design of the Caterpillar track-type tractor is continually changing and advancing. Today, Caterpillar, Inc., is the world leader in

The Best Model 25 tractor was an early small crawler. Like the Best 30, it was available only as a tailseat or orchard model.

RIGHT
Best marketed the Model 60 in two versions. The "Cruiser" version was a top seat Model 60 used in logging applications, while the standard 60 was a tailseat or agricultural model. The Best 30 was only available as a tailseat. *Literary Digest Vol. 57 No 1*

"Cruiser" (60)

Tracklayer "Thirty"

Tracklayer "Sixty"

Lower Costs

As an example of the way tractors are cutting costs for road builders, consider the rig pictured above. This shows a BEST TRACKLAYER "SIXTY" TRACTOR, pulling two graders—one 12 foot, the other 10 foot—thereby accomplishing two operations at one time.

This cutting of time in half is possible because the tractor can deliver the necessary power. Labor is also reduced because tractor power requires fewer hands. Good tractors provide compact, easily-managed, dependable, tireless power for graders, levelers, plows, scarifiers, etc. They reduce operating costs for the road-builder, and that is the big problem these days. And with the BEST you can work without hindrance in most any weather and on any sort of soil, on grades as well as on level ground. The long, wide tracks make this possible.

BEST TRACKLAYER TRACTORS have earned a splendid reputation for dependability, power and low cost of operation, not only on road work, but also on heavy-duty work of all kinds. BEST TRACTORS are the result of many years of successful tractor-building experience.

Better decide to look into the question of tractors. Let us send you full data, prices and the names of our nearest dealers. Address us

C. L. BEST TRACTOR CO.
SAN LEANDRO, CALIFORNIA

The Holt Midget was the smallest of the early Holt machines to be equipped with the front tiller wheel for steering.

track-type tractor production sales. With an eye on the future and a strong and impressive past, Caterpillar, Inc., will continue to be the world leader in track-type tractor technology.

Model 10

In late 1928, Caterpillar Tractor Company unveiled the Model 10 tractor. Weighing in at 4,500 pounds, it was the smallest tractor to be made by the company and, at the time, filled a gap in the small crawler-tractor marketplace. Unfortunately, the Model 10 was born with design problems, and from early on, its future was dim. When the tractor was discontinued in 1932, only 4,929 units had been made. This was a fairly sizable number of tractors when compared to other Caterpillar models marketed in the era, but not as impressive as some other models made by other manufacturers.

The tractor was available in standard- or narrow-gauge at 37 inches, wide-gauge at 44 inches, an orchard or tailseat version in both gauges, and a high-clearance model. A wide-gauge, high-clearance model recently surfaced in Canada and was supposedly designed for use in Hawaiian sugar cane operations. The standard high-clearance 10 was a 44-inch gauge. This is the same gauge width as the wide-gauge Low 10. It is unclear how many versions were made. All variations of the Model 10 carried the "PT" serial number prefix, and no additional designations were issued to the special units.

Model 10 Variants

The narrow-gauge has a fairly good survival rate, but it is also the most common ver-

RIGHT
During World War I, the Holt Manufacturing Company was a vital supplier to the war effort. While the Best machines were making strides in agriculture the Holt Machine was defending our country. *Literary Digest August 18, 1918*

With the front tiller wheel removed, the Holt Model 45 became a popular tractor. This new design was what became standard on all truck type tractors produced to present day.

sion. Each variation's scarcity is regional. For example, the wide-gauge 10 is scarce in the Midwest and northern states. It is far more common in the West but only in limited numbers. The orchard version is more rare than any other 10 variation, even the high-clearance model. It is difficult to support this with actual numbers, but

The Best Model 25 used an undercarriage very similar to early Cletrac tractors. This design was not used on later tractors made after the merger.

in talking to several collectors, far less orchard tractors have surfaced than high-clearance, and the high-clearance tractors have been found in most areas of the country, unlike the orchard.

The wide and orchard models are generally only found on the West Coast, and both are sought after by collectors. I estimate under 150 Model 10s were made into orchard units, and between 800 and 1,000 were made into wide-gauge. Again, there are no numbers to document this claim, but based on conversations with other collectors, these numbers seem reasonable.

Orchard Models

The orchard model was available in two styles. One was a standard 10 fitted with grove or orchard fenders and a top seat. The other had a lowered implement-style seat and full orchard fenders. The foot-operated clutch was replaced with a hand clutch, and the brake pedal linkages were extended. The orchard 10 is a rare tractor simply because it was an unnecessary design as with most other tractors of this period, the orchard equipment lowered the operator away from the delicate hanging limbs of the trees. The standard 10 was already a very low tractor, so lowering the operator further was not deemed necessary. I have not found any evidence that a made-to-order kit was available to convert a standard model to an orchard model, but you could order individual pieces from the parts catalog. It is reasonable to assume that some standard 10s were converted to orchard models by the owners over the years and that some orchard 10s were converted back to top seat machines once their orchard service ended. The orchard 10 was also available in wide-gauge.

Model 10 Wide-Gauge

The 10 wide-gauge was designed for use on hillsides and in areas where low ground pressure was needed. The Wide 10 is fitted with longer trunnion braces, pivot shaft, and main spring. The drive sprockets are cupped outward, or concave, and give the tractor a gauge of 44 inches to rail centers. The Wide 10 is more scarce than the standard or narrow 10 and is found more regionally in the Pacific states. It is also considered by collectors to be a very sought-after tractor.

RIGHT
The Holt Manufacturing Company continued to build a solid reputation through the years of World War I. *Literary Digest May 18, 1918*

HOLT
PEORIA···STOCKTON

"OVER THERE"—through roadless wastes of mud and sand—over rough ground torn up by shell-fire and covered with countless obstructions—able to travel and climb where no other form of power will go—"Caterpillar" Tractors are hauling the Allied heavy guns to firing positions. Since 1914—on every Front from Belgium to Palestine—they have met every call for power and endurance. Yet these are the same tractors Holt has been building for years—the product of American genius in times of Peace—and pre-eminent in agriculture and industry in thirty-five different countries.

Inspiration for the great fighting "tanks" is frankly credited by Major-General E. D. Swinton of the British War Cabinet to the "Caterpillar" Tractors furnished by Holt to the British Armies.

Towing the great howitzers and supply trains at the Front—tilling and harvesting the grain fields so that the world may be fed—hauling ore from the mines, logs from the forests—building roads, clearing land—*wherever* dependable power is needed, "Caterpillar" Tractors are found.

There is but one "CATERPILLAR"— Holt builds it. The name "CATERPILLAR" is the exclusive Registered Trademark of The Holt Manufacturing Company, Stockton, California and Peoria, Illinois. In Peace and War it stands alone by name, quality and record for successful performance.

Catalog will be sent upon request.

"CATERPILLAR" TRACTORS   REG. U.S. PAT. OFF.

High-Clearance Model 10

The high-clearance Model 10 has some indicators pointing toward its history, probably due more to its demand in collecting circles than anything. The high-clearance is a standard 10 raised up to have 24 inches of ground clearance for row crop work. The high-clearance components were the same as those used later on the high-clearance 15 1D Series. The high-clearance 10 has been found in most areas in limited numbers and is considered a rare tractor. It is, however, far more common than the high-clearance 15 or orchard Model 10. I estimate production at approximately 500 tractors based on the information gathered from surviving tractors. No separate designation was given to the serial number of the high-clearance. A made-to-order kit was made available to convert a standard 10 to a high-clearance model, but it is not known how many, if any, of these kits were sold. We can only speculate that few of these conversions took place since we are not finding

The Model 10 was also available as a winter model. This machine is equipped with a cab and lights. The tractor is not equipped with skeleton ice pads which is somewhat strange, as most winter models were. *Midland Press Corp.—Caterpillar, Inc., Licensee*

The Model 10 tractor was introduced in 1928 and was the smallest tractor produced by the company. The model shown is a wide-gauge.

The high-clearance Model 10 has a total ground clearance of 24 inches. This version of the Model 10 is quite rare and sought after.

high-clearance 10 tractors in the lower serial numbers. Those discovered have serial numbers greater than PT3500. If many conversions took place, we would be finding high-clearance models in all areas of the serial number span.

It is not clear when the high-clearance model made its debut. We are fairly certain that it was not available in the first years of the Model 10's manufacture. Through extensive research we have found most serial numbers issued to the high-clearance 10 fall in a group, beginning at approximately serial number PT3650 and running to approximately PT4150, a span of about 500 machines. When this span of numbers is archived, they show a manufacture date of 1930. By that time nearly 3,500 of the Model 10 had been made. It has been rumored that the high-clearance model had been drawn up in blueprints as early as 1928 but was deemed too costly and the project was tabled. It is possible that with sales doing as well as they were, 1930 was chosen to introduce the high-clearance. This theory helps explain the grouping of numbers so closely together. Since few standard 10 tractors fall in this span, it appears total 10 production was ded-

High-clearance Model 10. *Clark and Sons*

An arched spring along with lowered final drive housing help the high-clearance Model 10 achieve its height.

icated to the high-clearance for a few months during mid- to late-1930. The high-clearance first appeared in advertising in early 1931; production would have occurred in the middle of the previous year. Whether or not high-clearance machines were made until the end of the pro-

duction run is not known. The high-clearance serial numbers seem to end around PT4200, but I would not be surprised if serial numbers turn up on high machines all the way to the end of the production run at PT4929.

When checking casting numbers on the High 10, we have found that most of the casting dates come back in the early 1940s. Through extensive research we have not been able to justify the ten-year gap in the casting codes. Perhaps there was a different code used than the NUMERALCOD system. It is possible that the code was disguised, and by subtracting ten from the corresponding date you would arrive at the correct year of manufacture. Being that the model of the tractor was 10 and the difference in dates is ten years, one has to wonder. We have checked standard Model 10 and 7C 15 casting numbers, and they correspond to the NUMERALCOD system accurately, while the High 10 generally is the exception to the rule. Of 10 high-clearance 10 tractors checked, all 10 have castings of their high-clearance components in the 1941 to 1942 era. Currently we have no concrete explanation for this ten-year discrepancy. We have also checked sales and service literature

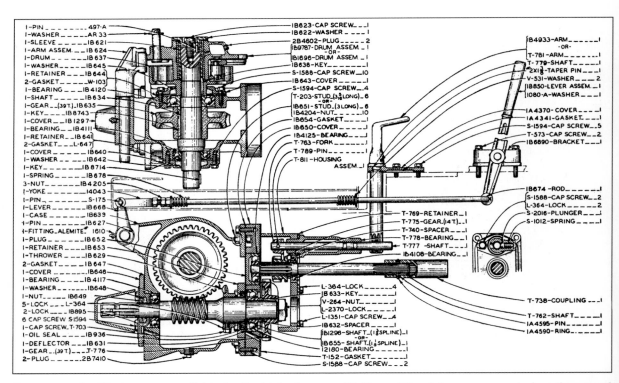

Four types of cultivators were available for the high-clearance 10. Two of the styles were mounted on the rear of the tractor and the remaining three was mounted on the front. The rock island model ric used a mechanical lift to raise and lower the shovels. *Midland Press Corp.—Caterpillar, Inc., Form P-1190*

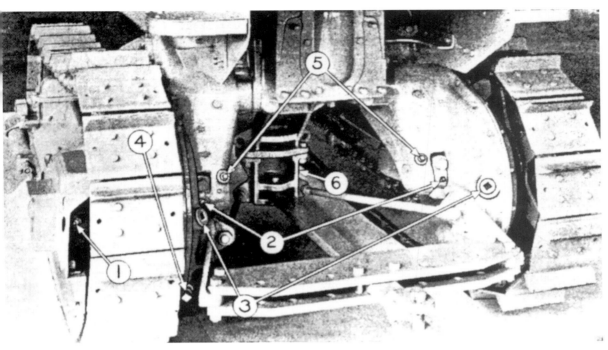

The high-clearance Model 10 was equipped with a wider drawbar. Many also were sold with a mechanical lift to operate a cultivator or other attachment.

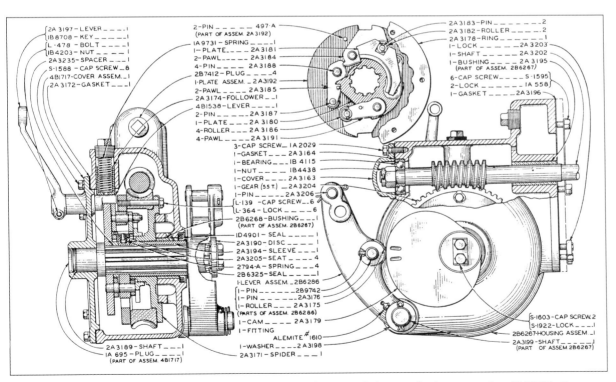

2A 3197 – LEVER ____ –_-.1
1B 8708 – KEY ____ –1
L·478 – BOLT ____ –1
1B 4203 – NUT __ _ _ –1
2A 3235 – SPACER __ ._.1
S-1588 – CAP SCREW__8
4B1717-COVER ASSEM._1
2A 3172 – GASKET ___ –1

2-PIN ____ ___ 497·A
(PART OF ASSEM. 2A 3192)
1A 9731 – SPRING ___ –1
1 – PLATE ___ _ 2A 3181
2 – PAWL ____ _ 2A 3184
4 – PIN ___ _ 2A 3188
2B7412 – PLUG _ _ _ _4
1 – PLATE ASSEM. _ 2A 3192
2 – PAWL ____ _ 2A 3185
2A 3174 – FOLLOWER _ _1
4B1538 – LEVER _ _ _ _1
2 – PIN ____ 2A 3187
1 – PLATE ___ _ 2A 3180
4 – ROLLER __ 2A 3186
4 – PAWL ____ 2A 3191

3 – CAP SCREW__ 1A 2029
1 – GASKET __ 2A 3164
1 – BEARING __ 1B 4115
1 – NUT ___ _ 1B4438
1 – COVER ___ _ 2A 3163
1 – GEAR (55 T.) _ 2A 3204
1 – PIN ____ 2A 3206
L-364 – CAP SCREW__6
L-364 – LOCK _ _ _ _6
2B6268 – BUSHING _ _ _1
(PART OF ASSEM. 2B6267)
1D 4901 – SEAL ____ 1
2A 3190 – DISC ____ 1
2A 3194 – SLEEVE _ _ _ 1
2A 3205 – SEAT _ _ _ 4
2794-A – SPRING___ 4
2B 6325 – SEAL _ _ _ _1
1 – LEVER ASSEM._2B6286
1 – PIN _____ 2B9742
1 – PIN _____ 2A3176
1 – ROLLER ___ 2A3175
(PARTS OF ASSEM. 2B6286)
1 – CAM ____ 2A 3179
1 – FITTING
ALEMITE # 1610
1 – WASHER ____ 2A 3198
2A 3171 – SPIDER ___ 1

2A 3183 – PIN ___ _ _ _ _2
2A 3182 – ROLLER ___ _2
2A 3178 – RING _ _ _ _ _1
1 – LOCK _ _ _ _ 2A 3203
1 – SHAFT _ _ _ _ 2A 3202
1 – BUSHING _ _ 2A 3195
(PART OF ASSEM. 2B6267)
6 – CAP SCREW_ _ _ S-1595
2 – LOCK _ _ _ _ _ _ 1A 558
1 – GASKET _ _ _ 2A 3196

S-1603 – CAP SCREW.2
S-1922 – LOCK _ _ _1
2B6267-HOUSING ASSEM _1
2A 3199 – SHAFT _ _ _ _ _ _1
(PART OF ASSEM 2B6267)

2A 3189 – SHAFT___1
1A 695 – PLUG _ _ _ _1
(PART OF ASSEM. 4B1717)

The mechanical lift mounts to the rear of the tractor in the area of the standard power take-off (PTO). It uses a handlever and linkage to activate a dog clutch to turn a rock shaft.

Vents were installed in the top of the fuel tank of the Model 10 to prevent vapor locking. An asbestos shield was also installed to deflect heat.

from the period featuring the High 10, and these publications generally show dates from 1930 through 1932, which also corresponds to the believed date of the High 10's debut.

Model 10 Troubles

All versions of the Model 10 have one thing in common: design problems. The mechanical problems began with the exhaust manifold being located too close to the gas tank. This lead to the gas expanding in the tank from the excessive heat, and vapor lock became a major problem. Servicegram number 58 was issued on June 2, 1930, and the owner could have had the dealer install an asbestos shield to help deflect the heat.

The gas tank was given two vents on the top surface, and two holes were placed in the hood to allow the vents to stick through it. This modification became standard on all later tractors and carried on until the end of production. The PV Series Model 15 had identical problem and the same modification was used. The 10 and PV Series 15 were the only models to use this design and it was never used again. Allis Chalmers duplicated the gas tank and manifold locations on its Model M crawler, and the same problems arose.

The next obstacle was the ease of operation on the tractor. The location of the throttle lever inside the right fender panel was awkward at best. It was arranged on a slide with notched grooves to set the throttle speed. In cold climates, the linkage often froze up and became inoperable. This design was also common to the PV 15.

Another operational inconvenience was the square seat back. It made operation of towed implements difficult, as the operator's arm had to reach over the top of the high seat back. A less important problem was the location of the brass instruction plate on the seat back. They seemed to get damaged easily or torn off completely from regular use and are damaged or missing on most tractors we see today.

The last problem was drawbar brackets. The brackets were made too lightly, and when the drawbar was unpinned, it slid abruptly and broke the brackets. On most tractors discovered today, the brackets have been welded or replaced with heavier ones.

Another concern was from a marketing perspective. The 10's four-cylinder, side-valve, L-head engine produced 15 horsepower. The 5 horsepower that was being "given" away was enough for Caterpillar to keep the engine but redesignate it as a 15 in the 7C Series. Thus, the 7C 15 is really a 10, given the previous changes in its design.

The Model 10 was also the subject of a 480-hour test run at Oregon State College. The test began on April 12, 1930, and ran for 21 days. In that time the tractor traveled 1,011 miles and consumed 724 gallons of gasoline. After the run, the tracks were found to have sixteen-hundredths of an inch in wear, and the cylinder taper was found to be worn by one-thousandth of an inch.

This test, in itself, is evidence of the longevity and quality built into every Caterpillar machine past and present.

The wide gauge Model 10 was 44 inches wide. The wide version is more rare than the 37-inch narrow gauge.

Models 15 7C Series and High-clearance 1D Series (Small 15s)

In 1932, Caterpillar introduced two "new" redesigned machines. The modifications made to the tractors were all lessons learned from the Model 10 and PV 15. The new tractors, known as the 8C 20, or Small 20, and the 7C 15, or Small 15, incorporated new technology that was to be used for several years.

When the Model 10 was discontinued, a small tractor was needed to replace it in the product line. Apparently, owing to the fact that the 10 was producing 15 horsepower, it was decided to correct the 10's problems but keep the basic design.

Model 15 7C Series

When the 7C 15 was introduced in 1932, it looked like a totally different tractor. The new tractor sported the bright Highway Yellow color and bold black decals. The old, over the engine location of the gas tank was moved ahead of the operator and served as the firewall. This allowed the exhaust outlet to pass through a hole in the hood rather than around the hood since the gas tank was now moved. This simple modification corrected the 10's old problem of heat transferring to the gas tank. Also, the delicate cast-iron dash of the Model 10 was eliminated.

In other changes, the drawbar brackets were made heavier. This design was used on the Model 22 and was a tremendous success. The throttle lever was moved to a location on top of the bell housing, near the gas tank base, and placed on a ratchet. This was a far more convenient location and was also adopted on other models. The seat back corners were angled, allowing the operator to control towed implements much more conveniently. Also, the two or three brass seat tags containing patent numbers and lubricating instructions were discontinued. These tags had a poor survival rate on the early models so the combination of tags was replaced with one brass tag containing only the patent numbers at the seat back top. This single

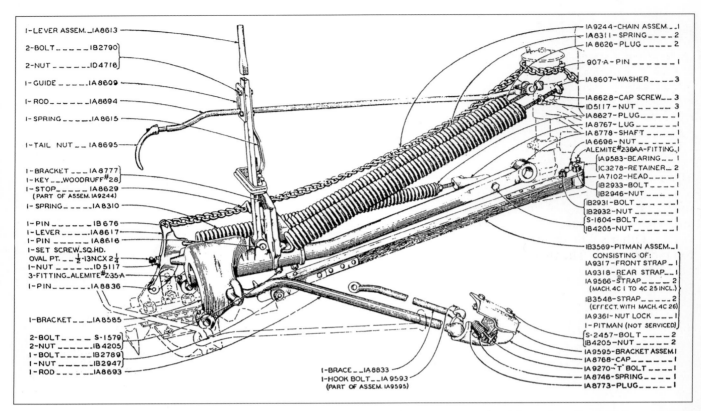

A mower was available for the Model 10 and similar models. It was issued serial numbers from 4C-1 to 4C-175. *Midland Press Corp.—Caterpillar, Inc., Form P-1190*

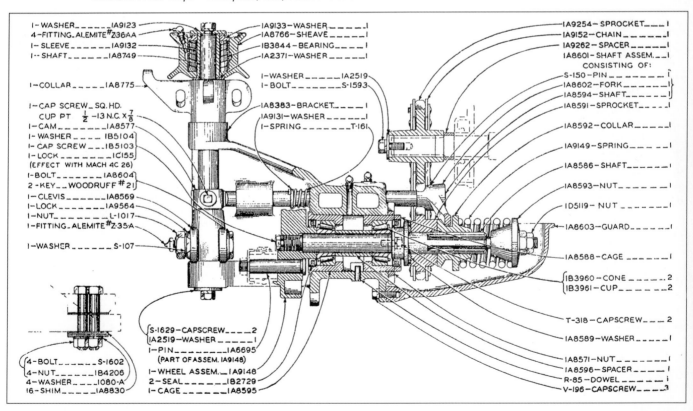

The drive assembly of the mower is chain driven off the tractor's PTO. *Midland Press Corp.—Caterpillar, Inc., Form P-1190*

tag was used on the seat back of all tractors made up into the early D Series tractors. The serial number location also changed with the Small 15. Since the brass seat tags that contained the serial number on early tractors had been replaced, the number was now placed on a small brass tag attached to the rear of the tractor on a flat boss near the right drawbar bracket. It was also placed on a brass tag above the carburetor on a raised plate on the left side of the engine. An arrangement similar to this is used today on most Caterpillar track-type tractors. The serial numbers are located on the rear-end housing and engine block but in different locations.

Other subtle changes are found on the top radiator tank. The two cradles that held the old gas tank on the 10 were removed. The carburetor is placed on an elbow that lowers it about 5 inches and allows it to act more as an updraft style and to aid gravity in feeding fuel from the new tank location. Perhaps this helped the performance of the carburetor. The carburetor itself had a redesigned cover, lowering it about an eighth of an inch, and thus using a shorter high-speed adjustment bolt.

Production

By all evidence the 7C 15 should have been a big success. It combined all the good aspects of the Model 10 and changed all its problems. When production ended in 1933, only 307 units were produced. The low production number makes the Small 15 a rare tractor.

The Small 15 was available in narrow- or standard-gauge at 37 inches and wide-gauge at 44 inches. Since the undercarriage is identical to the Model 10, the gauge widths are the same. One small change is that the Small 15 was equipped with cast-iron covers over the main spring that attached to the track frames. This was also used later on the Model 22.

Variants

The Small 15 was also available in an orchard or tailseat model and the high-clearance model. The high-clearance model was produced in the 44-inch gauge. The high-clearance 15 was the first version of a model to be given its own serial number. This variation was issued the serial number 1D. All units from 1D1 to 1D95 were definitely high-clearance machines and required those special parts. This had to make parts and service easier when using a serial number, and it sure helps us in researching these early machines.

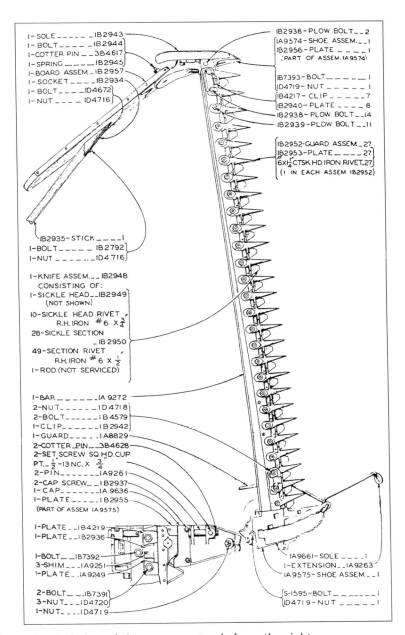

The sickle bar of the mower extends from the right side of the tractor. Several other brackets were attached to the tractor to accommodate the mower. *Midland Press Corp.—Caterpillar, Inc., Form P-1190*

One would assume that the company had learned from the mistake of not giving the High 10 its own serial number prefix. It could be that dealers and workers at the parts counters found it difficult to fill customers' parts orders. You can imagine calling the dealer and ordering a drive sprocket for a Cat 10 SN PT 4113 and getting a standard-gauge sprocket when the tractor was a high-clearance.

The wide gauge Model 10 utilized a longer pivot shaft and main spring. The drive sprockets were also concave or cupped outward.

The 7C or small 15 was really a Model 10 with various improvements. Only 307 of these tractors were produced and they are very sought after by collectors.

As you can tell from the numbers, all versions of the Small 15 are rare. But some variations of this model are plain scarce. The orchard model is again probably the most rare; personally, I have seen them only in sales literature. They probably exist only in the western states and will surface as the hobby grows. The wide-gauge appears in the Pacific states and the narrow-gauge in limited numbers in the Midwest and East. The high-clearance model is also rare and at this time less than a half dozen of the 95 produced have surfaced. The majority of those found have come from California, and some have appeared on the East Coast.

The high-clearance model is simply a Small 15 lifted to a total clearance of 24 inches with a High 10 undercarriage. It is unknown if any Small 15s were lifted by using a kit from a High 10 by anybody other than the factory. If you discover a High 15 with a 7C prefix, you probably have found a conversion. This was

Model	Production Number
TEN	(4,929)
FIFTEEN PV	(7,559)
TWENTY L & PL	(8,301)
TWENTY TWO	(15,154)
THIRTY PS	(14.294)
R-4	(4,507)
R-5 5E,4H,3R	(4,049)
SIXTY PA	(13,516)

the last attempt at a high-clearance crawler. It was rumored that a photo of a high-clearance 15 or 10 was seen hanging on the wall of a chief executive's office in the 1930s to remind him of how much money was lost with the high-clearance endeavor.

Why so few of this innovative little tractor were produced is a mystery. The engineering built into it paved the way for many other models to follow. Using much of this technology, the Model 22 was a huge success in the small tractor market.

The tractor was listed as having 18 horsepower, which was 3 more horsepower than the Model 10. Since by all evidence the engines are identical, I have no idea where the extra horsepower came from. It may have been from a new classification under test. It had been rumored that early 7C 15s used Model 10 radiators. It was thought that 10 radiators were left over so they just used them up at the factory until they were

gone. This seems unacceptable since the main purpose of creating the Small 15 and discontinuing the 10 was to market a tractor that more accurately advertised the horsepower it was producing. It makes more sense to say that an owner of a Small 15 may have replaced a damaged radiator with the more common and interchangeable Model 10 radiator. The radiator sides displaying the model designation may not have been changed, causing this misrepresentation. Rely on the serial number when in doubt.

Another interesting point is the use of the wavy logo on the top radiator tank of the 7C. Because the top radiator tank of this model did not significantly change from the 10, it was more cost-effective to continue using the same mold regardless of the new logo. In the movie *The Great Tractor Race*, the machines used all feature the new logo, even on tractors made well before this new logo became standard. Apparently the wavy logo

The Model 15 PV series was a larger version of the Model 10. It became the Model 20 8C series in 1932.

Model 15 PV Series.

was discontinued in December 1931, along with the gray paint.

In any case, the Small 15 in any version is a rare and desirable tractor for your collection and an important player in the evolution of later machines.

Model 15 PV Series (Big 15)

In 1929, Caterpillar introduced the Model 15 PV Series. The tractor was similar to the Model 10 in design but on a larger scale. The tractor was produced until 1932 with a total production of 7,559 units.

The Big 15 had the same design flaws as the Model 10. Its future looked bleak from the onset. When it was reintroduced in 1932 as the Small or 8C 20, it had undergone as complete of a modification as the 10 had gone through when it became the Small 15.

The Big 15 is common to several models. It has the design of a 10, the same main mechanical components as a Small 8C 20, and

Model 15 PV Series.

the same undercarriage as a 22. However, it should not be mistaken with the 7C Small 15.

Model 15 Variants

The tractor was available in narrow- or standard-gauge at 40 inches and wide-gauge at 50 inches. An orchard version was available in both gauges and is the rarest of the three styles. The orchard tractor or tailseat is equipped with full fenders, a lowered implement style seat, and a hand clutch. They are found in limited to moderate numbers on the West Coast. It is unknown how many orchard 15 tractors were made, but my guess is less than 1,000.

The wide-gauge model is also sought after by collectors. It is far more common than the orchard version and more common than a wide 10. Survival rates seem to be good and, unlike the wide 10, wide 15s are being found in most areas. It is difficult to tell how many wide-gauge 15 tractors were produced. It may be that nearly as many narrow 15s were produced as wide, but I am sure the wide-gauge is somewhat more rare.

The narrow-gauge, which is the most common, has an excellent survival rate. Many

Model 15 PV Series.

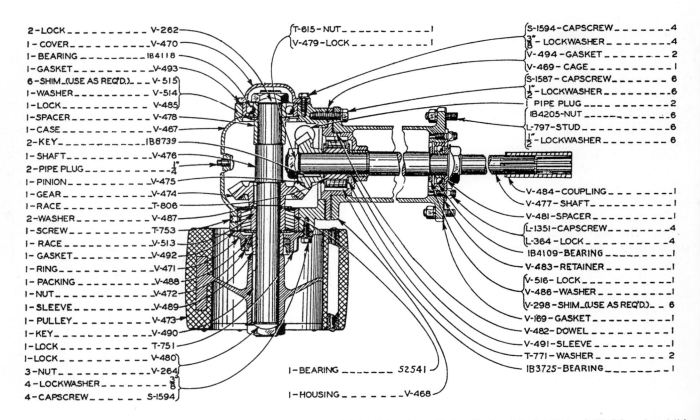

The belt pulley that was available for the Model 15 PV series will also fit the Model 22 and 20 8C series. *Midland Press Corp.—Caterpillar, Inc., Licensee*

that are found today are in good, usable condition and are still working in a limited capacity.

The 15 was slightly more popular than the 10, probably due to its increased horsepower. The 15 produced 22 horsepower and was approximately 1,000 pounds heavier than the Model 10.

Model 15 Problems

The 15 suffered from the same design problems as the 10. The gas tank was again located horizontally across the engine top and very close to the exhaust manifold. As with the 10, the heat from the manifold transferred to the gas tank, leading to vapor lock. After this problem was discovered, it too was equipped with an asbestos baffle and a vented gas tank. Neither the 10 nor the 15 was equipped with a fuel pump, so if it did vapor lock, it would not run.

Like the 10, the drawbar support brackets were made too light. When the drawbar swung abruptly under load, the brackets broke. Because of the flaw they were made heavier and used up through the Model 22.

Other problems with the Model 15 included a throttle level that froze up in cold climates; square seat back corners that made visualization and operation of towed implements difficult, and brass instruction tags that were easily damaged on the back of the seat. Minor changes were necessary for operator comfort and simplicity.

The major marketing problems of the 10 also haunted the 15. The horsepower of the 15 was 22, while it was marketed as the tractor with 7 less horsepower. The extra horsepower was virtually being given away. As with the 10, which was producing 15 horsepower, the tractor needed a new, more accurate designation. Thus in 1932, the old design was abandoned and the 15 became the 8C or Small 20.

Model 20 8C Series
(Small or Flathead 20)

In 1932, while the Model 10 became the 7C 15, the PV 15 was transformed into the Model 20 8C Series. The 8C 20 was given several names to differentiate it from the old Model 20 in the L and PL Series. The only thing similar between the two is their name. The 8C 20 is also known as the Small 20 and the Flathead 20.

The 8C is important for several reasons. Most important is that it is a transition model from the PV 15 to the Model 22. Also, along with the 7C 15, it was the first totally redesigned tractor to be painted the new Highway Yellow color with the black lettering and decals. The Model 25 was painted yellow in 1931 when it was introduced, but at that time it was really just a PL 20 with a different name. The C Series tractors were the first to undergo a major change and be painted a new color.

The 8C, like the 7C, was given a new smart design. All the problems from the PV 15 were remedied, even though the main components of the tractor were kept the same. The changes were mainly in appearance and design. The problems that the 7C solved for the Model 10 were the same ones the 8C solved for the PV 15.

The gas tank was moved behind the engine and ahead of the steering levers. With this relocation, the exhaust was allowed to pass through a hole in the hood rather than around it, as on the PV 15. The throttle lever was moved to a bracket on the bell housing and placed on a ratchet. This was improved from the old location inside the right fender. By doing this, operator comfort was improved and the problem of the linkage freezing up was overcome. The weak drawbar brackets were also replaced with a heavier style that did not break so easily. This was another problem found in the old Model 15. The square seat back corners of the 15 were replaced with tapered ones on the 8C 20 to ease the operation of towed implements.

The 8C 20 had cast-iron covers that fit over each end of the main spring. This not only made the tractor more attractive but also kept dirt from entering the spring mounting. These covers were used on the 7C 15 and Model 20. The engine side curtains on the 8C 20 had the louvers cut in them horizontally rather than vertically. This was changed from the Model 10 and PV Series 15.

With all of these modifications, the 8C should have been a popular small crawler. When production ended in 1934, only 638 units had been made. Why so few of these tractors were sold is somewhat of a mystery. Perhaps customers were focusing on other models and possibly even the use of diesels in crawlers.

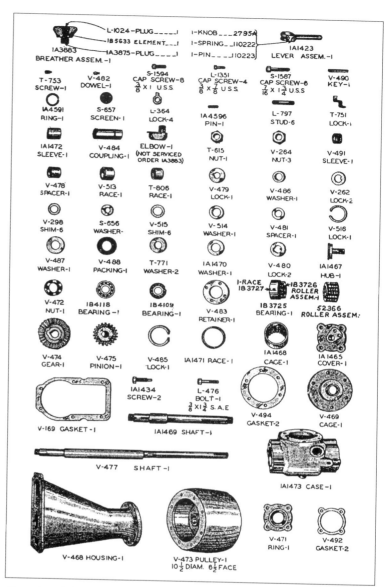

Parts breakdown of typical belt pulley drive. *Midland Press Corp.—Caterpillar, Inc., Licensee*

Model 20 Variants

The 8C 20 was available in 40-inch narrow-gauge and 50-inch wide-gauge as well as an orchard version in both gauges. It is not known how many of each type were made, but the orchard is the rarest, as with most other models. The narrow gauge is most common and is generally found in most areas but still in limited numbers. As with most wide-gauge models, they seem to be found generally on the West Coast. With few of these tractors made, you can see they are all quite rare.

Although the PV 15 was redesigned as the 8C 20, the two tractors still have a good

The Model 15 was also available in wide gauge. The early machines also came standard with engine side curtains that are often missing or damaged today.

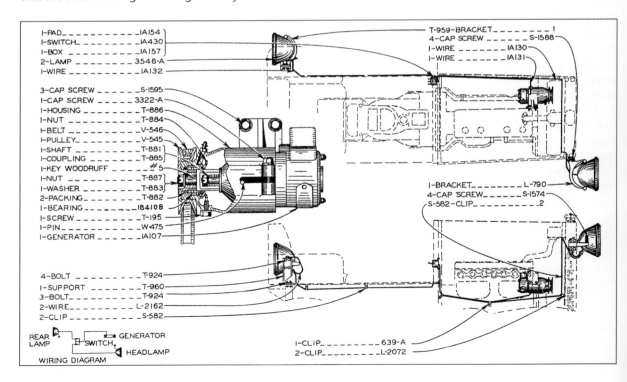

1-PAD _____ IA154
1-SWITCH _____ IA430
1-BOX _____ IA157
2-LAMP _____ 3548-A
1-WIRE _____ IA132

3-CAP SCREW _____ S-1595
1-CAP SCREW _____ 3322-A
1-HOUSING _____ T-886
1-NUT _____ T-884
1-BELT _____ V-546
1-PULLEY _____ V-545
1-SHAFT _____ T-881
1-COUPLING _____ T-885
1-KEY WOODRUFF ___ #5
1-NUT _____ T-887
1-WASHER _____ T-883
2-PACKING _____ T-882
1-BEARING _____ IB4108
1-SCREW _____ T-195
1-PIN _____ W-475
1-GENERATOR _____ IA107

4-BOLT _____ T-924
1-SUPPORT _____ T-960
3-BOLT _____ T-924
2-WIRE _____ L-2162
2-CLIP _____ S-582

REAR LAMP   GENERATOR
SWITCH   HEADLAMP
WIRING DIAGRAM

T-959-BRACKET _____ 1
4-CAP SCREW _____ S-1588
1-WIRE _____ IA130
1-WIRE _____ IA131

1-BRACKET _____ L-790
4-CAP SCREW _____ S-1574
S-582-CLIP _____ 2

1-CLIP _____ 639-A
2-CLIP _____ L-2072

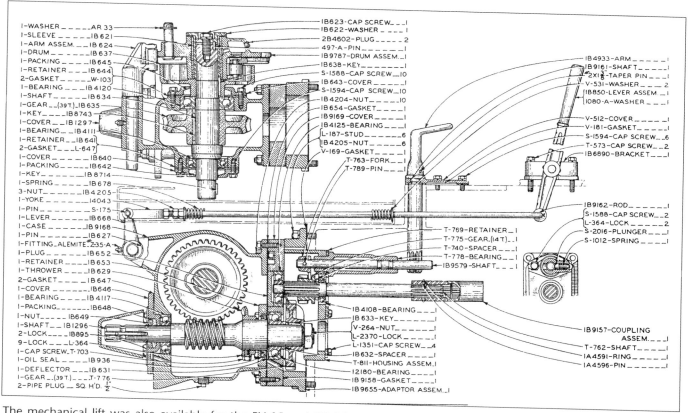

I-WASHER _ _ _ _AR 33	IB623-CAP SCREW_ _ _I	IB4933-ARM _ _ _ _ _I
I-SLEEVE _ _ _ _ _IB 621	IB622-WASHER _ _ _ _I	IB9161-SHAFT _ _ _ _I
I-ARM ASSEM. _ _ _IB 624	2B4602-PLUG _ _ _ _ _2	2XI 3/8-TAPER PIN _ _ _I
I-DRUM _ _ _ _ _IB 637	497-A-PIN _ _ _ _ _ _I	V-531-WASHER _ _ _2
I-PACKING _ _ _ _IB 645	IB9787-DRUM ASSEM._I	IB850-LEVER ASSEM _I
I-RETAINER _ _ _IB 644	IB638-KEY_ _ _ _ _ _I	I080-A-WASHER _ _ _I
2-GASKET _ _ _ _W-103)	S-1588-CAP SCREW_10	
I-BEARING _ _ _IB 4120	IB643-COVER _ _ _ _ I	V-512-COVER _ _ _ _I
I-SHAFT _ _ _ _IB 634	S-1594-CAP SCREW_10	V-181-GASKET _ _ _ _I
I-GEAR _ _(39T.)IB 635	IB4204-NUT_ _ _ _ _10	S-1594-CAP SCREW_ _6
I-KEY _ _ _ _IB8743	IB654-GASKET_ _ _ _I	T-573-CAP SCREW_ _2
I-COVER _ _ _IB 1297	IB9169-COVER _ _ _ _I	IB6890-BRACKET _ _ _I
I-BEARING _ _IB 4III	IB4125-BEARING _ _ _I	
I-RETAINER _ _ _IB 64I	L-187-STUD _ _ _ _ _6	
2-GASKET _ _ _L-647)	IB4205-NUT _ _ _ _ _6	
I-COVER _ _ _ _IB 640	V-169-GASKET _ _ _ _I	IB9162-ROD_ _ _ _ _I
I-PACKING _ _ _ _IB642	T-763-FORK _ _I	S-1588-CAP SCREW_2
I-KEY _ _ _ _ _IB 8714	T-789-PIN _ _I	L-364-LOCK _ _ _ _2
I-SPRING _ _ _ _IB 678		S-2016-PLUNGER _ _ _I
3-NUT _ _ _ _ _IB4 205		S-1012-SPRING _ _ _ _I
I-YOKE _ _ _ _ _ _I4043		
I-PIN _ _ _ _ _ _S-175	T-769-RETAINER _I	
I-LEVER _ _ _ _ _IB668	T-775-GEAR (I4 T.)_ _I	
I-CASE _ _ _ _IB 9168	T-740-SPACER _ _ _I	
I-PIN _ _ _ _ _ _IB627	T-778-BEARING _ _ _I	
I-FITTING,ALEMITE-235-A	IB9579-SHAFT_ _ _I	
I-PLUG _ _ _ _ _IB 652		IB9157-COUPLING
I-RETAINER _ _ _IB 653		ASSEM._ _ _I
I-THROWER _ _ _IB629	IB4108-BEARING_ _ _I	T-762-SHAFT _ _ _ _I
2-GASKET _ _ _ _IB647	IB 633-KEY_ _ _ _ _I	IA4591-RING _ _ _ _I
I-COVER _ _ _ _ _IB646	V-264-NUT_ _ _ _ _I	IA4596-PIN _ _ _ _ _I
I-BEARING _ _ _ _IB 4II7	L-2370-LOCK _ _ _ _I	
I-PACKING _ _ _ _IB648	L-1351-CAP SCREW_ _4	
I-NUT_ _ _ _IB649	IB632-SPACER _ _ _ _I	
I-SHAFT _ _ _ _IB 1296	T-8II-HOUSING ASSEM._I	
2-LOCK _ _ _ _IB895	I2I80-BEARING _ _ _ _I	
9-LOCK _ _ _L-364	IB 9158-GASKET _ _ _ _I	
I-CAP SCREW_T-703	IB9655-ADAPTOR ASSEM._I	
I-OIL SEAL _ _ _ _IB 936		
I-DEFLECTOR _ _ _IB 631		
I-GEAR _ _(39 T.) _ _ _T-776		
2-PIPE PLUG _ SQ. H'D. 2		

The mechanical lift was also available for the PV 15 and 8C 20. The linkages run under the seat to the lever mounted on the bell housing.

deal in common. The engine in the 8C 20 is the same as in the PV 15. Also, the transmission, final drives, and undercarriage are the same. The radiator core and bottom tank are the same, but the top tank and sides are changed. The carburetor is the same, but it is lowered on an elbow to achieve better gravitational flow from the gas tank. Ignition timing and most other adjustments are the same as the PV 15. Where the increase in horsepower came from is unknown, but it is probably from the way it was tested.

The 8C 20 and 7C 15 are two interesting and transitional tractors. They paved the way in design for many other models to follow. Until recently, with more organized collection and research, these two models were not known to exist by many collectors. I hope now these rare and interesting tractors will be sought out and preserved by many collectors.

LEFT
Auxiliary lighting assembly for use on Model 15 PV series without wooden cab.

Model 20 L and PL Series

In 1927, two years after the formation of the Caterpillar Tractor Company, the Model 20 was introduced. This tractor was the first totally new tractor to be manufactured by the company. In many respects the 20 borrowed much of its engineering from its big brother, the 30, which was a huge success.

The 20 was first manufactured in the San Leandro, California, plant. Later in 1928, production began in Peoria, Illinois, and eventually manufacturing ended in San Leandro with 1,970 units being produced. Meanwhile, in Peoria, production increased and when production of the 20 ended in 1931, a total of 6,319 units had been manufactured. It should also be noted that in 1931 a special order for 12 Model 20 tractors was placed, and numbers PL6587 through PL6598 were produced. It is not known why there is a gap between the two production runs or where these last 12 tractors went. Note that in *Caterpillar Magazine*, dated May 1930, a photo showing 12 Model 20 tractors belonging to one owner was featured. The owner was Eickhoff Farm Produce Corporation of Walla Walla,

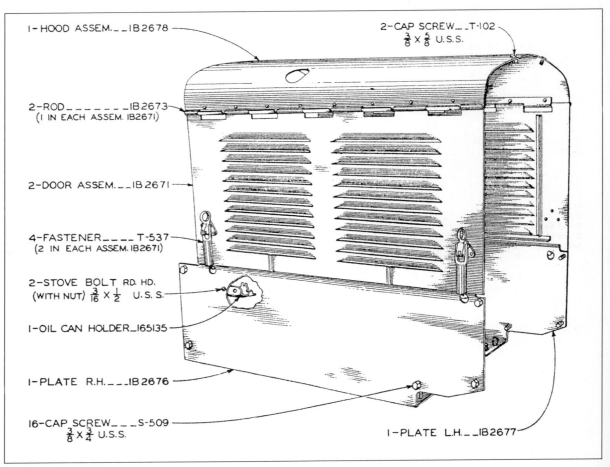

1—HOOD ASSEM.___IB 2678

2—CAP SCREW___T-102
$\frac{3}{8} \times \frac{5}{8}$ U.S.S.

2—ROD_____IB 2673
(1 IN EACH ASSEM. IB2671)

2—DOOR ASSEM.___IB 2671

4—FASTENER____T-537
(2 IN EACH ASSEM. IB2671)

2—STOVE BOLT RD. HD.
(WITH NUT) $\frac{3}{16} \times \frac{1}{2}$ U.S.S.

1—OIL CAN HOLDER_165135

1—PLATE R.H.___IB 2876

16—CAP SCREW___S-509
$\frac{3}{8} \times \frac{3}{4}$ U.S.S.

1—PLATE L.H.___IB 2677

Unlike the previous tractors, the side curtains of the Model 8C 20 had the louvers cut horizontally rather than vertically. The tractor was also painted highway yellow.

Washington. These 12 were apparently not the last 12 but it is possible that the owner ordered all of the machines.

The 20 was a fairly brave step for the new company since Caterpillar was basically experimenting with the introduction of this small tractor. Perhaps the 20 was meant to bridge the gap between the 2-Ton and the 30, both of which were very successful. The Model 20 was also the subject of a 408-hour nonstop run starting September 18, 1928. The run took place on the Hastings Ranch of the California Packing Company in Rio Vista, California. During the test, the tractor traveled more than 1,300 miles and worked 1,261 acres with an 8-foot disc harrow. This broke the previous record held by a Model 30 at 240 hours.

Model 20 Variants

As with most other tractors of this era, the 20 was available in several varia-

tions; the most common version is the 42-inch narrow-gauge, which is found in most areas of the county. This model was used by farmers and loggers, as well as in small construction applications. It was available in a tailseat or orchard model in both gauges, and these seem to be found in fair numbers in the orchard areas of the West Coast.

The wide-gauge model is the most scarce. Unlike the wide-gauge Model 10 and 15, the 20 did not have the concave rear sprocket. Instead, a spacer was placed between the rear-end housing of the tractor and the final drive housing. The main spring was also longer, giving the tractor its 55-inch wide-gauge. The 20 wide-gauge was made into a tailseat orchard mode. These are very rare and sought after by collectors.

Model 20 Problems

Like most of the early tractors, the 20 had its own share of problems. It was marketed

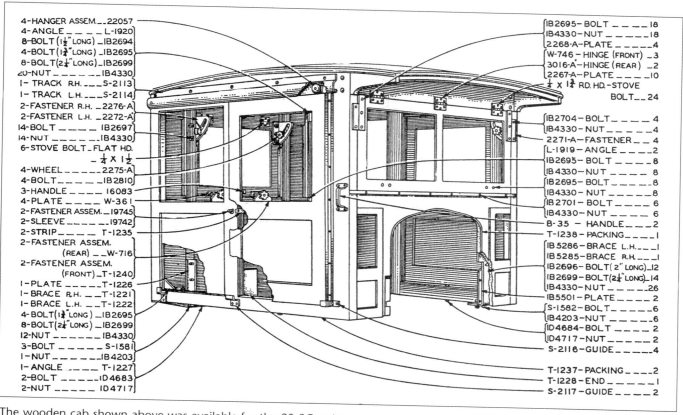

4-HANGER ASSEM.__22057
4-ANGLE____L-1920
8-BOLT (1½" LONG)_IB2694
4-BOLT (1¾" LONG)_IB2695
8-BOLT (2¼" LONG)_IB2699
20-NUT_____IB4330
1-TRACK R.H.___S-2113
1-TRACK L.H.___S-2114
2-FASTENER R.H._2276-A
2-FASTENER L.H._2272-A
14-BOLT_____IB2697
14-NUT_____IB4330
6-STOVE BOLT_FLAT HD.
_¼ X 1½
4-WHEEL_____2275-A
4-BOLT_____IB2810
3-HANDLE_____16083
4-PLATE_____W-361
2-FASTENER ASSEM._19745
2-SLEEVE_____19742
2-STRIP_____T-1235
2-FASTENER ASSEM.
(REAR)__W-716
2-FASTENER ASSEM.
(FRONT)_T-1240
1-PLATE_____T-1226
1-BRACE R.H.__T-1221
1-BRACE L.H.__T-1222
4-BOLT (1¾" LONG)_IB2695
8-BOLT (2¼" LONG)_IB2699
12-NUT_____IB4330
3-BOLT_____S-1581
1-NUT_____IB4203
1-ANGLE_____T-1227
2-BOLT_____ID4683
2-NUT_____ID4717

IB2695-BOLT_____18
IB4330-NUT_____18
2268-A-PLATE_____4
W-746-HINGE (FRONT)_3
3016-A-HINGE (REAR)_2
2267-A-PLATE_____10
¼ X 1½ RD. HD.-STOVE
BOLT__24
IB2704-BOLT_____4
IB4330-NUT_____4
2271-A-FASTENER__4
L-1919-ANGLE_____2
IB2695-BOLT_____8
IB4330-NUT_____8
IB2695-BOLT_____8
IB4330-NUT_____8
IB2701-BOLT_____6
IB4330-NUT_____6
B-35-HANDLE___2
T-1238-PACKING_____1
IB5286-BRACE L.H.___1
IB5285-BRACE R.H.___1
IB2696-BOLT (2" LONG)_12
IB2699-BOLT (2¼" LONG)_14
IB4330-NUT_____26
IB5501-PLATE_____2
S-1582-BOLT_____6
IB4203-NUT_____6
ID4684-BOLT_____2
ID4717-NUT_____2
S-2116-GUIDE_____4
T-1237-PACKING_____2
T-1228-END_____1
S-2117-GUIDE_____2

The wooden cab shown above was available for the 20 8C series when used in cold climates. Very few of these cabs are found intact today due to deterioration. *Midland Press Corp.—Caterpillar, Inc., Licensee*

as having less power than it actually produced. This was the case with several early tractors because design was based on engineering rather than testing in the field. The 20 was later reintroduced as the Model 25 to more accurately reflect the tractor's horsepower.

The first actual weakness in the machine itself was found in the ring and pinion drive system, a feature the 20 held in common with Model 30. The drive system usually held up to standard farm use, but it would typically fail when used for heavy construction or logging. The system was weak on both the Model 20 and 30.

Another problem was in the exhaust manifold. It is common to find the manifold in poor condition on many 20 tractors discovered today. The vertical updraft tube is usually cracked from moisture collecting inside it. In cold climates the moisture freezes and cracks the casing. The heat riser or hot box is also often found cracked or damaged. This manifold is difficult to repair and not easily found in usable condition on parts tractors.

Model 20 8C Series.

The 20 was painted gray in all of its variations. Some have said that the units made in San Leandro, California, were painted gray and highlighted with black lettering. It has also been said that the Peoria tractors were gray with red highlighting. I

Model 20 8C Series.

don't know if this is true; however, it's safe to say that all Model L and PL 20 tractors should be painted gray and highlighted in red.

On Saturday, December 5, 1931, the last Model 20 tractors were shipped. On Monday, December 7, 1931, the 20 was renamed the Model 25, to more accurately describe the horsepower of the tractor. Although it had its share of problems, the 20 was an admirable pioneer to all crawler machines produced by the company until today. When the 8C Series, or Small 20, was unveiled in 1932 with its small size and flathead engine, one can only imagine the strange looks and whispers. How did such a large tractor get such a different, modern look? Many probably did not realize the 8C 20 was really the old 15 and the old 20 was now the 25. It all may be confusing to us today, but it was probably more so back then.

In any case, the 20 is a very important piece in the history of the crawler tractor and a pleasure in any collection.

Model 22

In 1934, Caterpillar introduced the Model 22. When production ceased in 1939,

a total of 9,999 2F, or first series, and 5,157 1J Series tractors, or second series, were produced. Using a 26-horsepower, 4x5-inch OHV engine and a new updated design, the 22 was the company's most successful small gas crawler.

Model 22 Variants

The 22 was available in 40-inch standard-gauge with convex rear sprockets, 55-inch wide-gauge with concave rear sprockets, and an orchard-equipped model. All variations of the Model 22 seem to be in good supply. The orchard models are found generally on the West Coast but are still fairly common throughout the United States. Many are still in use today. A high-clearance model is shown in some of the original parts catalogs. Whether any of these versions were built is unknown. Some may have been equipped with tree harvesting and other specialty equipment, making them somewhat higher in clearance.

While most of the early gas crawlers had a myriad of problems, the 22 did not. It seemed to take the best from all of the earlier small machines, and with its operator-friendly

The 20 PL series or big 20 was the first new machine to be produced after the merger. The wide gauge is the most sought after. It utilized a spacer in the final drive. *Midland Press Corp.—Caterpillar, Inc., Form P-1190*

style and updated features, the 22 fast became a popular machine on the crawler tractor market.

When production of the 8C, or small 20, ended, apparently the company still had a market for a small crawler. Borrowing the chassis of a small 20 and even some main components of the PV Series 15, the 22 was given a redesigned sheet metal package and a new engine, making it a big success.

With the diesel crawler tractor coming of age, the gasoline-powered machines were starting to take a back seat. Yet the Model 22 sold better than any of the previous gas crawlers, and when production ended in 1939, 15,156 of the little tractors had been made. In the United States, as well as in other countries, the 22 sold well. Many 22 tractors are still working in the United Kingdom. The J Series R2 was also a common small gas crawler in the United Kingdom.

Model 22 Parts Interchange

Because the 22 borrowed so much of its engineering from earlier models, many of the parts are interchangeable. Basically, the undercarriage and drive components are common in the PV Series Model 15, the 8C Series 20, the 5E Series R-2, and the F and J Series Model 22. You can use parts from an unrestorable tractor to complete the better machine. The 22 also shares some common undercarriage components with the D-2 and J Series R-2, but the sprocket pitch is

	PRODUCTION NUMBERS					
	TRACTORS WITH LESS THAN 2,000 PRODUCED					
2,000					(1,728)	(1,808)
1,500			(1,171)			
1,000						
950						
900				(875)		
850						
800						
750						
700	(652)	(638)				
650						
600						
550						
	TWENTY	TWENTY	TWENTY	THIRTY	THIRTY	FIFTY
	8C	FIVE	EIGHT	6G	FIVE	

Model 20 orchard tractor.

the same; the center hub is splined on the D-2 rather than keyed. Unlike most of the early small crawlers, the 22 used a fuel pump. The fuel pump and gas caps were brass on the early 22, or 2F Series. On the later series, or 1J Series, they were made of pot metal. The latter fuel pump did not use a sediment bowl as was found on the brass pump. It may be that the pot metal versions of these were replacements installed over the years, but the later J model seems to have them on more consistently. Also, the J Series tractors more consistently display the 22 designations on brass tags at the base of the radiator sides. This is unlike the F Series with the model number across the top radiator tank. I have seen these combinations on both series of tractors.

Regardless of what version of the 22 you own or restore, you will find it to be a nice tractor, and when displayed, it is a machine many people will relate to.

Model R-2 5E Series

In 1934, the three-speed Caterpillar R-2, 5E Series tractor was released. Similar to the wide-gauge Model 22 tractor, the R-2 sold in

This Model 20 L-PL is undergoing restoration at Clark and Sons in Spokane, Washington.

limited numbers. The tractor was only available in wide-gauge at 50 inches and probably was a government-designed machine.

Production of the R-2 continued until 1937 with a total of 83 units being made. The R-2 is listed as having 25 horsepower, which is about .8 horsepower less than the 22. While the engines of the two tractors are the same, the transmission gearing is vastly different. The gearing was changed through different sized gears. At least six gearing combinations were available.

Apparently some government agencies would specify these gearing combinations for several different applications. Many of the tractors were sold to the Civilian Conservation Corps and ended up working forest fires. It is possible the high gearing was used to move the tractors rapidly out of danger. It is also known that some of the tractors were military machines. It is not known how many of the machines went to each government agency, but most were apparently used by forestry departments.

Another unique feature of the R-2 is the large cast-iron counterweights placed on each roller frame. Apparently this 350-pound casting was a government specification for either stability or traction. The castings are made in the shape of the dirt guards and have an indentation for the main spring to fit in. The military models were equipped with an odometer for either recording miles or speed. It was placed on a bracket near the clutch pedal with a hole drilled into the transmission bell housing. The forestry models have been found with a ring gear, starter, and lighting generator. These options may have been specified by the agencies ordering the tractors.

As you can tell by the numbers, this variation of the R-2 is rare. Even though orchard equipment was made available for this tractor, I doubt it was ever used. I presume all of the government models were top seat, unless they were used in some government agricultural operation. Also, it appears that from serial number 5E3501 to 5E3553, the R-2 designation was cast into the top radiator tank. On the last 30 tractors the R-2 designation was at the bottom of each radiator side on a brass plate. The last 30 are rarer, but they are appearing more than the style of the first 53. I have personally seen tractor numbers 5E3547 and 5E3548, and they both have "CATERPILLAR" cast across the top radiator tank and do not have the R-2 designation displayed anywhere on the tractor. However,

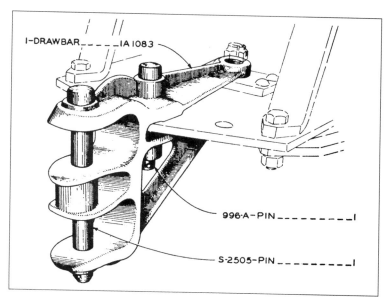

The adjustable height drawbar was a special order option on many of the tractors. *Midland Press Corp.— Caterpillar, Inc., Licensee*

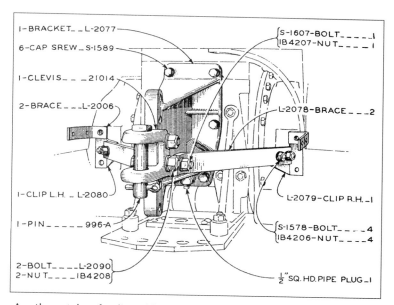

Another style of adjustable drawbar available as an option on the early tractors. *Midland Press Corp.— Caterpillar, Inc., Licensee*

tractor number 5E3553, which I own, does have the R-2 on the radiator top, as it should. As rare as these tractors are, we may never know which is more common. My advice is to rely on the serial number for authenticity when attempting to identify an unmarked machine.

The Model 22 was the most popular of the small crawlers. The wide-gauge version shown displays the Caterpillar name across the radiator top.

Model 25

On December 7, 1931, the Caterpillar Model 20 tractor was redesignated as the Model 25 tractor. Like the 20, the 25 still produced 28 horsepower. Basically, the two tractors were the same except for the radiator side plates, and in the later Model 25, the fenders were changed and there were other slight modifications.

When production ended in 1933, only 638 units had been produced. This tractor, in wide-gauge at 55 inches, narrow-gauge at 42 inches, and tailseat versions, is one of the most sought by collectors.

It is hard to find because only a small number were produced. There are more narrow-gauges, but the other variations are very rare, including the wide-gauge orchard model. The survival rate of Model 25 is quite good, however all variations of the Model 25 are given the same 3C serial number prefix, from 3C1 to 3C638. Therefore, as with most early models, it is impossible to find out how many of each version was produced.

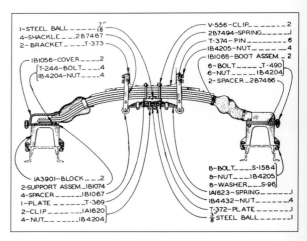

A high-clearance equalizer spring for the Model 22. It is not known how many high-clearance Model 22 tractors were produced. *Midland Press Corp.—Caterpillar, Inc., Licensee*

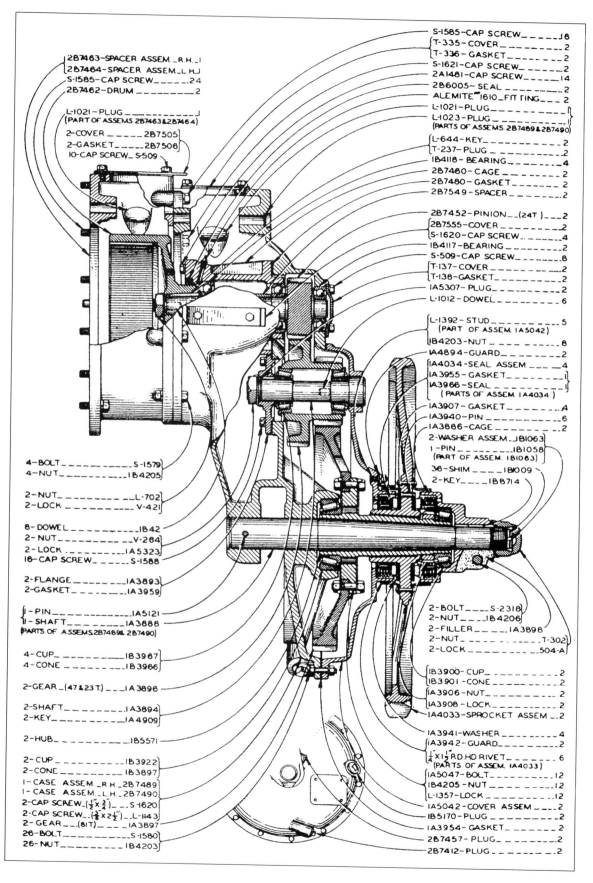

2B7463—SPACER ASSEM.—R.H.—1
2B7464—SPACER ASSEM.—L.H.J
S-1585—CAP SCREW_____24
2B7462—DRUM _____2

L-1021—PLUG _____J
(PART OF ASSEMS 2B7463&2B7464)
2-COVER _____2B7505J
2-GASKET____2B7506J
10-CAP SCREW_ S-509

S-1585—CAP SCREW_____J8
T-335-COVER _____2
T-336—GASKET _____2
S-1621—CAP SCREW_____2
2A1481—CAP SCREW_____14
2B6005— SEAL _____2
ALEMITE "1610_FITTING___2
L-1021—PLUG _____J
L-1023—PLUG _____J
(PARTS OF ASSEMS 2B7489&2B7490)
L-644—KEY _____2
T-237—PLUG _____2
1B4118—BEARING_____4
2B7480—CAGE _____2
2B7480—GASKET _____2
2B7549—SPACER _____2

2B7452—PINION__(24T)___2
2B7555—COVER _____2
S-1620—CAP SCREW_____4
1B4117—BEARING _____2
S-509—CAP SCREW_____8
T-137—COVER _____2
T-138-GASKET_____2
1A5307—PLUG _____2
L-1012—DOWEL _____6

L-1392—STUD _____5
(PART OF ASSEM 1A5042)
1B4203—NUT _____8
1A4894—GUARD _____2
1A4034—SEAL ASSEM____4
1A3955—GASKET_____J
1A3966—SEAL _____J
(PARTS OF ASSEM 1A4034)
1A3907—GASKET _____4
1A3940—PIN _____6
1A3886—CAGE _____2
2-WASHER ASSEM._1B1063J
1—PIN_____1B1058J
(PART OF ASSEM 1B1063)
36—SHIM____1B1009
2—KEY____1B8714

4—BOLT_____S-1579J
4—NUT_____1B4205J

2—NUT_____L-702J
2—LOCK_____V-421J

8—DOWEL_____1B42J
2—NUT_____V-264J
2—LOCK_____1A5323J
18—CAP SCREW_____S-1588

2—FLANGE_____1A3893J
2—GASKET_____1A3959J

1—PIN_____1A5121J
1—SHAFT_____1A3888
(PARTS OF ASSEMS 2B7489&2B7490)

4—CUP_____1B3967J
4—CONE_____1B3966J

2—GEAR_(47&23T.)___1A3896

2—SHAFT_____1A3894J
2—KEY_____1A4909J

2—HUB_____1B5571J

2—CUP_____1B3922J
2—CONE_____1B3897J
1—CASE ASSEM.R.H. 2B7489
1—CASE ASSEM.L.H. 2B7490
2—CAP SCREW_(½x¾)__S-1620
2—CAP SCREW_(½x2½)__L-1143
2—GEAR__(81T)____1A3897
26—BOLT_____S-1580J
26—NUT_____1B4203J

2—BOLT____S-2318J
2—NUT____1B4206J
2—FILLER_____1A3898
2—NUT_____T-302J
2—LOCK_____504-AJ

1B3900—CUP_____2
1B3901-CONE_____2
1A3906—NUT_____2
1A3908—LOCK_____2
1A4033—SPROCKET ASSEM._2

1A3941—WASHER_____4
1A3942—GUARD _____2
¼x1½"RD.HD.RIVET_____6
(PARTS OF ASSEM. 1A4033)
1A5047—BOLT _____12
1B4205-NUT _____12
L-1357—LOCK _____12
1A5042—COVER ASSEM____2
1B5170—PLUG _____2
1A3954—GASKET _____2
2B7457—PLUG _____2
2B7412—PLUG _____2

The high-clearance
Model 22 has a final
drive that is quite
similar to that of the
high-clearance
Model 10. *Midland
Press Corp.—Cater-
pillar, Inc., Liscensee*

35

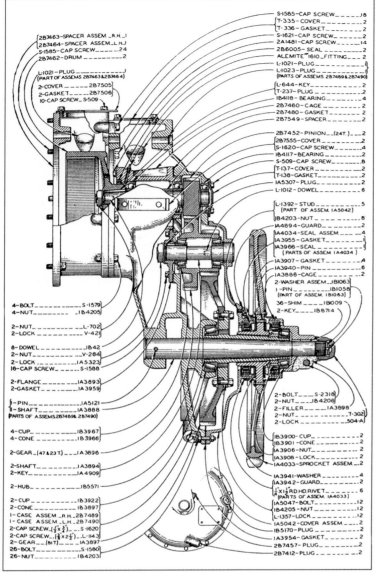

Although similar to that of the high-clearance 10, the final drive cross section for the Model 22 high-clearance has some differences. Only one high-clearance Model 22 is known to exist as of 1996. *Midland Press Corp.— Caterpillar, Inc., Licensee*

Model 25 Parts Interchange

Since the Model 25 is nearly identical to the PL Model 20, most parts are interchangeable. On the early Model 25 the curved rear fenders were used, as on the 20. About the last 400 Model 25 tractors had straight fenders. The later models also had a slightly different exhaust manifold. On the intake portion, the priming cups were placed on elbows that came directly out of the face of the manifold rather than the top on the Model 20 and early 25.

The Model 20 tractors on the assembly line were changed to the 25 only by serial number and designation. Later, as parts were used up in the warehouse, new parts were produced specific to the 25. These parts include the fenders, radiator castings, and final drive components. These characteristic parts are found on tractors made after serial number 3C250 or so.

Model 25 Serial Number Locations

The serial number locations of the 25 are located on the vertical column on the left side of the front of the engine block. There should be a brass tag riveted to the casting. The serial number is also located on the small tag riveted to the boss on the rear housing by the right drawbar bracket. The number is not found on the rear seat tag.

The 25 is not only interesting to collectors because of its rarity, but also because of its importance and history. The 25 was the saving grace for the Model 20. The 20 was the first totally new joint accomplishment by the newly formed company. It was important that this tractor not fail; therefore, it was redesigned twice and marketed as three different models.

Being the second tractor in the chain, the 25 marked a new appearance for the company. On December 7, 1931, not only did the 20 become a 25, but the look of road machinery changed too, forever. The popular gray-and-red color scheme of Caterpillar tractors was replaced with Highway Yellow. At the same time the wavy, crawling "Caterpillar" insignia, was replaced with a no-nonsense block print. This was used on radiator and engine block castings, as well as on the three-piece decal sets. The old gray color could be special ordered along with silver gray. For any tractors made after this date, it is possible to find them in any of these three colors. The Highway Yellow should be used on all Model 25 restorations. I doubt few were special ordered in gray, but it is your tractor and your preference.

Another point with the Model 25 is that the early or low serial-numbered tractors have been found with the wavy logo cast on the top radiator tank. These were apparently left from the 20 production run and were used up until the supply ran out. On later Model 25s, or the ones with straight fenders, most have the block print on the top radiator tank. These are either replacement radiator tanks, or the tractors were made late enough in the production

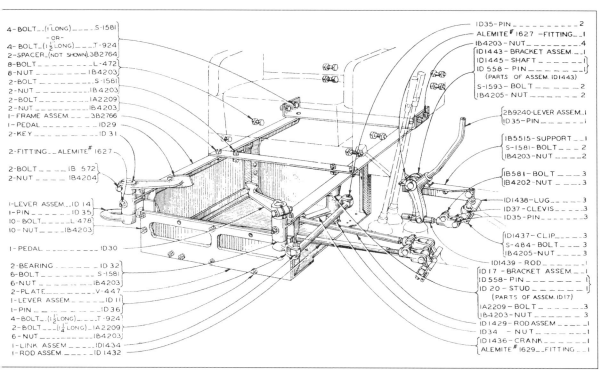

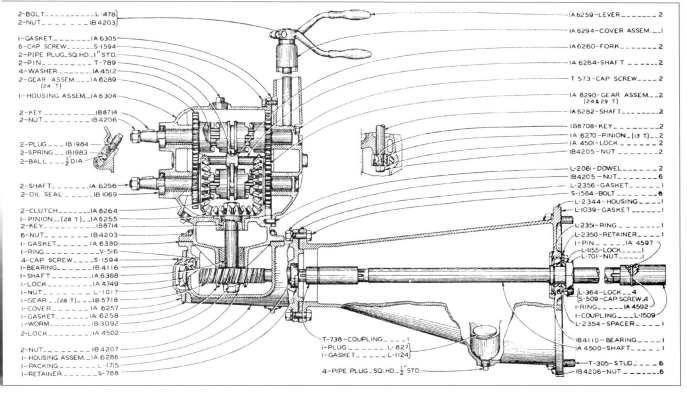

A unique variation of the Model 22 is the side seat. It was designed to ease the operator in the task of pulling a road patrol grader. Any side seat equipped tractor is very rare.

The side seat tractors were made to ease the operator's view of a towed grader. Often the grader unit was controlled by a double power take-off assembly. *Midland Press Corp.—Caterpillar, Inc., Form P-1190*

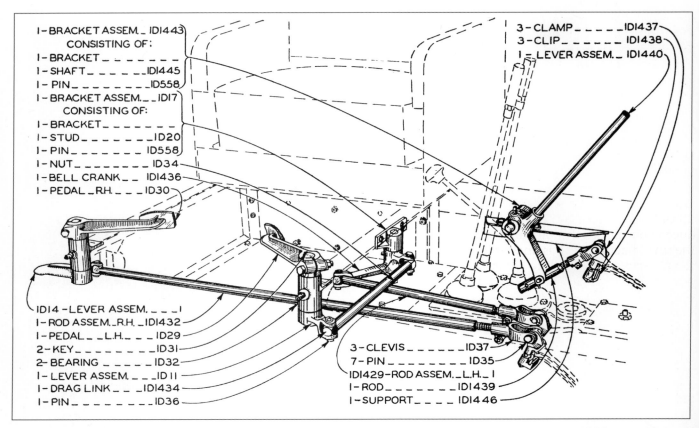

1 - BRACKET ASSEM. _ ID1443
    CONSISTING OF:
1 - BRACKET _ _ _ _ _ _ _
1 - SHAFT _ _ _ _ _ ID1445
1 - PIN_ _ _ _ _ _ _ _ ID558
1 - BRACKET ASSEM. _ _ ID17
    CONSISTING OF:
1 - BRACKET_ _ _ _ _ _ _
1 - STUD _ _ _ _ _ _ ID20
1 - PIN _ _ _ _ _ _ ID558
1 - NUT_ _ _ _ _ _ _ ID34
1 - BELL CRANK _ _ ID1436
1 - PEDAL _ R.H. _ _ _ ID30

3 - CLAMP_ _ _ _ _ ID1437
3 - CLIP _ _ _ _ _ ID1438
1 _ LEVER ASSEM. _ ID1440

ID14 - LEVER ASSEM. _ _ _ 1
1 - ROD ASSEM._ R.H. _ ID1432
1 - PEDAL _ _ L.H. _ _ _ ID29
2 - KEY _ _ _ _ _ _ _ ID31
2 - BEARING _ _ _ _ _ ID32
1 - LEVER ASSEM. _ _ _ ID11
1 - DRAG LINK _ _ _ ID1434
1 - PIN _ _ _ _ _ _ _ ID36

3 - CLEVIS _ _ _ _ _ ID37
7 - PIN _ _ _ _ _ _ _ ID35
ID1429 - ROD ASSEM._ L.H._ 1
1 - ROD _ _ _ _ _ _ ID1439
1 - SUPPORT_ _ _ _ ID1446

The side seat control package is a very complicated assembly of linkages and rods. It was available as an optional kit. *Midland Press Corp.—Caterpillar, Inc., Form P-1190*

run that this tank and logo design were standard. The 7C 15 and 8C 20 were being made at the same time as the 25. Yet both of these tractors used the wavy logo on the top radiator tank like the early tractors, but they also had the Highway Yellow paint and block decal lettering. It is most acceptable to assume the old logo was used until the other design became standard.

When restoring the Model 25 tractor it is important to realize that many parts can be interchanged from the Model 20 L and PL Series. Many parts are also in common with the Model 28, so these three tractors can borrow quite a bit from each other.

The 25, although rare and somewhat unknown, is an important tractor in the evolution of crawler tractors. Restored along with a 20 and 28, they are a historical and interesting line-up.

Model 28

In 1933, Caterpillar gave Models 20 and 25 another update with the Model 28. When production of the Model 28 ended in 1935, only

1,171 units had been produced. The Model 28 was marketed in standard-gauge at 42 inches, wide-gauge at 55 inches, and an orchard model.

As is shown by the relatively low number produced, the 28 is moderately rare. The wide-gauge and orchard models are more rare than the standard version. It is not known how many of these special variations were made, but they seem as scarce as with many other models.

The 28 has most parts in common with the model 25 tractors made after 3C269. Some parts such as the track rails are common clear back to the Model 20. Like the later Model 25, the 28 used the straight fenders next to the seat rather than the curved style from the Model 20.

The gas tank of the 28 is rounded on the front side, similar to a 22. The Model 20 gas tank is set inward with a lip running around the perimeter. Another change that occurred with the 28 is that it was one of the first models to use the SP prefix after the serial number. Depending on who you talk to, this designates either "special purpose" or "special part." Either way means the tractor received some modification or option at the factory. These options could range from electric start to orchard equipment. Other designations such as "W" were used, indicating a wide-gauge tractor. The Model 28 was the last major attempt at updating the Model 20.

Model R-3

In 1934, while the Model 28 tractor was being produced, a close companion to it, the Model R-3, was introduced. The Model R-3 was manufactured until 1935, with a total of 60 units produced. The serial numbers run from 5E2500 to 5E2560. By the small number produced you can see this probably is the rarest of the small tractor line. It is unclear why so few of there tractors were produced, but it is probably due to a special government order. As with other unique models of limited production, such as the R-2 5E Series, Diesel 70, 9M D-5, and R-6, this may have been a government-originated design. The R-3 was available only in the 55-inch wide-gauge, which was also the same width of the wide-gauge 28.

The R-3 was listed as producing 36 horsepower. This was six more horsepower than the Model 28. The increase in horsepower was due to an increase in engine bore from 4 3/16 inches to 4 1/2 inches. The stroke of both tractors was 5 1/2 inches. The engine crankshaft is the same in both models, but the manifold, cylinders, block, and head differ. The exhaust leaves the tractor at number one cylinder instead of the center of the manifold, as with Model 28.

Another specific addition to the R-3 was the use of cast-iron weights on top of each roller frame. Cast in the shape of dirt guards, the weights apparently were designed to add stability to the tractor and increase traction. The castings weigh approximately 400 pounds each and are a fairly smooth casting. The only other machine known to use these castings in that manner is the 5E Series R-2, which also is a government-originated machine.

Also, whether the R-3 was ever sold as a wide-gauge or an orchard model is not known. Assuming that it is a machine built of government specifications, it was probably made in only one version. The R-3 engine was used in some Auto Patrol graders. Perhaps the engine was first designed for the grader and then installed in a Model 28 tractor chassis. An individual can speculate, but it all ends up with the fact that the R-3 is an extremely rare and desirable tractor.

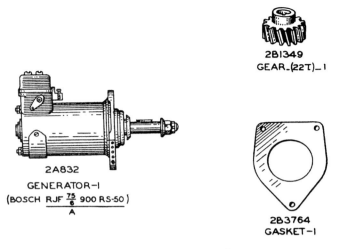

2B1349
GEAR-(22T)-1

2A832
GENERATOR-1
(BOSCH RJF 75/6 900 RS-50)
A

2B3764
GASKET-1

2B7094 LIGHTING GENERATOR GROUP
(6 Volt—For Use Without Battery)
(For Machines 2F1 & Up)

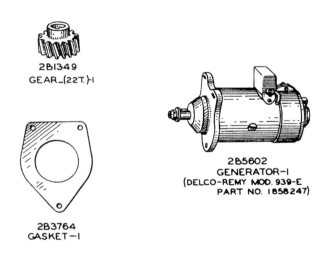

2B1349
GEAR-(22T)-1

2B3764
GASKET-1

2B5602
GENERATOR-1
(DELCO-REMY MOD. 939-E
PART NO. 1858247)

Two styles of lighting generator were made available for the Model 22. *Midland Press Corp.—Caterpillar, Inc., Licensee*

Model 30 S and PS Series

When the Caterpillar Tractor Company was formed in 1925, the Model 30 was held over from the Best Tractor Company product line. The Model 30 was first produced in 1921 in the S Series and continued until 1932 when it was discontinued as the PS Series. I will cover the Model 30 of post-1925 production.

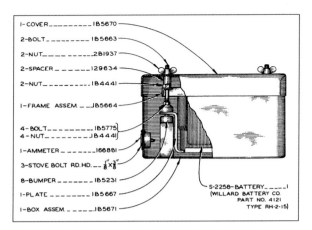

I—COVER	IB5670
2—BOLT	IB5663
2—NUT	2BI937
2—SPACER	I29634
2—NUT	IB4441
I—FRAME ASSEM	JB5664
4—BOLT	IB5775
4—NUT	JB4441
I—AMMETER	I6888I
3—STOVE BOLT RD.HD.	⅛"X¾"
8—BUMPER	IB523I
I—PLATE	IB5667
I—BOX ASSEM	IB567I
S-2258—BATTERY	I
(WILLARD BATTERY CO. PART NO. 4121 TYPE RH-2-15)	

Battery box for use on Model 22 tractor. *Midland Press Corp.*

The Model S tractors were produced in the San Leandro, California, plant until 1930 with production ending at serial number S10536. This indicates that approximately 7,000 Model S 30s were produced under the Caterpillar name from 1925 to 1930. The PS Series tractors were made from 1927 until 1932 at the Peoria, Illinois, plant with a total production of 14,294 machines.

The Model 30 was a successful tractor for both Best and later Caterpillar.

Model 30 Variants

The 30 was available in standard- or narrow-gauge at 43 3/4 inches, wide-gauge at 60 3/4 inches, and an orchard model. The wide-gauge version is the rarest of the three styles and the orchard is next. The standard 30 is in good supply in most areas of the country. The orchard style is most generally found on the West Coast and in moderate numbers.

The 30's engine is a 4 3/4-inch bore by 6 1/2-inch stroke, valve-in-head, producing 25 drawbar horsepower and 30 belt horsepower. Shipping weight of the tractor was approximately 10,000 pounds.

Model 30 Problems

As with most of the early tractors, the 30 did have problems. One of the most common problems was in the final drive system. Apparently the ring and pinion were not strong enough, and often they failed. Today many collectors are in need of good gears for a Model 30 they are restoring and are searching for them. The gears were a problem common to the L and PL 20, which were similar to the 30. Also, like the early Model 20, the 30 had rounded rear fenders

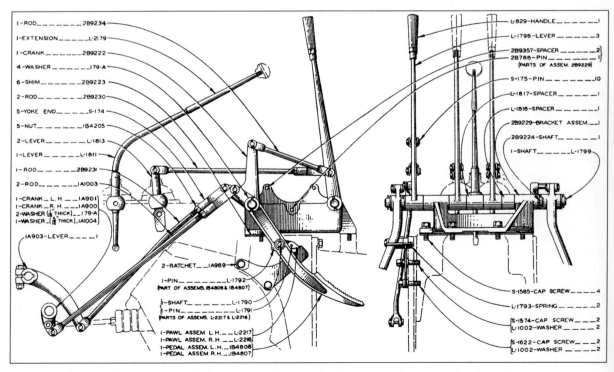

The control group above was needed to convert the standard top seat 22 to an orchard model.

PRODUCTION NUMBERS
TRACTORS WITH LESS THAN 600 PRODUCED

	FIFTEEN 7C	R-2 5E	R-3	FORTY	SIXTY-FIVE	SEVENTY
600				(584)		
550					(521)	
500						
450						
400						
350	(307)					
300						(266)
250						
200						
150		(83)				
100			(60)			
50						

that often became damaged from routine use. Many of these fenders have been cut down by previous owners when they became bent up or dented. It is also important to note that the fenders are the location of the instruction plates and are also often found to be missing.

The Model 60, which was also a Best holdover, has much in common to its little brother, the 30. They are nearly identical in appearance, only on a far different scale. These two machines, when used in farming and crop harvesting applications, were most often equipped with the familiar corrugated tin canopy. When displayed together, they make an interesting pair of the two most widely known models of the legendary Caterpillar tractor product line.

The Model 30 was the subject of a record 240-hour nonstop test run that was established April 21, 1928. The test was run at the Battaglia Brothers Ranch of San Jose, California, and broke the 168.5-hour record held by a 2-Ton from New Zealand.

Over the course of its production, the 30 underwent many changes in design. Over time it transformed into the 6G Series 30 and the Model R-4. These tractors are closely related to the extremely popular diesel RD-4 and D-4 tractors. Thus, the 30 paved the way for many other advancing machines to follow.

Caterpillar Model 30 6G Series and R-4

In 1935, a totally redesigned Model 30 was introduced in the 6G Series. This model was introduced three years after the old PS Series 30 was discontinued, and it had a totally new look. Only 874 units were produced carrying the 30 name. After that the model was redesignated as the Model R-4. The tractor weighed in at just over 9,000 pounds.

The tractors were available in narrow- or standard-gauge at 44 inches, wide-gauge at 60 inches, and the orchard-equipped model. All variations of the machines carrying the 30 name over the radiator are quite rare and sought after. The R-4-designated machines are far more common and are found in most areas. Total production of both machines combined was 5,383 units, with 4,508 units carrying the R-4 designation.

Many of the R-4 tractors found today seem to be retired from some branch of government service. They are often equipped with electric start and either a cable blade or early

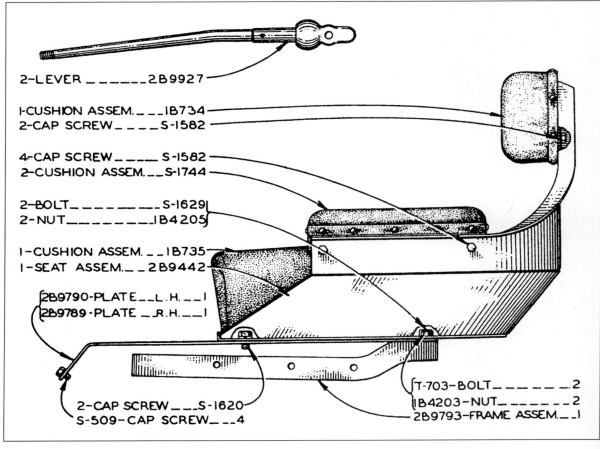

2-LEVER _ _ _ _ _ _2B9927

1-CUSHION ASSEM._ _ _1B734
2-CAP SCREW_ _ _ _ S-1582

4-CAP SCREW_ _ _ _ _ S-1582
2-CUSHION ASSEM._ _S-1744

2-BOLT_ _ _ _ _ _ _S-1629
2-NUT_ _ _ _ _ _ _ 1B4205

1-CUSHION ASSEM._ _1B735
1-SEAT ASSEM._ _ 2B9442

2B9790-PLATE_ _L.H._ _ 1
2B9789-PLATE _ _R.H._ _ 1

2-CAP SCREW _ _ _S-1620
S-509-CAP SCREW_ _ _4

T-703-BOLT_ _ _ _ _ _2
1B4203-NUT_ _ _ _ _ _ 2
2B9793-FRAME ASSEM._ _1

Seat assembly used on orchard or tailseat Model 22.

This is a Caterpillar Model 22 "camel-back" used for nursery work.

LaPlant Choate hydraulic dozer. It is not clear what percent were used by the government, but I bet the number is quite high.

The 30 and R-4 are handsome tractors that contain styling and engineering used into the RD and D Series machines introduced later the same decade. These tractors also used much of the design of a 22 but on a larger scale. When the RD-4 was introduced a year later, it was nicknamed the diesel R-4 in some areas due to the identical components of the machines. As changes in the design of the RD-4 were made, the same changes were made to the R-4. A similar situation took place with the early D-2 and J Series R-2, which had many identical components but differently fueled engines. Production of the R-4 ended in 1944, three years before the last 5T D-4 was produced. Apparently by this time the diesel had become accepted as the choice for powering new tractors.

The 6G Series 30 and R-4 should be painted Highway Yellow and highlighted in black. If your machine was a tractor owned by a

This Model 22 is a wide gauge version.

specific branch of government, you may wish to restore it to that application. Please keep in mind the extensive interchangeability of these models, and when in doubt, identify them by serial number. These tractors are important in the evolution of crawler tractors going from the spark ignition to diesel fuel and are desirable in any collection.

Models 35, 40, and R-5

In 1932, the Model 35 tractor was introduced to fill the void left by the Model 30 PS Series. The tractor was equipped with basically the same engine and undercarriage as the old 30 but was given a more up-to-date look. When production ended in 1934, only 1,728 machines had been made.

The 30 was available in narrow- or standard-gauge at 53 inches, wide-gauge at 74 inches, and an orchard model. All variations of the 35 are quite rare. The narrow-gauge model is the most common and few of the wide and orchard models have surfaced at this time. Why such a

The Model 22 wide gauge and R-2 SE series have much in common. The R-2 had large weights placed on each track frame. Shown is a Model 22 wide gauge which is far more common than the Model R-2.

The Model R-2 "J" series was the gas version of the D-2. It was very popular in the United Kingdom.

limited number of these tractors where produced is unclear, but it was probably due to the introduction of the diesel engine for crawler tractors.

The 4 7/8x6 1/2-inch four cylinder engine produced 38 drawbar horsepower and 46 belt horsepower. Weighing in at 12,280 pounds, it was slightly heavier than the Model 30 it replaced. It also differed from the 30 with its enclosure of the engine compartment. The 35 was equipped with a hood and side curtains with the gas tank being located in front of the operator. Like many other models in production at this time, the louvers of the side curtains run horizontally instead of vertically. All variations of the 35 were painted Highway Yellow, highlighted in black with the block decals that were introduced in 1931.

In 1934, the Model 40 replaced the 35 in the product line. The 40 was produced until 1936 with a total number of 584 machines. Three versions of the 40 were available. These included the standard- or narrow-

gauge at 56 inches, wide-gauge at 74 inches, and orchard model. All variations of the 40 are rare and sought after by collectors. As with most of the early machines, no separate serial number was given to the special variations, making it difficult to tell how many of each were produced. The gauge widths of these tractors were 74-inch, wide-gauge, and 56-inch, narrow-gauge.

Apparently due to the severe competition from the diesel engine, the larger spark ignition tractors were no longer selling as well as they had. Even though the horsepower was increased to 44, the fuel economy of the diesel was a far better choice. The serial numbers of the Model 40 run from 5G1 to 5G584. All versions should be painted Highway Yellow with the later decals. The styling of the 40 was similar to that of the 35, with the gas tank located ahead of the operator with a hood and side curtains containing the engine compartment. This design stayed standard for many of the tractors that followed.

The orchard version of the R-2 is a rare machine. It is not to be confused with the R-2 5E series which used a three-speed rather than five-speed transmission.

The Model R-5 was introduced in 1934 during the end of the production run of the 35 and at the beginning of the 40's production. The R-5 was made in three batches with a total production of 1,549 machines. The first series of the R-5 was given the serial number prefix 5E, of which 500 units were produced. These first series machines had the most parts in common with the 35. The second series was the 4H Series, of which 1,000 units were produced. The tractors of this series likely have the most components in common with the Model 40. The third series tractors were given the 3R serial number prefix, of which 49 units were produced. These machines, along with a portion of the 4H-designated machines, became the gasoline-fueled alternative to the RD-6 tractor being produced at part of the same time. The R-5 weighed approximately 13,200 pounds.

All variations of the R-5 are moderately rare. I am not sure if the different serial number prefix groups are any more valuable than the other.

The Model 25 is the tractor that replaced the 20 PL series. The 25 is very sought after by collectors.

What's this "Caterpillar" pulling?

A deep-set plow?...a hardwood log?...a road grader?
Maybe there's a load of ore behind it...or a house that's
being moved. Perhaps it's pulling a circus wagon out of
the mud...or hauling a load of sealskins on an Alaskan
Island...wattle poles in Africa...or yanking out a stump.
It might be any one of these, *for the chain is taut* and
"Caterpillar" Tractors are used the world over for out-
door tasks where plentiful power and generous traction
are necessary.

SIXTY - $4600
THIRTY - $2650
TWENTY $2175

F. O. B. San Leandro
or Peoria

2-TON - $1675

F. O. B. Peoria

CATERPILLAR TRACTOR CO.

Executive Offices: San Leandro, California, U.S.A.
Sales Offices and Factories:
Peoria, Illinois   San Leandro, California
New York Office: 50 Church Street
Successor to

BEST C. L. Best   The Holt Manufac- HOLT
      Tractor Co.   turing Company

CATERPILLAR

REG. U.S.   PAT. OFF.

TRACTOR

The Model 28 was the last update for the Model 20 PL series. Although not as rare as the Model 25 it replaced, they are still quite rare.

LEFT
The belt pulley used on the Model 25 will also fit the PL series Model 20 and 28.

I believe if the machines had a vastly different design from one to the other this may be true. It is obvious that the 3R Series machines are the rarest, but it is unknown if they demand a higher value.

Like so many other of the early tractors, the R-5 has some history with a government order or specification. It is known that about 175 machines were part of a government order at about serial number 5E3135. These machines were ordered with a foot-operated master clutch with steering brakes engaged with the steering clutch levers. Machines found with these changes are very rare and sought after.

All variations of the R-5 were painted Highway Yellow unless by special order. The tractor in its restored condition is a handsome and welcome addition to any collection.

Model R-6

The most mysterious tractor ever made may be the Model R-6. Little is known about the machine except it was designed as the spark-ignition or gas-powered version of the Model RD-6. Produced in 1941, it is not known if this tractor was issued a serial number. It is not known how many were produced or if they were ever sold commercially. It is possible that the government is behind the origins of this machine.

It has been reported that some of these may have seen some service in the armed forces during World War II. In fact, two R-6 tractors

47

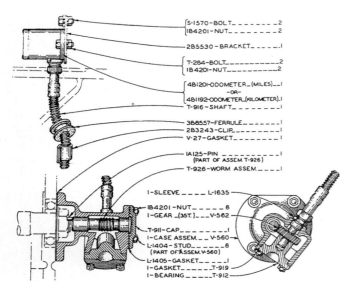

```
S-1570-BOLT_____2
IB4201-NUT_____2
2B5530-BRACKET_____1
T-284-BOLT_____2
IB420I-NUT_____2
4B1201-ODOMETER_(MILES)___1
     -OR-
4BI192-ODOMETER_(KILOMETER)_1
T-916-SHAFT_____1
3B8557-FERRULE_____1
2B3243-CLIP_____1
V-27-GASKET_____1
IA125-PIN_____1
(PART OF ASSEM. T-926)
T-926-WORM ASSEM_____1
```

```
I-SLEEVE_____L-1635
IB4201-NUT_____8
I-GEAR_(3ST.)___V-562
T-911-CAP_____1
I-CASE ASSEM.___V-560
L-1404-STUD_____8
(PART OF ASSEM.V-560)
L-1405-GASKET____1
I-GASKET_____T-919
I-BEARING____T-912
```

The R-3 as well as the R-2 "5E" series have been found equipped with an odometer. This may have been a government specification. *Midland Press Corp.—Caterpillar, Inc., Licensee*

were possibly used in a logging operation on the West Coast some years back but were sold for scrap and apparently destroyed. It is not known if any survive at this time.

Weighing approximately 16,000 pounds, the R-6 was available in 74-inch wide-gauge and 60-inch narrow-gauge. The tractor produced 55 drawbar horsepower and 65 belt horsepower with a 4 1/4x5 1/2-inch engine.

The sheet metal of the R-6 is rounded, similar to the R-2 J Series. It is not known if the R-6 was painted the Highway Yellow of the period or some color from a special branch of the service. The R-6 is the rarest tractor covered in this book, and if one is discovered it should be thoroughly studied and photographed.

Model 50

The Model 50 was introduced in 1931 to take its place in the product line as one of the company's larger tractors, weighing in at 18,080 pounds. When production ended in 1937,

The Model 30 is a smaller version of the Model 60. Originally a Best Tractor Company Design, the Model 30 remained a standard in the product line for many years.

This is a Model 30 S-PS orchard. *Clark and Sons*

1,808 of the tractors had been produced. Serials numbers ran from 5A1 to 5A1808.

The Model 50 was available in standard- or narrow-gauge at 60 inches as well as wide-gauge at 74 inches. It is unknown if any orchard models were produced. All variations of the 50 are somewhat rare. The machines that are found missing parts or other components specific to this tractor are difficult to restore because this machine had many unique parts.

Some of the Model 50 tractors had the 50 designation located on the radiator sides, while others had it located on the top. The model designation has also been found on the radiator top tank. Early Model 50s, or machines made before 5A757, had the gas tank ahead of the operator. Machines made after that time had the fuel tank under the seat. The Model 50 should be painted Highway Yellow with black decals and highlights.

The OHV engine produced 52 horsepower with a 5 1/2x6 1/2-inch bore and stroke. The cylinder heads of this tractor were individual, and the intake and exhaust manifolds were located on opposites sides. This was a unique design at the time of this tractor's debut and makes the task of locating used parts difficult now.

It is also important to know that the 50 was made at the same time as the Diesel 50. In fact, the 50 was made one year later than the Diesel version. By the mid-1930s, several diesel tractors were in production. This may have led to the relatively small amount of model 50 tractors produced.

Model 60

The Caterpillar 60 is one of the most widely known and recognized tractors of all time. Original production began in 1919 by the C. L. Best Company as a rival machine to the Holt 10-Ton. The 60 quickly moved Best to the lead of the large crawler tractor market. In 1925, with the merger of these two companies, the Caterpillar 60 remained the leader in large crawler tractor sales. When production ended in 1931, 13,516 tractors had been produced at the Peoria, Illinois, factory, and 5,431 units were produced at the San Leandro, California, plant.

The 60 was available in 72-inch standard-gauge and as a logging cruiser and snow special model. Weighing in at 20,500 pounds, it was the largest tractor to be produced by the company at that time. The 60 was powered by a 6 1/2x8 1/2-inch four-cylinder engine that produced 65 drawbar horsepower.

The tractor was similar in design to its smaller companion, the Model 30. Often these tractors were equipped with an optional corrugated tin canopy over the entire length of the tractor. All styles of the Caterpillar 60 should be

RIGHT
The Best 30 was only available in a tailseat model. Best also dealt mainly west of the Mississippi River. *Engineers and Contracting Vol. 57, No. 18*

painted Battleship Gray with the red wavy decals that were standard at the time.

The Model 60 has a good survival rate, probably due in part to its large size. Its popularity and appealing design make it quite sought after by collectors. Few extensive changes were made to the 60 over its vast production run.

The Model 60 is a legendary and well-respected tractor in collecting circles as well as a welcomed addition to any collection.

Models 65 and 70

The 65 tractor was introduced in 1932 as a modified version of the Model 60. The tractor was issued the serial number prefix 2D to 2D521. When production ceased in 1933, only 521 units had been produced. By the small

This is a Model 30 PS orchard.

BEST TRACTORS

PARTS AND SERVICE

BEST "SIXTY"

BEST "THIRTY"

BEST "CRUISER" (60)

In formulating the dealer organization to represent BEST Tractors a policy was created that insured service to purchasers—service in tractor stocks, parts and accessories.

This policy has been rigidly enforced with BEST distributors, who must maintain both parts and service departments, and has been strengthened by the addition of warehouses at logical distributing centers. These factory warhouses maintain adequate stocks of parts and tractors that can be drawn upon by distributors in the serving radius of the warehouse, warehouse stocks are continually replenished direct from the factory.

These warehouses also maintain factory service experts who are continually calling upon the service departments of distributors, helping in the constant aim of better service to purchasers.

The best of material and workmanship are built into BEST Tractors; this, combined with a practical knowledge of tractor requirements, insures maximum service of the product itself and the policy of parts service insures to the purchaser a minimum of delay if parts or accessories are required.

C. L. BEST TRACTOR CO.

Factory and General Offices:
SAN LEANDRO, CALIFORNIA

Distributing Warehouses:

ST. LOUIS, MISSOURI   SPOKANE, WASHINGTON

The Model 30 was also available in an orchard or tailseat version. Although the wide gauge 30 is considered the rarest, the orchard model is also quite desirable.

amount produced, you can see that the tractor is rare, and it is sought after by collectors.

The tractor weighed in at just over 24,000 pounds with a 6 1/8x9 1/4-inch bore and stroke. The machine produced 68 drawbar horsepower and 79 belt horsepower. Standard track shoe width was 16 inches with other sizes available. The one gauge it was available in was 72 inches.

As part of the update from the Model 60, the 65 was given a rounder radiator shell to give it a different look. Hood and engine side curtains were installed to complete the update. Some will speculate this radical new look was meant to detract and direct attention over to the new diesel. With the new Highway Yellow paint color, the machine looked very up-to-date and different from the previous models. Others consider these changes unattractive and harmful to the look of the tractor. Some characteristics of the Model 60 remained the same, including the handlebar steering clutch levers and the flywheel starting setup.

Apparently, even with its many updates, the 65 fell victim to the diesel engine, which was coming of age at the same time.

In 1933, the year that the Model 65 was discontinued, the Model 70 was introduced. While the machine was produced for four years, only 266 units were produced. With this machine the company resorted back to the old appearance of the machines and abandoned the new look that was given to the 65.

Like the Model 65, the 70 is also a rare tractor. This machine was a victim of the new diesel engine that was slowly putting an end to the use of the spark-ignition engine in the large crawler tractors. The engine used was a 7x8 1/2-inch bore and stroke four-cycle that still used the flywheel starting system.

The Model 70 weighed in at approximately 31,000 pounds and produced 77 drawbar horsepower with test number 213 at the Nebraska test site. Gauge to track center was 78 inches with a standard 20-inch track shoe, or grouser. It was also painted the now standard Highway Yellow and highlighted in black. The 70 was available in only 78-inch gauge.

Both of these machines are a proud addition to any collection and show the end of gasoline power in the larger crawler tractors.

The 6G series 30 was a more modern version of the old 30. It later became the Model R-4 and eventually was replaced the by diesel RD-4 and D-4.

LINE	SIZE	SERIAL NUMBER IDENTIFICATION	MAXIMUM DRAWBAR HORSE POWER (a)	MAXIMUM BELT HORSE POWER (a)	SHIPPING WEIGHT (Pounds) (d)	SPEED IN M. P. H. AT FULL LOAD GOVERNED ENGINE R. P. M.							
						First	Second	Third	Fourth	Fifth	Sixth	Reverse Low	Reverse High
1	10-Ton	15001, 34001	55.30	60.90	20500	1.67(c)	2.2	3.0	X	X	X	1.25	X
2	5-Ton	19001, 40001	35.60	38.20	9400	1.51(c)	3.0	5.71	X	X	X	1.09	X
3	5-Ton	43001	35.60	38.20	11200	1.75	3.0	4.25	X	X	X	2.0	X
4	2-Ton	25003, 70001	19.40	27.20	5370	2.12	3.0	5.25	X	X	X	2.37	X
5	Diesel Seventy-Five	2E1	83.23	98.01	32600	1.7	2.4	2.8	3.2	3.9	5.3	1.7	2.8
6	Diesel Seventy	3E3	76.00	87.00	30800	1.7	2.3	2.7	3.1	3.7	5.0	1.7	2.7
7	Seventy	8D1	77.07	89.43	31070	1.7	2.3	2.7	3.1	3.7	5.0	1.7	2.7
8	Diesel Sixty-Five	1C1	70.25	83.86	24390	2.1	2.8	4.7	X	X	X	2.3	X
9	Sixty-Five	2D1	73.33	83.66	23010	1.9	2.6	4.4	X	X	X	2.1	X
10	D7 (RD7)	5E7501, 9G1	69.41	82.04	20490	1.6	2.4	3.4	4.7	X	X	1.9	X
11	Sixty	101A, PA1	65.60	77.10	20500	1.9	2.6	3.7	X	X	X	1.4	X
12	R6 (RD6)	5E8501, 2H1	44.75	51.86	15210	1.7	2.5	3.2	4.6	X	X	1.9	X
13	D6	4R1, 5R1	55.00	65.00	16695	1.4	2.3	3.2	4.4	5.8	X	1.8	5.4
14	Diesel Fifty	1E1	56.03	65.60	20250	1.6	2.4	3.4	4.7	X	X	1.9	X
15	Fifty	5A1	51.96	60.75	18080	1.6	2.4	3.4	4.7	X	X	1.9	X
16	D5	9M1	45.00	52.00	11230	1.7	2.4	3.0	3.7	5.4	X	1.9	X
17	R5	5E3001, 4H501, 3R1	54.99	64.28	13840	1.9	2.8	3.6	5.1	X	X	2.1	X
18	Diesel Forty	3G1	44.00	49.00	14700	1.7	2.5	3.2	4.6	X	X	1.9	X
19	Forty	5G1	44.19	51.53	13310	1.7	2.5	3.2	4.6	X	X	1.9	X
20	Diesel Thirty-Five	6E1	40.95	46.15	13900	1.7	2.5	3.2	4.6	X	X	1.9	X
21	Thirty-Five	5C1	38.6	46.08	12480	1.7	2.5	3.2	4.6	X	X	1.9	X
22	Thirty	S5001, PS1	35.6	40.2	9910	1.7	2.6	3.6	X	X	X	2.0	X
23	D4 (RD4)	4G1-2T1, 7J1-5T1	35.68	41.17	10195	1.7	2.4	3.0	3.7	5.4	X	1.9	X
24	R4	6G1	35.33–32.39(a)	40.83–37.97(a)	9390	1.7	2.4	3.0	3.7	5.4	X	1.9	X
25	Twenty-Eight	4F1	30.49–25.00(a)	37.47–31.00(a)	7830	1.8	2.6	3.6	X	X	X	2.0	X
26	Twenty-Five	3C1	28.63	35.18	7707	1.8	2.6	3.6	X	X	X	2.0	X
27	Twenty-Two	2F1, 1J1	25.79–25.15(a)	31.96–31.47(a)	6210	2.0	2.6	3.6	X	X	X	2.1	X
28	R3	5E2501	36.61	43.88	9130	1.8	2.6	3.6	X	X	X	2.0	X
29	R2	5E3501, 6J1, 4J1	25.06–24.66(a)	31.07–30.82(a)	6130	1.7	2.5	3.0	3.6	5.1	X	2.1	X
30	D2	3J1, 5J1	25.86	31.99	6710	1.7	2.5	3.0	3.6	5.1	X	2.1	X
31	Twenty	L1, PL1	28.03	31.16	7740	1.8 (c)	2.6	3.6	X	X	X	2.0	X
32	Twenty (Repl. Fifteen)	8C1	23.69	28.39	5933	2.0	2.6	3.6	X	X	X	2.1	X
33	Fifteen	PV1	22.77	25.94	5790	2.0	2.6	3.6	X	X	X	2.1	X
34	Fifteen (Replaced Ten)	7C1	18.03	21.63	4480	2.0	2.6	3.5	X	X	X	2.1	X
35	High-Clearance Fifteen	1D1	18.03	21.63	5050	2.0	2.6	3.5	X	X	X	2.1	X
36	Ten	PT1	15.15	18.72	4420	2.0	2.6	3.5	X	X	X	2.1	X
37	High-Clearance Ten	PT1	15.15	18.72	5020	2.0	2.6	3.5	X	X	X	2.1	X
38	DW10	1N2001, 6V5001	100	X	15180	2.7	5.0	8.0	12.1	18.1	X	3.3	X

(a) These values are maximum load test data corrected to sea level barometric pressure (29.92" Hg.) and standard temperature of 60° F. as outlined in the A.S.A.E. and S.A.E. test codes. University of Nebraska official tractor test report data have been used where available. Where two figures are given the first one refers to operation on gasoline and the second to operation on tractor fuels.

(b) Not tested at University of Nebraska.
(c) Speeds different than when machine was tested.
(d) Standard or narrow gauge.

NOTE: (.......X....... signifies information not available because of machine design.

YPE TRACTORS

MAXIMUM DRAWBAR PULL POUNDS AT RATED ENGINE SPEED (e)						NEBRASKA TEST NO.	GAUGES (f)	ENGINE			LINE
First	Second	Third	Fourth	Fifth	Sixth			Type	No. Cylinders @ Bore x Stroke	R. P. M. Governed at Full Load	
9756	9426	6912	X	X	X	61	60½"	V. I. H.	4@6½"x7"	750	1
5558	3773	2340	X	X	X	59	48¾"	V. I. H.	4@4¾"x6"	1050	2
6620	3773	3141	X	X	X	(b)	45"	V. I. H.	4@4¾"x6"	1000	3
3275	2397	1325	X	X	X	86	52"–38"	V. I. H.	4@4 "x5½"	1000	4
18697	13334	10985	9311	7346	5196	218	78"	V. I. H.	6@5¼"x8"	850 (g)	5
17200	12400	10410	8690	6975	4630	(b)	78"	V. I. H.	4@6⅛"x9¼"	820	6
16796	11790	9528	8228	6453	4403	213	78"	V. I. H.	4@7 "x8½"	700	7
11991	8817	4449	X	X	X	208	72"	V. I. H.	4@6⅛"x9¼"	700	8
13597	9906	4950	X	X	X	209	72"	V. I. H.	4@7 "x8½"	650	9
16098	10236	6792	4564	X	X	254 (h)	74"–60"	V. I. H.	4@5¾"x8"	850	10
12360	9155	6240	X	X	X	105	72"	V. I. H.	4@6½"x8½"	650	11
10753	7238	5230	3261	X	X	243	74"–56"	V. I. H.	3@5¼"x8"	850	12
15850	10100	6880	4440	2950	X	(b)	74"–60"	V. I. H.	6@4¼"x5½"	1400	13
12765	7751	5145	3305	X	X	214	74"–60"	V. I. H.	4@5¼"x8"	850	14
12061	7457	4996	3337	X	X	204	74"–60"	V. I. H.	4@5½"x6½"	850	15
11300	7900	6400	4900	3200	X	(b)	60"–44"	V. I. H.	6@4¼"x5½"	1400	16
10384	6778	5049	3288	X	X	224	74"–56"	V. I. H.	4@5½"x6½"	950	17
9692	6524	4714	2939	X	X	243	74"–56"	V. I. H.	3@5¼"x8"	850	18
9496	6321	4613	3086	X	X	244	74"–56"	V. I. H.	4@5⅛"x6½"	850	19
9135	5966	4303	2716	X	X	217	74"–56"	V. I. H.	3@5¼"x8"	850	20
8169	5542	4005	2574	X	X	206	74"–56"	V. I. H.	4@4⅞"x6½"	850	21
7563	4823	3343	X	X	X	104	60¾"–43¾"	V. I. H.	4@4¾"x6½"	850	22
8637	6392	4955	3818	2453	X	273	60"–44"	V. I. H.	4@4¼"x5½"	1400	23
7211–6120(a)	5186–4264(a)	4105–3642(a)	3147–2536(a)	2045–1680(a)	X	272–271	60"–44"	V. I. H.	4@4¼"x5½"	1400	24
810–5880(a)	4578–3750(a)	3100–2550(a)	X	X	X	(b)	55"–42"	V. I. H.	4@4 3/16"x5½"	1100	25
6011	4068	2746	X	X	X	203	55"–42"	V. I. H.	4@4 "x5½"	1100	26
4900–4534(a)	3705–3294(a)	2448–2214(a)	X	X	X	228–226(a)	50"–40"	V. I. H.	4@4 "x5"	1250	27
7927	5459	3712	X	X	X	227	55"	V. I. H.	4@4½x5½"	1100	28
6150–5150(a)	4380–4270(a)	3570–3330(a)	2970–2760(a)	1860–1740(a)	X	320–321	50"–40"	V. I. H.	4@3¾"x5"	1525	29
6680	4420	3570	2890	1840	X	322	50"–40"	V. I. H.	4@3¾"x5"	1525	30
6259	4208	2851	X	X	X	150	55"–42"	V. I. H.	4@4 "x5½"	1100	31
4572	3486	2375	X	X	X	205	50"–40"	L-Head	4@3¾"x5"	1250	32
4166	3175	2039	X	X	X	159	50"–40"	L-Head	4@3¾"x5"	1250	33
3315	2657	1818	X	X	X	207	44"–37"	L-Head	4@3⅜"x4"	1500	34
3315	2657	1818	X	X	X	(b)	44"	L-Head	4@3⅜"x4"	1500	35
2816	2087	1455	X	X	X	160	44"–37"	L-Head	4@3⅜"x4"	1500	36
2947	2197	1521	X	X	X	(b)	44"	L-Head	4@3⅜"x4"	1500	37
12000	6390	4040	2660	1780	X	X	X	V. I. H.	6@4¼"x5½"	1800	38

Observed drawbar pull as reported in Nebraska Tractor Tests except where later tractors had different gear ratios with same engine as the machine tested, or where tractors were not tested. In these cases the maximum drawbar pounds pull is based on maximum drawbar horsepower.

(f) Center to center of tracks—the figure or figures are the gauge or gauges in which the tractor was available.
(g) Speed changed since tested at Nebraska.
(h) See also Tests Nos. 253 and 255.

The Model 35-40 and R-5 tractor are all very similar. The Model 35 pictured was available in narrow gauge at 53 inches and wide gauge at 74 inches.

The Caterpillar Model 35.

The Model 60 is the most popular of all the early gas crawlers. Most collectors do not consider a collection complete without the 60 in it.

The 60 was also originally produced by the Best Tractor Company. It was held over during the merger and became a very popular machine. Many Model 60 tractors were equipped with the corrugated canopy top.

The radiator side badge on the front of the muscular Model 60.

A Model 60 pulls a scraper.

This Model 60 is a cruiser model and is equipped with ice tracks.

The Model 65 was introduced with a newly designed rounded radiator shell. Only 521 of the units were produced and they are considered rare.

Begun With One BEST
—Ended With Ten!

Through swampy mud and muck—through gulleys and deep fissures, this BEST TRACTOR and nine more like it pulled plows, scrapers and levelers—doing the hardest kind of a job a tractor can be called upon to do. Here a fleet of ten BESTS worked a miracle of reclamation— and made a profit for the owners every day.

Five Years Work in One

In undertaking the gigantic task of reclaiming Bay Farm Island, the owners tackled a five year job, but BEST TRACTORS finished it in less than fourteen months! The first BEST was purchased as an experiment, only to be followed by two and later by seven more. The fleet of ten BESTS was from that time on in continuous operation until the job was done. A circular describing in greater detail this work of reclamation will be sent on request.

BESTS are moving dirt for contractors everywhere. They are helping counties and individuals construct good roads. They are skidding logs in the woods, hauling sugar cane in Cuba; helping the world do its work easier and cheaper.

Write for the name of nearest distributor.

C. L. BEST TRACTOR CO.
Factory and General Office
SAN LEANDRO, CALIFORNIA

Distributing Warehouses
SPOKANE, WASH.
ST. LOUIS, MO.

Best "Sixty"

Best "Thirty"

Best "Cruiser" (60)

BEST TRACTORS

Advertisement for Best Model 60 tractor published in April of 1922. *Engineers and Contracting*

A Model 65 sits in a line of restored tractors, with a logging arch.

The last of the big spark ignition tractors was the Model 70. Production ended with only 266 units being produced, making it a very rare tractor.

CHAPTER TWO

PURCHASING AN ANTIQUE CATERPILLAR TRACTOR

If you are buying a tractor for the first time, it is best to purchase a tractor that is somewhat common and small. The Model 22, which is the most common of the small tractors, is easy to store and it is quite easy to find parts for it. Tractors of this model can be found in good condition in most areas of the country without spending a large amount of money.

You first must decide from whom you are going to purchase the tractor. If you are in an area with many old tractors around, it is more interesting and fun to hunt for the tractor and purchase the tractor from the original owner or a pri-

The Model 22 is a good choice for a new collector. Due to the large amount that were made, they can be bought reasonably and parts are easy to find.

The Model 30 is also a popular tractor for many collectors. In many ways, it is simply a down-sized Model 60.

vate party. These people can often tell you of other tractors in the area that may be for sale, and they are generally happy to see that someone will restore the tractor that they have used for many years. Many times they are eager to share the interesting history that goes with the tractor.

If you are in an area where there are salvage yards, it is worth your time to hunt around and ask if any tractors were sold for scrap when iron prices were high. Many collectors have found rare and desirable tractors in salvage yards that eventually would have been cut up. These machines are usually in poor condition and become parts machines. However, you may just find that part you need for your tractor. Some dealers will trade you the tractor for an even amount of junk that most likely you would have to get rid of anyway. Also, some individuals will ask scrap price for an old tractor

they have sitting around. This is a good way to bargain for a tractor if the owner doesn't know the value or can't decide on a price. Keep in mind the current price of scrap iron when negotiating the price. It is possible you may pay more for the tractor than it is worth.

Another source for purchasing antique tractors is from other collectors. Most collectors can accurately describe the condition of the tractor and are often willing to trade for machines they do not have. Some collectors who live in areas with large amounts of tractors may be able to find the machine you are looking for and in the right price range. Buying a tractor from a fellow collector is also beneficial in that the collector knows the current values of the machines and would not have purchased them at a high price. They also can be a good source for used parts and information on machines they may not want or need.

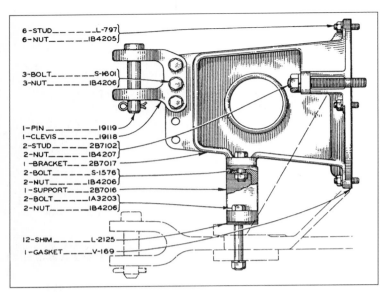

6 -STUD	L-797
6 -NUT	IB4205
3 -BOLT	S-I60I
3 -NUT	IB4206
I -PIN	I9II9
I -CLEVIS	I9II8
2 -STUD	2B7I02
2 -NUT	IB4207
I -BRACKET	2B7017
2 -BOLT	S-1576
2 -NUT	IB4206
I -SUPPORT	2B7016
2 -BOLT	IA3203
2 -NUT	IB4206
12 -SHIM	L-2125
I -GASKET	V-169

Options such as an adjustable height drawbar add value and character to a restored tractor. *Midland Press Corp.—Caterpillar, Inc., Licensee*

A final source is tractor hunters or brokers. These are usually people who deal only in buying and selling the machines and not collecting or restoring them. It is possible to give the person a list of the tractors you are looking for at prices you are willing to pay and have them find the machine for you. Generally, they do not know the in-depth details of many of these machines but will send photos and a brief description of what they have found. I have had good luck in using these services and recommend them to a collector looking for a specific machine or accessory.

Crawler Evaluation

After you have found the tractor that you want to buy, you have to assess its condition. The first step is to find out if the tractor's engine is loose or if it is frozen. If the exhaust or spark plug holes have been left open and the engine is stuck, you can plan on extensive internal engine work. If the exhaust and any openings to the engine have been covered and the engine is still stuck, you may be able to loosen up the engine with transmission or diesel fluid. You still may have to remove the cylinder head and use other means to free the engine. Depending on rarity of the tractor, this condition alone may separate a salvageable machine from one that is not.

The high-clearance 10 is a rare and desirable tractor. Many new collectors have been lucky enough to find a rare tractor early in the hobby.

The 7C series or small 15 is very desirable and a welcome addition to any collection.

If the engine is loose upon initial inspection, you have a far better chance of saving the tractor than if it is stuck. While you still may have extensive engine work ahead of you; the engine was probably not exposed to the harsh elements. By shining a small flashlight down into the spark plug holes, you may be able to tell the condition of the cylinders. If the engine is a side or overhead valve, you can remove the valve cover to see if the valves are stuck. If they move, your next step should be a compression test with a gauge or at least by holding your thumb over the spark plug hole while someone turns the engine over. This will help you in determining if the piston rings or valves are in poor condition.

If you are purchasing the tractor in a cold-weather climate, you may want to check for

The "J" series Model R-2 is not as rare as the "5E" series. New collectors should try to educate themselves to the differences in machines with the same model number.

Both the gas and diesel Model 35s are considered desirable by collectors. Interest in the larger tractors is starting to grow.

evidence of a cracked block. Other than an internal inspection of the engine, there is no definite way to tell if there is a crack, but an easy test is to pull the dipstick out of the crankcase and see if

the oil is gray or milky. Water in the oil will give it the gray appearance. You can also check the bottom radiator tank and see if the drain plug has been removed. If the plug is gone, chances are the engine has been drained. You can also remove the drain plug on the oil pan, and if water comes out before the oil in a moderate quantity, chances are there is a crack in the block. It doesn't take much water to make the oil look bad. Condensation in the oil pan may give you this gray or milky appearance.

Once you have determined the condition of the engine, you should direct your attention to the undercarriage. Not only can you tell much about the amount of use the tractor had, but you may be able to get an indication on how the tractor was maintained. On the crawler tractor, the undercarriage is the part of the machine that is made to wear out and be replaced. If the undercarriage is in poor condition, chances are the rest of the machine was maintained the same way. It is feasible that the tractor was retired when the undercarriage became inadequate. Usually, a responsible owner would not let these components wear out.

The condition of the undercarriage is determined by a percentage, with 100 percent being a tractor showing no wear. The scale goes down usually to 50 percent, with any number below that being unserviceable. It is best to have an undercarriage in the 80 percent and above range.

The main components of the undercarriage are the rails, pins, bushings, sprockets, idler wheels, grousers, and rollers. Many of these components are interchangeable, so you may decide to use the better parts on a rarer machine. The undercarriage is a costly area to replace, so keep this in mind when negotiating the price.

The final area of inspection is the overall completeness of the machine. Many Caterpillar models have specific parts to that machine, the cast-iron weights on the track frames on the R-3 and R-2 5E Series, for example. These parts are difficult to find because of their large size and few of these tractors were made. The value of the machine drops considerably when these distinguishing parts are missing. It is common for the large air cleaner on the 2-Ton to be missing, and these are nearly impossible to find. Therefore, a 2-Ton with a complete air cleaner assembly will demand a much higher price.

Other frequently damaged or missing items are the fenders and sheet metal of most of the tractors. There are many pieces to the sheet metal package of a tractor. The upper dirt guards

The Model 28 is a moderately rare tractor. A collector who finds one with original factory lighting equipment has found a good tractor with a rare option.

The Model 70 is a very rare tractor. Although this tractor is missing a few parts, it is very restorable.

over the roller frames and the lower engine shields and side curtains are the most commonly missing items. These pieces are difficult to find in usable condition on parts tractors and are costly to reproduce. This is the part of the tractor you will be most dissatisfied with after your restoration if you do not take the time to properly prepare it before your final paint job. Again, keep in mind the cost involved in replacing or repairing these key pieces when arriving at a price.

Pricing and Other Notes

Here are a few things to keep in mind when negotiating the purchase of a machine. When buying the machine from a private party,

Although the Model 22 is very common, a unique variation such as the side seat model is very rare and desirable.

If the owner of the tractor you find followed this advice from a company service magazine, you may find a restorable tractor. *Midland Press Corp.—Caterpillar, Inc., Licensee*

try to find out how long they have owned the machine. Also find out if they got their use out of it. This lets you know what has been done with the tractor and clues you in on how it was taken care of. If the seller feels he or she has done enough work with it, you can usually arrive at a much lower purchase price. If the seller asks you to make an offer, do not insult him or her by trying to "steal" the tractor. I prefer to let the seller name the price and negotiate from there. If you know the value of the machine and you sincerely want the tractor for your collection, make an offer the seller won't refuse. It is possible that no matter what you do, you will not be able to buy the machine. In this case, record the name of the owner and machine and occasionally follow up on it so the seller knows you are serious about it.

If you are purchasing tractors from fellow collectors or tractor hunters, they usually have a pretty good idea of the value of the

The 8C or small 20 is a rare tractor. It is much more desirable when found with the original side curtains and track shields.

machine. Most of the time the prices are near what they are worth and you may not get any great deal. But if you are looking to fill a void in your collection and want a tractor that has been inspected by a fellow collector, this is your best bet. You may be able to work out a trade with a tractor that you have more than one of.

Prices are regional. In areas where there are few collectors and the hobby is relatively unknown, the tractors generally have a lower value. This is especially true in an area where there are more tractors than collectors. The opposite is also true; when there are more collectors than machines, tractors demand a higher price. Overall the tractor is worth whatever you are willing to pay for it. As the hobby grows and the tractors become less and less available, the values will continue to climb and later models will become more sought after.

Many collectors shy away from the larger tractors due to the difficulty in hauling and storing them. Some of the larger models are quite collectible, such as this Model 50.

CHAPTER THREE

ENGINES AND SPECIFICATIONS

At a time when most tractor producers were using engines made by other manufacturers, Caterpillar was designing its own engines. This trait has been the mark of this company for over half a century. Today, Caterpillar, Inc., is a leader in diesel engine manufacturing and design.

All of the early gas tractors were powered with four-cylinder, four-cycle engines. These engines, like the machines they were installed in, became the object of continued change and modification. Many engines were redesigned after testing due to the horsepower they produced. These design changes and classifications can be confusing when first encountered but are easily understood with some research.

Models 10 and 15 7C Series

These two machines use the same engine. Internally, the engine is a four-cylinder 3 3/8x4-inch, side-valve, L-head. It used in the high-clearance Model 10 and the high-clearance 15 1D Series. While this engine is identical from one machine to the other, it was listed as producing less horsepower in the Model 10 than in the 15. The only explanation for this discrepancy is a reclassification under test. The Model 10 was listed as producing 15 horsepower and the 15 that replaced it as having 18 horsepower. The only visible difference between the engines was on the exterior.

The carburetor on the 15 7C was moved to an elbow about 5 inches lower than on the

The valve mechanism of the side valve engines is accessed by removing the small valve covers. The valve clearance is .008-inch when hot. *Midland Press Corp.—Caterpillar, Inc., Licensee*

Model 10. Also, a flat boss measuring approximately 1 1/2x3 inches was now cast into the left side of the block above the carburetor on the new 15. This flat plate was now the location of the serial number tag. In all other respects, the engines are mechanically the same.

If the tractor is unrestored, you will want to remove the cylinder head and valve covers to assess the condition of the valves and cylinders. If the valves and valve seats are in poor condition, you will want to remove the valves.

To remove the valves, first place rags below the valve rack of the cylinder you are working on to prevent the retainers from falling through to the oil pan. Use a valve spring compressor and remove the locks from the base of the spring around the valve stem. Once you remove the valves from the engine, place them in order on a valve stick or sheet of paper. This will keep the valves in order when being ground. Now check the condition of the valve seats. If the seats are in poor condition and you are not removing the block from the tractor, you will have to bring a portable seat grinder to your location. I generally try to do a three-angle valve job on the outer edge of the seat, on the seat itself, and off the edge of the guides. You will have to take the valves to an appropriate

The Model 10 exhaust manifold passed around the side of the gas tank causing vapor locking. When the 10 was discontinued, the problem was remedied with its replacement, the 7C 15.

facility to be ground. You can check the condition of the valve guides when you insert the pilot into them when you grind the seats. Try to insert a .001-inch or .002-inch pilot into the guide to determine the extent of the wear. If the valves or guides need to be replaced, try to match up a current production component

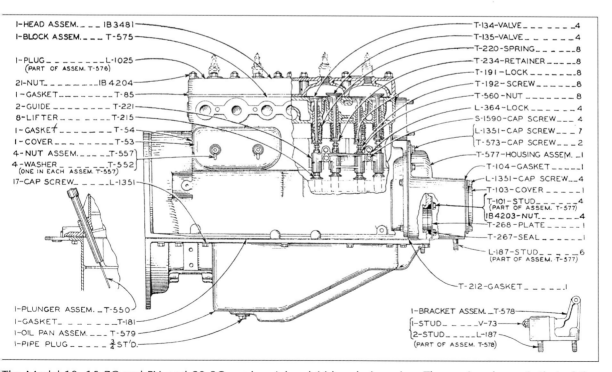

The Model 10, 15 7C and PV, and 20 8C used an L-head (side-valve) engine. The engine shown is that of the 10. *Midland Press Corp.—Caterpillar, Inc., Form P-1190*

This photo shows the locations of the serial number tags on a Model 10. *Clark and Sons*

through the engine part specification guides that some auto parts stores use. I have had good luck using the *Perfect Circle* specification book. You may have to do some minor machining, but the end result is worth it.

After you have the valve components in good condition you can replace them in the block. Again, place a clean rag below the valve rack to keep the retainers from falling into the oil pan when you install them. To adjust the valves use a blade-type feeler gauge to set them at .010 inch when cold and in their closed position. You should adjust the valve clearance to .008 inch when the engine is at operating temperature.

If you have decided to completely rebuild the engine, do not reinstall the valves. You will want to remove the oil pan next. You can do this by either removing the entire engine from the tractor or by jacking the front of the tractor up and first removing the equalizer spring. You now can remove the oil pan to inspect the crankshaft and bearings.

If you decide to remove the connecting rods and pistons, take them out in one piece.

Remove the oil sump and pipe and then remove the bearing caps. When doing so make note of the marks on the rods and caps so they are reassembled in the same fashion. Remove the rod and piston out from the top.

To adjust the main and rod bearings, remove the cap if more than .012 inch of play is found. Remove an equal amount of shims from each side and replace the cap. You should have .003 inch of movement to be adequate. To assure the proper fit of the babbitted bearings, coat the shaft journals with Prussian blue dye and replace the bearing cap. Turn the crankshaft and then remove the cap and scrape any high spots down. Repeat this until the fit is uniform. Take extra care when scraping the main bearings because the proper fit of these is crucial.

Reassemble the engine with new gaskets obtained from whatever supplier you choose. I use 30-weight non-detergent oil in my tractors. Torque specifications are standard for the stud size you are using.

Models 15 PV Series and 20 8C Series

The engines used on these tractors follow the same lines as the style used on the Models 10 and 15 7C Series but on a larger scale. The four-cylinder, side-valve engine of the Model 15 produced 22 horsepower at 1250 rpm. When the 8C 20 replaced Model 15, the 3 3/4x5-inch engine remained the same internally. Externally, the carburetor was lowered on the elbow and the flat boss was placed on the left side of the block for the serial number to appear.

When the 20 8C was marketed, it was advertised as having 23 horsepower. This is 1 horsepower more than the old Model 15, which used the same engine. It is possible the increase in horsepower was from a new test classification or fuel type.

All of the adjustment specifications and repair procedures are the same as for the Model 10 listed previously. The engines are identical in principle and theory but differ in bore and stroke and dimensions.

Model 22 and R-2 5E Series

Model 22 is the most common of the early small gas tractors. The tractor it has the most in common with, the R-2 5E Series, however, is one of the rarest. A great deal of credit for the success of the Model 22 must be given to the engine it was equipped with.

The engine was a four-cylinder, valve-in-head, producing 25 horsepower at 1250rpm. The

The 7C 15 had the relocated gas tank but used the same engine as the Model 10. The exhaust passed through a hole in the hood.

cylinder head and valve cover can be removed independently. The cylinder jugs are also removable and are cast with two cylinders per casting.

To adjust the valves, get the tractor to operating temperature. Remove the valve cover and loosen the adjusting screws. You can now adjust the intake valves to a clearance of .005 inch and the exhaust valves to .015 inch. The adjusting procedure is to be performed with the valves in the closed position.

While there is no service reference book available for Model 22, one can assume the bottom end repair and adjustment procedures are relatively the same as those for Model 15 or 10.

Models 20, 25, 28, and R-3

These tractors all use an engine that is similar in design to the old style Model 30. The 20 and 25 tractors used a valve-in-head, 4x5 1/2-inch four-cycle engine. These tractors produced 28 horsepower at the drawbar with a maximum 1100rpm. The Model 28 replaced the 25 in 1933, at which time the engine was increased to 4 3/16x5 inches and produced 30 drawbar horsepower. The Model R-3, which is similar to the Model 28, had its bore increased

Machines such as the Model 30 and 35 have removable cylinder jugs and large inspection covers to access the crankshaft.

73

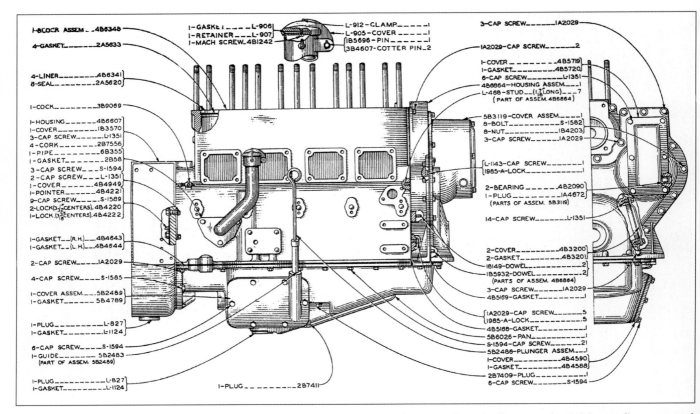

1-BLOCK ASSEM _ 4B6348
4-GASKET _____ 2A5633

4-LINER _____ 4B6341
8-SEAL _____ 2A5620

I-COCK _____ 3B9069
I-HOUSING _____ 4B6607
I-COVER _____ IB3570
3-CAP SCREW _____ L-1351
4-CORK _____ 2B7556
I-PIPE _____ 6B355
I-GASKET _____ 2B58
3-CAP SCREW _____ S-1594
2-CAP SCREW _____ L-1351
I-COVER _____ 4B4949
I-POINTER _____ 4B4221
9-CAP SCREW _____ S-1589
2-LOCK(3½CENTERS) 4B4220
I-LOCK(3½CENTERS) 4B4222

I-GASKET __(R.H.) 4B4643
I-GASKET __(L.H.) 4B4644

2-CAP SCREW _____ IA2029

4-CAP SCREW _____ S-1585

I-COVER ASSEM _____ 5B2489
I-GASKET _____ 5B4789

I-PLUG _____ L-827
I-GASKET _____ L-1124

6-CAP SCREW _____ S-1594
I-GUIDE _____ 5B2483
(PART OF ASSEM. 5B2489)

I-PLUG _____ L-827
I-GASKET _____ L-1124

I-GASKET _____ L-906
I-RETAINER _____ L-907
I-MACH SCREW 4B1242

L-912-CLAMP _____
L-905-COVER _____
IB5696-PIN _____
3B4607-COTTER PIN-2

3-CAP SCREW _____ IA2029
IA2029-CAP SCREW _____ 2
I-COVER _____ 4B5719
I-GASKET _____ 4B5720
6-CAP SCREW _____ L-1351
4B6864-HOUSING ASSEM _____ I
L-468-STUD__(1⅞LONG)___7
(PART OF ASSEM.4B6864)

5B3119-COVER ASSEM _____ I
8-BOLT _____ S-1582
8-NUT _____ IB4203
3-CAP SCREW _____ IA2029

L-1143-CAP SCREW _____ I
1985-A-LOCK _____ I

2-BEARING _____ 4B2090
I-PLUG _____ IA4672
(PARTS OF ASSEM. 5B3119)

14-CAP SCREW _____ L-1351

2-COVER _____ 4B3200
2-GASKET _____ 4B3201
IB149-DOWEL _____ 2
IB5932-DOWEL _____ 2
(PARTS OF ASSEM. 4B6864)
3-CAP SCREW _____ IA2029
4B5169-GASKET _____ I

IA2029-CAP SCREW _____ 5
1985-A-LOCK _____ 5
4B5168-GASKET _____ I
5B6026-PAN _____ I
S-1594-CAP SCREW _____ 2
5B2486-PLUNGER ASSEM _____ I
I-COVER _____ 4B4590
I-GASKET _____ 4B4588
2B7409-PLUG _____ I
6-CAP SCREW _____ S-1594

I-PLUG _____ 2B7411

The block of the Model R-2 "J series" is identical to that of the D-2 "J series," except the R-2 is gasoline powered rather than diesel. *Midland Press Corp.—Caterpillar, Inc., Form P-1190*

to 4 1/2 inches, while the stroke remained at 5 1/2 inches. A similar engine was used in the Auto Patrol No. 11 in the 9D, 7D, and 1F Series. This engine differed from the type used in the other models because its exhaust outlet was at the number one cylinder.

To adjust the valves on these tractors, first get the tractor up to operating temperature. Remove the valve cover and, using a blade-type feeler gauge, adjust the exhaust valves to .015 inch and the intake valves to .005 inch. If the valves are in poor condition, use a spring compressor to depress the spring and remove the retaining lock. The valve can now be removed from the head. Keep the valves in order, and take them to an appropriate facility to be ground. You can check the wear of the valve guides by inserting a pilot the size of the valve stem into the valve guide and moving it from side to side. Increase the size of the pilot by .001 inch until you find one that fits snugly. You may have to install new valve guides in the head. This can also be done at the machine shop you use to grind or replace the valve seats.

It is possible to remove the cylinders independently from the crankcase. First, you must remove the cylinder head and the water manifold that connects the cylinders. The cylinders then can be removed individually by lifting them off. If you have decided to remove the connecting rods and pistons, continue by removing the lower inspection covers. Remove the rod bearing cap, turn the crank shaft out of the way, and pull the piston down through and out the piston hole.

If you have replaced the bearings of the connecting rods or mains, you will need to fit them properly. Remove an equal number of shims from each side of the cap and tighten the cap back to the connecting rod. You should have approximately .003 inch of clearance and no more than .012 inch. Some of the shims are .003 of an inch thick, so you can make your adjustments very slight. It is also good to paint the journals of the crankshaft with Prussian blue dye, and after replacing the cap, slightly turn the crankshaft. Remove the bearing cap and scrape the babbitt from the high spots and then refit.

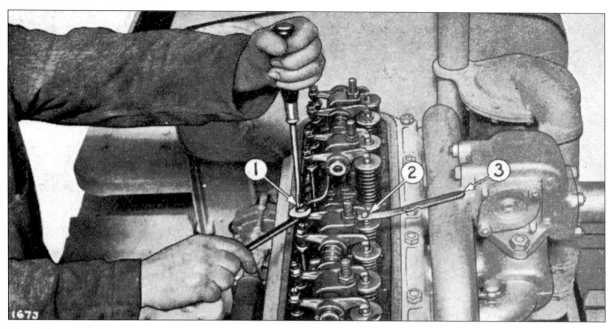

The valvetrain of overhead-valve engines can be accessed through the top valve cover. This is common to machines such as the Model 20 PL series, 25, and 28. *Midland Press Corp.—Caterpillar, Inc., Licensee*

As you reassemble the engine, use new gaskets that are available from one of the reproduction vendors.

Models 30 6G Series and R-4

Models 30 of the 6G Series and R-4 are the same except for their designation. The engine that is used has little in common with the old style Model 30, which shares the same name. The valve-in-head, 4 1/4x5 1/2-inch engine produces 35 drawbar horsepower at 1400rpm. This engine had many modern advancements similar to the updated engine of the Model 22.

Valve adjustment should be completed when the engine is at a burning temperature. Remove the valve cover and use a blade-type feeler gauge to adjust both the exhaust and intake valve to .012 inch. Do this with the valve closed and by loosening the adjusting screw on the rocker. After the correct clearance is obtained, tighten the adjusting screw and recheck the gap.

Unlike many models made prior to this time, the R-4 was equipped with an oil filter. The filter was meant to be removed and discarded at the time of the oil change. It is unclear if these filters are still available, but perhaps there is a modern filter that is similar.

Models 35, 40, and R-5

The above three tractors have much in common with each other with the design of their engines. While the bore and stroke of each was different, thus the horsepower each produced was different, many of the technical procedures remained the same. Model 35 produced 38 drawbar horsepower with a 4 7/8x6 1/2-inch at 850rpm. The 40 produced 44 drawbar horsepower using an engine with a 5 1/8x6 1/2-inch bore and stroke with the same rpms. The final model, the R-5, produced 55 horsepower with a 5 1/2x6 1/2-inch engine at 950rpm.

To adjust the valves, run the machine until it is at operating temperature. Remove the valve cover and with the valve in its closed position, loosen the adjusting screw on the rocker arm and adjust it to the proper clearance. Adjust both the intake and exhaust valves to a clearance of .015 inch. After the adjustment has been made, tighten the lock nut on the adjusting screw and recheck the adjustment.

If the valves are in poor condition and need to be removed, remove the valve cover and cylinder heads. By using a spring compressor, you can compress the valve springs and remove the locks, then the valves will come out. At this point, you can also check the position of the valve seat to determine whether or not it needs to be replaced. Many of the auto parts stores offer machine shop

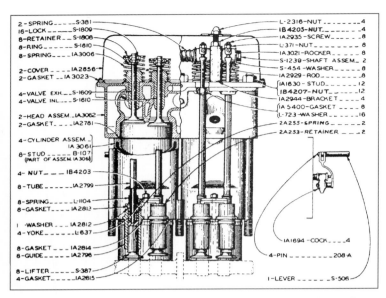

2 - SPRING ____ S-381	L-2316-NUT _____4
16-LOCK ____ S-1809	1B4205-NUT _____4
8-RETAINER _ S-1808	1A2935-SCREW____8
8-RING _____ S-1810	L-371-NUT _____8
8-SPRING ____ 1A3006	1A3021-ROCKER _____8
	S-1239-SHAFT ASSEM._ 2
2-COVER ____ 1A2856	S-454-WASHER ____8
2-GASKET __ 1A 3023	1A2929-ROD _____8
	1A1630-STUD____12
4-VALVE EXH._ S-1609	1B4207-NUT____12
4-VALVE INL._ S-1610	1A2944-BRACKET __ 4
	1A 5400-GASKET __ 8
2-HEAD ASSEM._1A3062	L-723-WASHER ____16
2-GASKET ____1A2781	2A2255-SPRING _____2
	2A253-RETAINER __ 2
4-CYLINDER ASSEM.	
1A 3061	
8-STUD _____ B-107	
(PART OF ASSEM 1A3061)	
4- NUT____ 1B4203	
8-TUBE _____ 1A2799	
8-SPRING ____ L-1104	
8-GASKET ____ 1A2813	
1 -WASHER ___ 1A2812	
4-YOKE _____ L-637	
8-GASKET ___ 1A2814	1A1694 -COCK____4
8-GUIDE ____ 1A2798	4-PIN _____208-A
8-LIFTER ____ S-387	
4-GASKET ____1A2815	1-LEVER _____ S-506

The valve mechanism of the PS series 30 is basically an individual unit for each head. This is common to the split-head Model 30 tractors and Model 35. *Midland Press Corp.—Caterpillar, Inc., Licensee*

services and are able to find replacement valves using the dimensions from the originals. It is possible that the valves located may be too long or use a different retainer lock combination, but often a machinist can correct these problems.

If the engine is in poor condition internally, you may decide to remove the pistons and connecting rods. For number one and two cylinders, first remove the crankcase inspection covers from the left side of the engine. You will also need to remove the fuel pump and cover from the front right side. You will then have access to the connecting rods caps. Remove the nuts from the bearing caps, and remove the cap and connecting rod from the crankshaft. Lower the connecting rod to the bottom of the crankcase, and turn the piston so the pin is facing crossways. Drive out the piston pin retaining pins with a small punch, and push out the piston pin.

To remove the piston and connecting rod assemblies from the number three and four cylinders, you may choose to remove the scavenge pump and tube from the crankcase. On these cylinders, the piston and connecting rod do not need to be disassembled, and it is possible to get a socket on the nuts of the connecting rod if the oil pump scavenge pieces are removed.

In installing piston rings, minimum gap should be no less than .007 inch. The ring diameter for oversized bores should be no less than .010 inch under the bore size or over .010 inch. If the rings are .010 inch over the bore size, they should be filled to a minimum of .007 inch.

To test the adjustment of the main and connecting rod bearing, lift up on the crankshaft. The bearings should have no less than .003 inch of clearance nor more than .012 inch. The bearings can be adjusted by removing an equal amount of shims from each side of the bearing cap. Replace the cap onto the bearing and check for uniform clearance on the crankshaft before going on to the next bearing.

Use appropriate lubrication in assembling the new parts and new gaskets obtained from one of the reproduction gasket vendors.

Model 50

The Model 50 tractor was equipped with a 5 1/2x6 1/2-inch engine that produced 52 horsepower at 850rpm. This tractor used a crossflow engine that allowed each cylinder and head to be removed independently. A valve rocker box was used to house the rocker arm shaft and valve sleeves. This box was attached to the top of the cylinder heads.

To remove the rocker box, remove the hood and disconnect the oil line leading to that box. The box can then be removed by loosening the nuts and, if needed, disassembled. To remove the cylinder heads, remove the water and intake manifolds. The head can then be removed by pulling straight up off the studs. If you have decided to remove the valves from the head, you must first remove the hairpin locks from the valve stems from the retainers. Use a valve spring compressor to depress the springs and remove the retainers. You can then lift the springs off and pull the valves out of the head. If you decide to have new valve guides placed into the head or have the seats ground or replaced, you can get good service from most machine shops. Often an aftermarket valve or seat with similar dimensions can be made to work. Check the condition of the valve guides by moving the valves side to side and checking for wear. If any wear is found, the guide should be replaced. You can also use a valve with a larger diameter stem if the guides are not available.

To remove the connecting rods and pistons from cylinders one and two, remove the lower engine inspection covers. Next, remove the nuts that hold the cap to the bearing. Remove the cap and lift the rod off the crankshaft. Slide the connecting rod to the bottom of

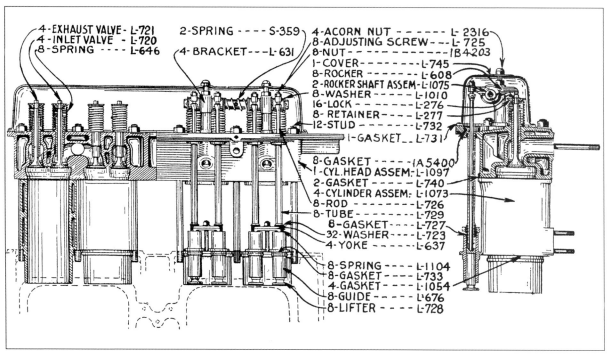

The Model 20 PL series also used a system with a single cylinder head over all four cylinders. *Midland Press Corp.— Caterpillar, Inc., Licensee*

the crankcase and turn it so you have access to the piston pin. Remove the retaining plugs and pull the piston pin out. After disassembly, remove the two pieces from the inspection hole. The piston and rod from cylinders three and four can be removed without disassembly because they can be lowered into the deeper portion of the pan.

You can check the wear of the main and rod bearings by prying slightly upward with a bar. Bearing play should be no less than .003 inch nor more than .012 inch. Remove the bearing caps and adjust by subtracting an equal number of shims from each side of the bear cap. Place the cap back on the bearing and check for uniform fit and clearance with the gap gauge. Reassemble the engine with the proper lubricants and gaskets.

Model 60, 65, and 70

For many years the Model 60 tractor was the largest in the production line. After several years, Models 65 and 70 were introduced to replace the 60 as the large tractor of the product line. Unlike the 60, these two models were short-lived because of increased use of diesel engines and large track-type tractors.

The Model 60 produced 65 horsepower with a 6 1/2xby 8 1/2-inch engine at 650rpm.

The model 65 that replaced it produced 73 horsepower with a 7x8 1/2-inch engine at 650rpm. The 70, which was the last of the big gasoline-powered tractors, produced 77 horsepower with an engine that had the same bore and stroke as the 65 with an increased rpm of 700.

The engines of these models used a valve rocker box over the cylinder head. Along with this component, the cylinder heads could be removed individually. To remove the valves, first remove the small hairpin from the grooves at the upper part of the valve stem. Use a valve spring compressor to depress the spring, then remove the retainers and locks, and pull the valves from the head. If the valves can be moved side to side inside the valve guides, they should be replaced. You will first have to soak the outer perimeter of the valve guide with penetrating oil and then drive the valve guide out with a hammer and punch. You may find it necessary to use a valve or valve guide with similar dimensions in the antique tractor.

To remove the connecting rods and pistons, first remove the lower inspection covers from the crankcase. Remove the cotter pins from the nuts that hold the bearing caps to the connecting rod. Turn the piston so that the wrist pin is facing across the engine. Drive out the retainer plugs and pull out the piston pin. Raise the con-

Cylinder head and valve mechanism of a Model R-4 tractor. This is also used with the Model 30 6G series which the R-4 replaced. *Midland Press Corp.—Caterpillar, Inc., Licensee*

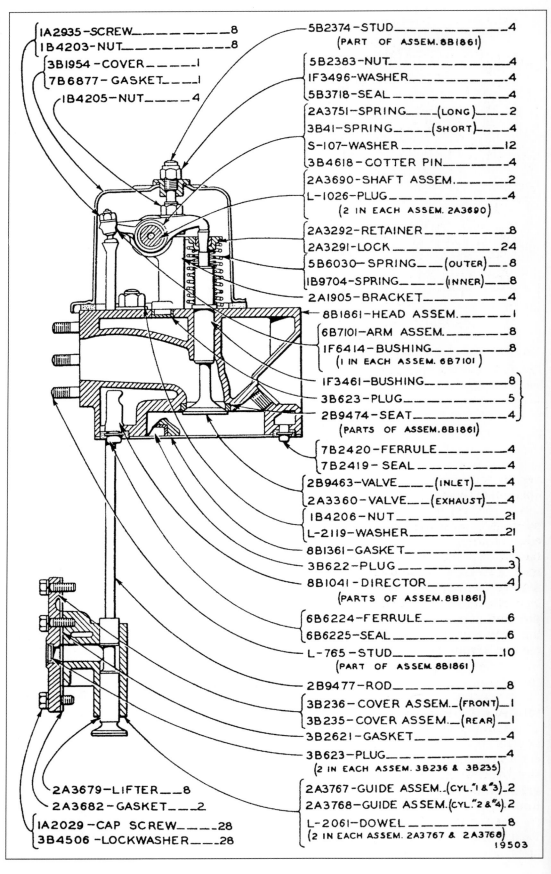

IA2935—SCREW _____8
IB4203—NUT _____8
3B1954—COVER _____1
7B6877—GASKET ____1
IB4205—NUT ____4

5B2374—STUD _____4
(PART OF ASSEM. 8B1861)
5B2383—NUT _____4
IF3496—WASHER _____4
5B3718—SEAL _____4
2A3751—SPRING ___(LONG)____2
3B41—SPRING ____(SHORT)___4
S-107—WASHER _____12
3B4618—COTTER PIN_____4
2A3690—SHAFT ASSEM._____2
L-1026—PLUG _____4
(2 IN EACH ASSEM. 2A3690)
2A3292—RETAINER _____8
2A3291—LOCK _____24
5B6030—SPRING ___(OUTER)__8
IB9704—SPRING _____(INNER)___8
2A1905—BRACKET _____4
8B1861—HEAD ASSEM._____1
6B7101—ARM ASSEM._____8
IF6414—BUSHING _____8
(1 IN EACH ASSEM. 6B7101)
IF3461—BUSHING _____8
3B623—PLUG_____5
2B9474—SEAT_____4
(PARTS OF ASSEM. 8B1861)
7B2420—FERRULE _____4
7B2419—SEAL _____4
2B9463—VALVE ____(INLET)___4
2A3360—VALVE ___(EXHAUST)___4
IB4206—NUT __ _____21
L-2119—WASHER_____21
8B1361—GASKET _____1
3B622—PLUG _____3
8B1041—DIRECTOR_____4
(PARTS OF ASSEM. 8B1861)
6B6224—FERRULE _____6
6B6225—SEAL _____6
L-765—STUD_____10
(PART OF ASSEM. 8B1861)
2B9477—ROD _____8
3B236—COVER ASSEM._(FRONT)_1
3B235—COVER ASSEM._(REAR)_1
3B2621—GASKET_____4
3B623—PLUG_____4
(2 IN EACH ASSEM. 3B236 & 3B235)
2A3767—GUIDE ASSEM._(CYL.1 & 3)_2
2A3768—GUIDE ASSEM.(CYL.2 & 4)_2
L-2061—DOWEL_____8
(2 IN EACH ASSEM. 2A3767 & 2A3768)
19503

2A3679—LIFTER ___8
2A3682—GASKET ___2
IA2029—CAP SCREW____28
3B4506—LOCKWASHER___28

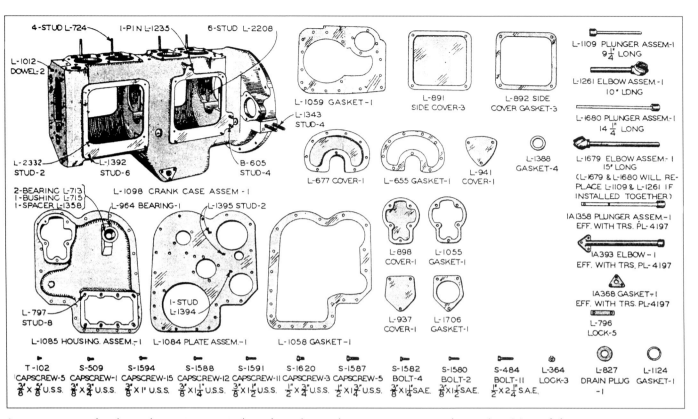

It was common for the early gas tractors to have large inspection covers to access the engine. Most of the components were removable for repair or replacement. *Midland Press Corp.—Caterpillar, Inc., Licensee*

necting rod back and then pull it through the opening in the crankcase.

To test the connecting rod and main bearings for wear, use a pry bar to lift up on the edge of the crankshaft. The bearings should have no less than .003 inch nor more than .012 inch of clearance. If adjustment is needed, first remove the screw that fastens the oil line to the bearing cap. You can then take out the cotter pins and nuts, which hold the cap to the bearing. You can now pry the cap upward and remove it from the exposed studs.

Once the bearings are removed from the tractor, you will be able to add or remove the laminated shims from either side of the cap. Add or subtract the same amount of shims from both sides to ensure the proper fit. Replace the babbitted bearing back on the crankshaft and check for uniform fit. Make sure the clearance is no less than .003 inch nor greater than .012 inch. When the proper fit is found, place the cotter pins back into the nuts to keep them from unthreading. Upon reassembly, remember to use new gaskets and appropriate lubrication.

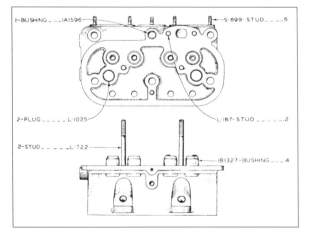

Check the condition of the valve guides and valve seats in the head. Most machine shops will be able to replace these components if they are in poor condition. *Midland Press Corp.—Caterpillar, Inc., Licensee*

CHAPTER FOUR

IGNITION SYSTEMS AND TIMING

The ignition systems used on the early Caterpillar gas tractors are all somewhat similar in principle. The components of the system include the magneto, ignition wires, and spark plugs, each important in the proper performance of the ignition system. All of these systems must be in adequate condition for the tractor to run smoothly and produce the power it should.

The easiest components to troubleshoot are the plugs and wires. A spark plug should be properly gapped upon installation. The gap is the distance in thousandths of an inch between the electrodes of the spark plug and is measured with a blade-type feeler gauge. The gap is important for the proper burning of fuel at the point of combustion. Most of the early gas tractors use an AC Delco C75 spark plug or an equivalent. Some collectors prefer the W14 Champion plug, but it is your preference. If the tractor is equipped with the Eisemann CT-4 magneto, the spark plug gap should be set at .025 inch. If equipped with the Eisemann GV-2Q or GV-4 magneto, the spark plug gap should be set at .022 inch. With the exception of the 2-Ton, all of the gas Caterpillar tractors have a firing order of 1-3-4-2.

The ignition wires used on these early tractors are a solid core copper or alloy wire. It is important not to use the more modern carbon core wires because of the continuity of the high-tension spark. Performance will be seriously compromised if you use this type of wire. I prefer to buy wire in bulk at my local auto parts store and make my own set of wires. The crimp-on ends work well and some older style ones are still available. These add to the original

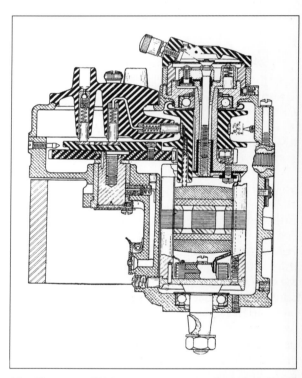

The Eisemann GV-4 magneto was used on virtually all of the early models. *Eisemann Magneto*

look of the tractor while giving good service to the ignition system.

The most common original magneto used on these early machines is the Eisemann, which was almost exclusively used with the exception of an occasional American Bosch. On the earliest model, the Eisemann GV-4 was the magneto most commonly used. It is easily identified by the large horseshoe magnet over its top. The GV-4 replaced the G-4, which was used on tractors made early in the years after the merger. The Bosch ZR-4 magneto was standard on the Model 60 and 30 tractors for a portion of their production run.

The next magneto to be used was the Eisemann Model CT-4. It was formally introduced March 2, 1934, as a replacement on all current production models. These machines included the Model 22, 28, 35 5C1404 and up, 50 5A810 and up, and 70 8D66 and up. On August 15, 1935, this magneto was offered as a replacement group on the models originally sold with the GV-4. The Model 10, 15 PV and 7C, and 20 8C were the only machines that could not use the CT-4 replacement group.

The Model CT-4 used a rotor to replace the armature with one tungsten and one platinum breaker point. This magneto was larger than the previous types and was updated internally. On June 23, 1936, the CM-4 replaced the CT-4 on all spark-ignition tractors and remained on all versions through the end of production. While the exterior of the magneto seemed the same, the interior was modified to provide greater spark. This magneto was now equipped with two tungsten breaker points.

Models 10, 15 PV and 7C, and 20 8C

To time the above tractors, first remove the front valve cover. Put the number one cylinder on top dead center of the exhaust stroke. The exhaust valve will begin to close. Next, turn the engine over until the crankshaft pulley mark MAG is in line with the boss on the block. Top dead center can also be confirmed with the pulley mark TDC and the mark on the block. The breaker points should open and the rotor should be inline with the brush for the number one cylinder. The point gap should be set at .012 inch, and the spark plugs should be set at .025 inch. Install the magneto now and fine tune with the coupling on the splined shaft. Make your adjustments slight, and use caution when cranking any tractor for the first time.

Models 20 PL Series, 25, 28, and R-3

To time the above tractors, first remove the spark plug on the number one cylinder. Place your thumb over the hole while someone turns the engine over slowly. When you feel air push against your thumb, the piston is coming up on the compression stroke. Remove the inspection cover from the left side of the engine covering

This magneto is covered with a protective shroud. It is lubricated through a top plug. This is the application used on a Model 30 PS series. *Midland Press Corp.— Caterpillar, Inc., Licensee*

WIRING TO SPARK PLUGS

The magneto used on "Caterpillar" Tractors is of Clockwise rotation—as indicated by arrow stamped in magneto housing at the drive end and the order of firing, or spark sequence, of Distributor is as shown in the drawing at Right.

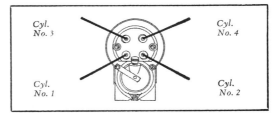

Firing order of Engine must be considered in connecting Cables to Plugs. Above is shown **cable** arrangement for an Engine firing 1-3-4-2; **below,** the arrangement for 1-2-4-3 firing order.

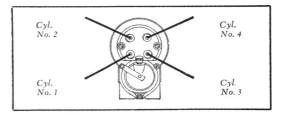

The firing order of the early gas engines is 1-3-4-2 with cylinder number one located at the front of the engine. *Eisemann*

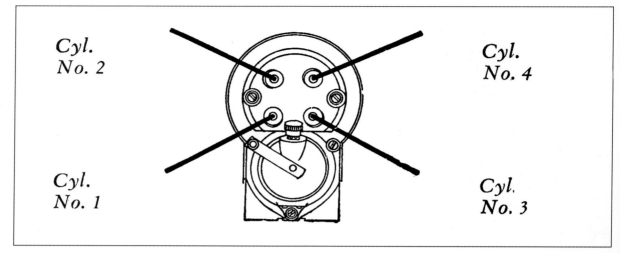

Proper positioning of plug wires to magneto cap. *Eisemann*

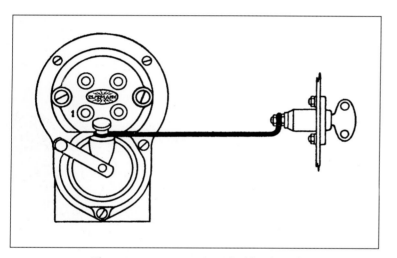

The tractors were equipped with a keyed ignition switch to ground out and kill the magneto spark. *Eisemann*

the flywheel. Turn the engine over until the mark on the flywheel MAG is inline with the mark on the edge of the crankcase. If the tractor is equipped with the CT-4 magneto, you can check the magneto timing by checking the magneto plug at the top of the housing. The short tooth of the gear should be inline with the mark on the inside the housing.

If the tractor is equipped with the CT-4 magneto, set the contact points at .020 inch. If equipped with the GV-4 magneto, set the contact points at .012 inch. The spark plug gap should be set at .025 inch and checked fairly regularly.

Be sure to fine tune the timing by adjusting the splined coupling on the magneto shaft. Make the adjustment slight, and use caution when starting the tractor for the first time.

Model 22 and R-2 5E Series

Remove the spark plug at the number one cylinder and place your finger over the hole. Have a helper slowly turn the engine over until you feel a rush of air from the cylinder. This will indicate that the piston is on its way up on the compression stroke, which is the correct position for the cylinder to be in for the timing procedure.

Now look at the crankshaft pulley while standing at the left side of the tractor. Note a mark on the pulley with the word MAG next to it. Line the MAG up with the boss on the side of the engine block.

Next remove the plug on the top of the magneto and line the short tooth up with the line made on the magneto housing. This method is for use with the original Eisemann CT-4 magneto. Make sure the spark plugs are gapped at .025 inch and gap the breaker points at .020 inch. On June 17, 1935, the louvered spark plug cover was introduced for these models. Also, fiber tubes were placed over the plug wires for added protection. All machines shipped after January 4, 1935, had these improvements.

You can make minor adjustments with the coupling on the splined shaft attached to the magneto. Make your adjustments slight, and use caution when starting the tractor for the first time after timing.

Model 30 PS and S Series

When timing the Model 30, first identify the magneto as an Eisemann GV-4 or Bosch ZR-4. Put the number one cylinder at top dead

Timing marks for the Model 10, 15 PV and 7C, and 20 8C tractors. *Midland Press Corp.—Caterpillar, Inc., Licensee*

Flywheel timing mark location on the tractors timed by this method. *Midland Press Corp.—Caterpillar, Inc., Licensee*

center of the compression stroke, which is found by holding your finger over the spark plug hole as the engine is turned over. You will feel a rush of air escape when the piston is in the correct position.

If the tractor is equipped with a Bosch ZR-4 magneto, time it as follows. First, remove the inspection cover on the master clutch housing and line up the mark on the flywheel with the one on the edge of the casting. Be sure the engine is on the compression stroke as described above.

Next, place a mark on the flywheel 6 13/32 inches to the left of the original mark on

Timing marks found on the flywheel of the Model 60. *Midland Press Corp.—Caterpillar, Inc., Licensee*

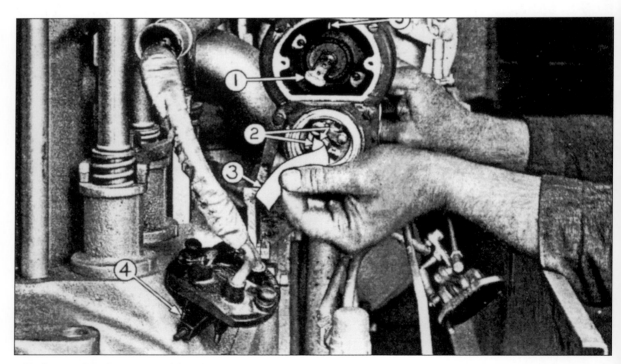

Distributor plate location and breaker point locations on Eisemann GV-4 magneto. *Midland Press Corp.—Caterpillar, Inc., Licensee*

Distributor plate and breaker point positions with flywheel on "MAG" mark.

Top dead center and cam shaft timing marks on the large flywheel timed tractors. *Midland Press Corp.—Caterpillar, Inc., Licensee*

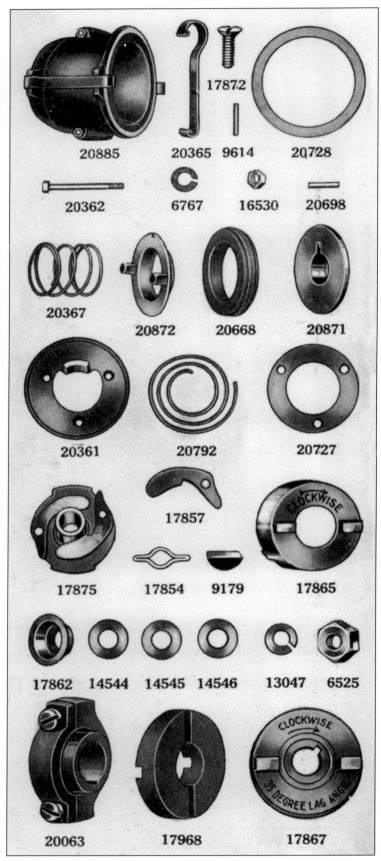

20885	20365	9614	20728
20362	6767	16530	20698
20367	20872	20668	20871
20361	20792		20727
17875	17857 17854 9179		17865
17862 14544 14545 14546		13047	6525
20063	17968		17867

Magneto coupling device as used on GV-4 magneto. *Midland Press Corp.—Caterpillar, Inc., Licensee*

the flywheel. Turn the flywheel 1 or 2 inches beyond this mark, and then turn it back to the mark you have made. This will take up the lash in the timing gears.

Place the magneto at the position where the rotor is inline with the brush-on the number one cylinder. You now can replace the magneto on the tractor. Be careful when starting the tractor for the first time, as it may kick if the timing is incorrect.

If the tractor is equipped with an Eisemann GV-4 magneto, you can follow these guidelines for timing it. First, follow the above procedure for arriving at top dead center on the number one cylinder.

You will now need to remove the inspection cover from the clutch compartment. Lineup the mark on the flywheel with the mark on the outer clutch housing. From the mark on the flywheel measure 5 1/2 inches to the left and make another mark. Turn the flywheel 1 or 2 inches beyond this mark and then turn it back to the mark you have made. This will take up any lash in the timing gears.

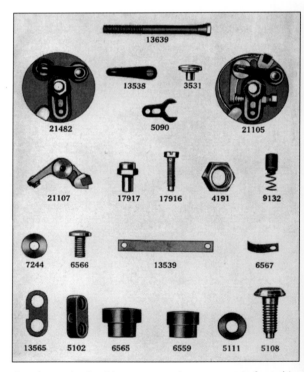

Breaker point ignition parts and components found in the GV-4 magneto. *Eisemann*

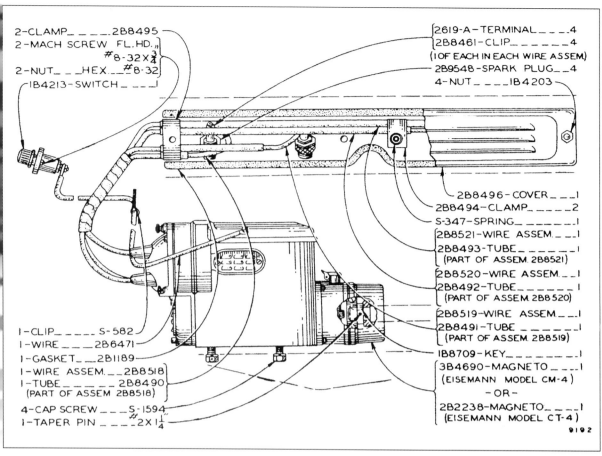

2-CLAMP_ _ _ _ _ .2B8495
2-MACH SCREW FL.HD. "
    #8-32X¾
2-NUT_ _ _HEX _#8-32
-1B4213-SWITCH_ _ _ _ _

2619-A—TERMINAL_ _ _ _4
2B8461-CLIP_ _ _ _ _ _4
(1 OF EACH IN EACH WIRE ASSEM.)
2B9548-SPARK PLUG_ _4
4-NUT_ _ _ _1B4203

2B8496—COVER_ _ _ _1
2B8494—CLAMP_ _ _ _ _2
S-347—SPRING_ _ _ _ _ _ _1
2B8521-WIRE ASSEM._ _ _1
2B8493-TUBE_ _ _ _ _ _1
(PART OF ASSEM. 2B8521)
2B8520-WIRE ASSEM._ _1
2B8492-TUBE_ _ _ _ _ _1
(PART OF ASSEM. 2B8520)
2B8519-WIRE ASSEM._ _ _1
2B8491-TUBE _ _ _ _ _ _1
(PART OF ASSEM. 2B8519)
1B8709-KEY_ _ _ _ _ _ _1
3B4690-MAGNETO _ _ _ _1
(EISEMANN MODEL CM-4)
—OR—
2B2238-MAGNETO_ _ _ _1
(EISEMANN MODEL CT-4)

1-CLIP_ _ _ _ _ S-582
1-WIRE _ _ _ 2B6471
1-GASKET_ _ _2B1189
1-WIRE ASSEM._ _2B8518
1-TUBE_ _ _ _ _ 2B8490
(PART OF ASSEM 2B8518)
4-CAP SCREW _ _ _ S-1594
1-TAPER PIN _ _ _ _2X1¼"

9192

Magneto of the CM-4 or CT-4 Eisemann magneto design. *Midland Press Corp.—Caterpillar, Inc., Licensee*

Now place the magneto so that the segment is lined-up with the brush on the number one cylinder. You can now replace the magneto on the tractor. Use caution when cranking the tractor for the first time since it may kick if the timing is not correct.

Model 30 6G, R-4, and R-2 J Series

These tractors listed above were all equipped with the Eisemann CM-4 magneto. Time the machines by removing the spark plug from the number one cylinder and turning the engine over until the rush of air is felt. Next, remove the valve cover and confirm TDC by checking valve position. A quick way is to see if the eighth valve from the front or last valve on the head is closed. If it is, you have the number one cylinder at TDC on the compression stroke.

Now remove the inspection cover from the left side of the flywheel housing and line the flywheel mark, MA, up with the line on the housing. You can now remove the plug from the top of the magneto and line-up the short tooth of the gear with the line on the housing. Replace the magneto on the tractor and use caution when starting the tractor for the first time.

Models 35, 40, 50, and R-5

To time the above models, first set the ignition points at .012 inch. Remove the cover from the flywheel housing at the left side of the engine. Also remove the valve cover over the number one cylinder and have someone turn the engine over until this cylinder is at top dead center of the compression stroke. The intake and exhaust valves of this cylinder will be closed when in the correct position. You can confirm this position by lining-up the mark, TC 1, on the flywheel with the mark on the edge of the inspection hole.

While standing on the left side of the engine, turn the flywheel backward with the fan until the word, MAG, appears and line-up this mark with the line on the edge of the opening. You can turn it a little past the mark with

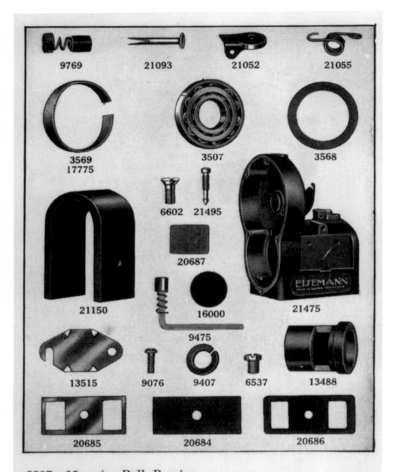

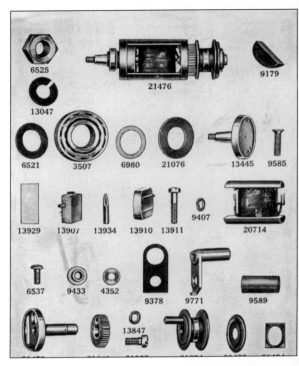

Armature components found in the GV-4 Eisemann magneto. *Eisemann*

3507	15 m/m Ball Bearing.
3568	Insulating Washer. For Part No. 3507.
3569	.011" Insulating Strip. For Part No. 3507.
6537	4 m/m Screw. For Part No. 13515.
6602	Fastening Screw. For Part No. 21150.
9076	Stop Screw. For Part No. 13488.
9407	Lock Washer. For Part No. 13515.
9475	Oil Wick. For Eccentric Bearing.
9769	Ground Carbon, with Spring and Cap.
13488	Eccentric Bearing, with Stop Screw No. 9076.
13515	Clamp Plate. For Part No. 13488.
16000	Felt Disc. For Part No. 13488.
17775	.015" Insulating Strip (Oversize). For Part No. 3507.
20684	Ventilating Screen. For Base of Housing.
20685	Cover Plate. For Part No. 20684.
20686	Gasket. For Part No. 20684.
20687	Felt Plug. For Base of Housing.
21052	Oil Duct Cover. Drive End.
21055	Spiral Spring. For Part No. 21052.
21093	Pin. For Part No. 21052.
21150	Magnet.
21475	Housing, complete.
21495	Timing Marker Screw.

the fan, then line it up using the starting crank to take the lash out of the timing gears.

In the tractors equipped with the Eisemann GV-4 magneto, remove the cap and line the disk segment up with the brush for the number one cylinder. If equipped with an Eisemann CM-4 or CT-4 magneto, remove the plug from the top of the housing and line the short tooth of the gear up with the mark. You can now replace the magneto to the tractor. Use caution when cranking any tractor for the first time. The firing order is 1-2-4-3. The spark plug gap is .023 inch.

Models 60, 65, and 70

In timing the above tractors you must first determine whether the tractor is equipped with a Bosch or Eisemann magneto. The 60 was most commonly equipped with the ZR-4 Bosch magneto. The Eisemann GV-4 was used on the Model 65 exclusively and on the 70 from 8D1 to 8D65, when it was most likely replaced with the Eisemann CM-4. If equipped

LEFT
Housing components of Eisemann GV-4 magneto. *Eisemann*

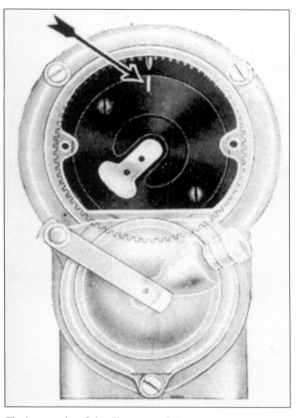

Timing marks of the Eisemann GV-4 magneto. *Eisemann*

21062
17956
21345
21144
21081
21091
6537
6767
21145
13452
21148
21033
21547
20950
21479
21082
3569
17775
3507
3568

Cap and rotor parts of the GV-4 model magneto. *Eisemann*

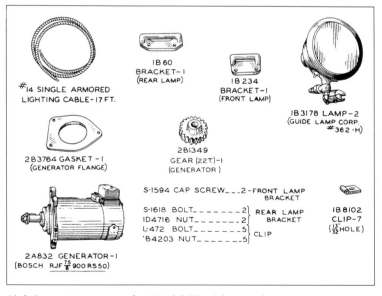

IB 60
BRACKET-1
(REAR LAMP)
IB 234
BRACKET-1
(FRONT LAMP)
IB 3178 LAMP-2
(GUIDE LAMP CORP.
#362-H)
#14 SINGLE ARMORED
LIGHTING CABLE-17 FT.
2B3349
GEAR (22T)-1
(GENERATOR)
2B3764 GASKET-1
(GENERATOR FLANGE)
S-1594 CAP SCREW___2-FRONT LAMP
BRACKET
S-1618 BOLT_____2
ID4716 NUT_____2
L-472 BOLT_____5
'B4203 NUT_____5
REAR LAMP
BRACKET
CLIP
IB 8102
CLIP-7
(13/32HOLE)
2A832 GENERATOR-1
(BOSCH RJF 75/8 900 RS50)

Lighting system group for Model 22 without cab.

with the Eisemann magneto, the following instructions are to be used.

First, turn the flywheel until the number one cylinder is at top dead center of the compression stroke. Top dead center is located by lining-up the mark on the flywheel with the letters TC 1 with the pointer that is located near the oil pressure gauge. If the pointer is missing, the compression stroke can be determined by the position of the valves. You will also find on the flywheel, the letters MAG. Turn the flywheel 1 or 2 inches beyond this mark and then back to it. This will take the lash out of the timing gears.

Now set the magneto so that the disk is in line with the brush for the number one cylinder. Replace the magneto on the tractor, and use caution when starting the tractor for the first time.

If the tractor is equipped with a Bosch magneto, place cylinder number one at top dead center. Line the M on the flywheel up with the pointer and confirm the compression stroke

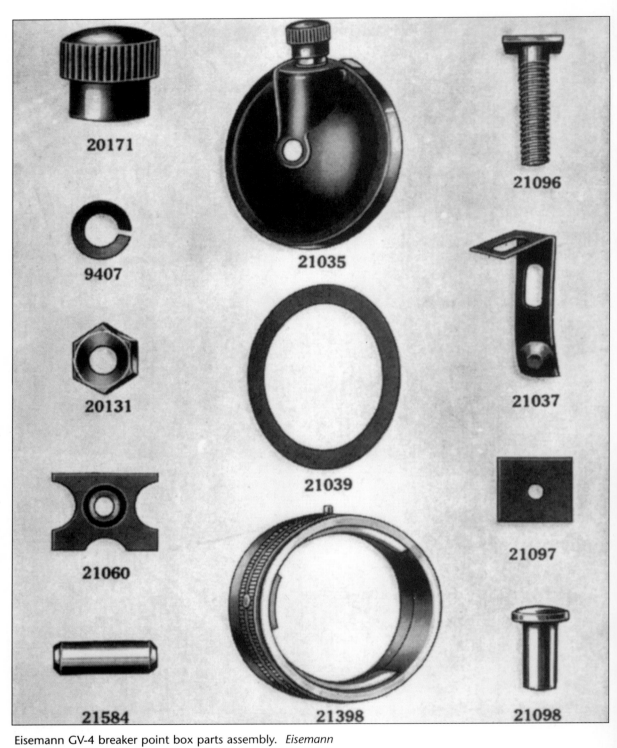

20171

9407

20131

21060

21584

21035

21039

21398

21096

21037

21097

21098

Eisemann GV-4 breaker point box parts assembly. *Eisemann*

Magneto Interchange

Caterpillar Model / Part	Ten	Fifteen 7C	Fifteen PV	Twenty PL	Twenty 8C	Twenty Two	Twenty Five	Twenty Eight	Thirty PS	Thirty 6G	R2-5E	Thirty Five	Forty	Sixty	Sixty Five	Seventy
Eisemann GV4	X	X	X	X	X		X								X	X
Eisemann CT 4						X		X		X	X	X	X			
Bosch ZR4									X					X		

by the position of the valves. Another mark on the flywheel is located approximately 8 1/2 inches to the left of the M. Turn the flywheel 1 or 2 inches beyond this mark and then back to it to take the lash out of the timing gears. You can now set the magneto so the brush for the number one cylinder is in-line with the segment on the disk. Replace the magneto on the tractor and use caution when starting it for the first time. The firing order is 1-3-4-2. Spark plug gap is .023 inch. Breaker point gap should be set at .013 inch.

Remember, at 1250rpm, the tractor produces 40 sparks per second. In a 10-hour day, this adds up to 1,500,000 sparks. The two main reasons for magneto failure are a poor electrical circuit outside the magneto, such as too wide a spark plug gap or loose or damaged ignition wires; and dust or other foreign particles entering the inside of the magneto. It is important to keep the magneto properly lubricated and free of dust. If you store the tractor in a building where you may be grinding, sandblasting, or painting, cover the magnetos on all your tractors in the area.

CHAPTER FIVE

FUEL SYSTEMS AND CARBURETION

Models 10, 15 PV, 7C, 1D and, 20 8C

The carburetor used on the above tractors as well as the fuel system that they were equipped with are all similar. The 10 and 15 PV Series tractors were the only machines to use the over-the-engine-style gas tank. These machines were not equipped with a fuel pump, as gravity was used to feed the fuel down to the carburetor. Usually, the gas tanks were equipped with a front and rear shut-off, with two copper lines running from each valve to one line that leads to the carburetor.

Due to the close proximity of the exhaust manifold to the gas tank, vapor lock became a problem. A service bulletin was issued and an asbestos shield was placed between the

Breakdown of parts used in the Ensign BeT-1-inch carburetor for the Model 10, 7C 15, 8C 20, and PV 15. (*Midland Press Corp.—Caterpillar, Inc., Licensee*

tank and the manifold to deflect the heat. Also, two vents were installed on the top of the gas tank to release pressure. These actions most certainly improved the situation; however, this fuel system was never used again.

With the two shut off on either end of the fuel tank, the tractor could be operated at steep angles and still obtain an adequate fuel supply. If the tractor had some type of fuel pump, one petcock may have been sufficient and the vapor locking might have been alleviated.

The fuel enters the pot metal Ensign BeT-one-inch carburetor through a brass banjo fitting that is placed over a small screen. The fuel then enters the needle and seat area which contacts a brass arm attached to the cork float. The float is nearly round and circles the throat of the carburetor. At the rear of the carburetor, there is a jet screwed into the body with another one beneath it. These jets seem to be the only difference between the carburetor of the 10 and PV Series.

When servicing this carburetor, take great care in handling it. Use a delicate hand when tightening and loosening the acorn nut holding the banjo fitting to the top of the carburetor. This is the weakest point of the carburetor, and many have stripped the threads at the fuel inlet. The exterior adjustments of the carburetor include the high-speed adjusting jet, the low-speed or idle adjusting jet, and the idle speed screw. There is also a drain at the bottom of the carburetor to permit excess fuel to flow from the float bowl.

On the 15 7C and 1D Series, along with the 20 8C, the carburetor is placed on an elbow, lowering it about 5 inches from its old location. This carburetor was the model BeT-R-1 inch.

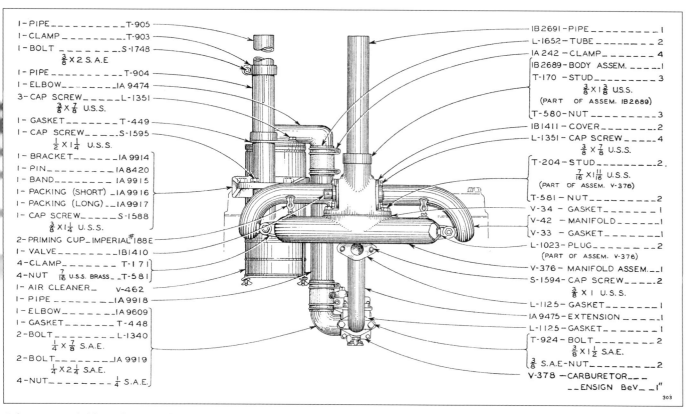

Left column of diagram labels:
```
1-PIPE _____T-905
1-CLAMP _____T-903
1-BOLT _____S-1748
    3/8 X 2 S.A.E
1-PIPE _____T-904
1-ELBOW_____IA 9474
3-CAP SCREW_____L-1351
    3/8 X 7/8 U.S.S.
1-GASKET _____T-449
1-CAP SCREW_____S-1595
    1/2 X 1 1/4 U.S.S.
1-BRACKET_____IA 9914
1-PIN_____IA 8420
1-BAND_____IA 9915
1-PACKING (SHORT)_IA 9916
1-PACKING (LONG)__IA 9917
1-CAP SCREW_____S-1588
    3/8 X 1 1/4 U.S.S.
2-PRIMING CUP_IMPERIAL #188E
1-VALVE_____IB1410
4-CLAMP _____T-171
4-NUT 7/16 U.S.S. BRASS__T-581
1-AIR CLEANER_   V-462
1-PIPE _____IA 9918
1-ELBOW_____IA 9609
1-GASKET_____T-448
2-BOLT _____L-1340
    1/4 X 7/8 S.A.E.
2-BOLT_____IA 9919
    1/4 X 2 1/4 S.A.E.
4-NUT_____1/4 S.A.E.
```

Right column of diagram labels:
```
IB 2691-PIPE _____1
L-1652-TUBE _____ _ _2
IA 242-CLAMP_____4
IB 2689-BODY ASSEM.____1
T-170 -STUD_____3
    3/8 X 1 3/8 U.S.S.
    (PART OF ASSEM. IB 2689)
T-580-NUT _____3
IB 1411-COVER_____2
L-1351-CAP SCREW____4
    3/8 X 7/8 U.S.S.
T-204-STUD_____2.
    7/16 X 1 11/16 U.S.S.
    (PART OF ASSEM. V-376)
T-581-NUT_____2
V-34 - GASKET_____1
V-42 - MANIFOLD_____1
V-33 - GASKET_____1
L-1023-PLUG_____2
    (PART OF ASSEM. V-376)
V-376 - MANIFOLD ASSEM.__1
S-1594-CAP SCREW____2
    3/8 X 1 U.S.S.
L-1125-GASKET_____1
IA 9475-EXTENSION____1
L-1125-GASKET_____1
T-924 - BOLT_____2
    3/8 X 1 1/2 S.A.E.
3/8 S.A.E.-NUT_____2
V-378 -CARBURETOR__
    __ENSIGN BeV__1"
```

303

Exhaust manifold used on Model 20 8C series. *Midland Press Corp.—Caterpillar, Inc., Licensee*

Due to the new location of the gas tank, this carburetor was relocated there to assist gravity with the fuel flow. The top cover of the carburetor used on these tractors is slightly shorter than those on the previous machines. Therefore, it takes a high-speed screw about 1/8 inch shorter than previous models. Some of these carburetors have been found with small brass tags attached to the top containing its make and model. Some late Model 10 tractors were equipped with this second type of carburetor.

When adjusting these carburetors, many have found that regardless of how they adjust it, the machine will run with little or no improvement. It is first important to carefully dismantle the carburetor and clean it thoroughly with a carburetor cleaner. A cutting torch tip cleaner works well for cleaning out the jets. Next try floating the cork float in a small pail of gasoline. If it stays afloat overnight, it should be in good shape. If not, you may have to lightly sand the exterior of the float and shellac it. After you are certain that it will float, next direct your attention to the needle and seat. You can test the needle and seat by blowing lightly down the fuel inlet and seeing if you can stop the air flow by

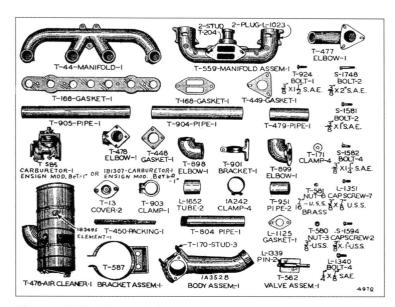

The manifold of the Model 10 is different than that of the 7C Model 15. The exhaust outlet of the 10 passes around the gas tank rather than through the hood. *Midland Press Corp.—Caterpillar, Inc., Licensee*

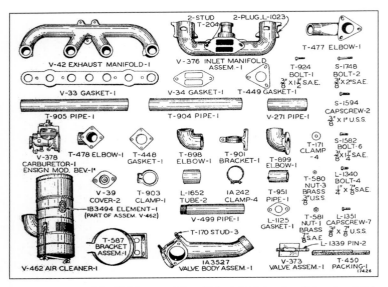

Manifold assembly of Model 15 tractor PV series. *Midland Press Corp.—Caterpillar, Inc., Licensee*

pushing the needle against the seat. You may be able to clean up the end of the needle valve with some fine sandpaper. This may be enough to seal up the worn components.

As you reassemble the carburetor, make sure to level the float inside the bowl. Be sure the bottom of the float is 3/8 of an inch below the fuel bowl cover flange around the whole float. To adjust the float, remove the fuel bowl cover and turn it upside down. Hold the piece

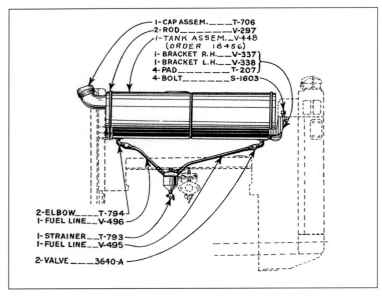

Fuel tank and strainer system used on PV series Model 15. *Midland Press Corp.—Caterpillar, Inc., Licensee*

upside down and carefully bend the float lever upward, keeping the float level. Bend it until the float drops to the correct height. When the cover is put back on the carburetor, the float should now lift the valve when the fuel lifts it to this height.

After the carburetor is installed back on the tractor, turn the high-speed screw located on the top of the carburetor one turn from its closed position. Turn the idle screw located on the side of the carburetor a half turn from the closed position. After the engine has warmed up, turn the high-speed screw out to make richer and in to make leaner. The idle mixture screw should be turned in to be richer and out to be leaner. In the course of your collecting you may come across one of these models with an Ensign Type H kerosene converter carburetor. This carburetor was made to use with kerosene or other white fuels. It cannot be used with diesel or furnace oil. This carburetor consists of a metering system that produces the correct fuel-air ratio and a combustion chamber that converts the fuel to a gas. In this carburetor, fuel passes through an orifice located in the fuel chamber and passes into the mixing chamber. It then enters a passage where it is discharged to the intake manifold. This carburetor is also equipped with a priming valve. The gasoline is supplied to this valve from a small tank and is activated by a button located on the instrument panel. When this button is pulled out, gas flows into this valve for use in starting in cold weather. Unlike the pot metal construction of the standard carburetor, this style is made of brass and was probably far more durable. This carburetor, if found, is considered quite rare but not very practical to use if it is not working properly.

Models 20 PL, 25, 28, and R-3

The fuel system of these machines is based on the location of the fuel tank ahead of the operator. As with other tractors being produced at this time, no fuel pump was placed on these tractors. Once again, gravity was used to feed fuel to the carburetor through a copper line after passing through the fuel strainer. The exhaust manifolds of these tractors changed little over the production run, with the exception of the R-3. The main difference in the R-3 manifold was that the exhaust was released from the machine at the number one cylinder. The manifolds used on all of these tractors are often in poor condition and are difficult to repair.

All L Series and PL machines to PL4112 were equipped with the Ensign 1 1/4-inch Model

AeL carburetor. This early model was not furnished with an actual choke but with a primer button. The front portion of this model was equipped with a brass air intake and a pot metal rear float.

The second type of carburetor, the Ensign Model AeLC 1 1/4-inch, was installed on the tractors made after PL4112 and on tractors that followed the Model 20. The "C" referred to the choke assembly on this carburetor. The priming button remained, but the choke assembly was a welcome addition for the operator.

The fuel entered both carburetors through a brass banjo fitting and then passed into the float chamber. The float was in two pieces attached to the brass float arm, one on each side. Cork was again varnished and used as the float material. A valve was also usually placed just before the banjo fitting at the union of the lines from the main and auxiliary tanks.

When initially cleaning the fuel system, it is important to clean the two sediment screens. The first is located in the brass sediment bowl before the carburetor and the other is located below the banjo fitting on the carburetor itself. Use caution when turning the acorn nut to remove or replace the fuel line on the inlet area. The threaded housing is pot metal and may strip if overtightened.

There are three exterior adjustments of the carburetor. The first is the idle mixture screw that threads into the brass air intake portion of the carburetor. The next is the high-speed or load adjustment screw located on top of the pot metal float chamber next to the fuel inlet. Finally, the idle speed screw is located on the front of the brass air intake portion facing the air cleaner.

The starting mixture for the carburetor should be with the high-speed adjusting screw one and an eighth turn from close. The idle mixture screw should be turned a half turn from close. After the engine warms up, the high-speed screw can be turned out to make richer and in to make leaner. The idle mixture screw can be turned in to be leaner and out to be richer. The idle speed screw can be turned in to speed up and out to slow down. Make the adjustments slight and monitor the engine's performance as you go.

Model 22 and R-2 5E Series

The Model 22 and R-2 5E Series tractors are nearly identical in the components of their fuel systems. The fuel tank used was a double-chambered tank with the smaller tank being used for gasoline or a high-grade starting fuel. The smaller auxiliary tank was not connected to

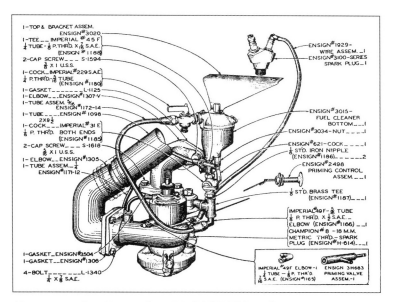

Kerosene carburetor used on Model 15. This carburetor is of brass construction. *Midland Press Corp.— Caterpillar, Inc., Licensee*

the carburetor on tractors that were shipped from the factory before December 13, 1934. A kit to pipe this tank into the carburetor was made available July 31, 1935. Many operators used this tank as a reserve fuel supply and as the starting fuel tank. These tractors were also the first small machine to be equipped with a fuel pump. The manifold assembly of these tractors stayed virtually the same through the production run.

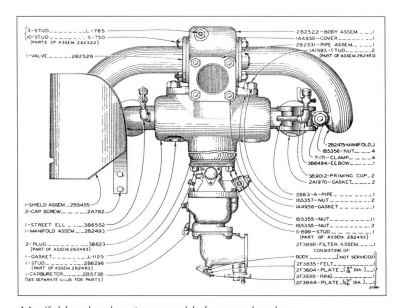

Manifold and carburetor assembly for use when burning tractor fuel on Model 22 tractor. *Midland Press Corp.—Caterpillar, Inc., Licensee*

Ensign carburetor with three external adjustments: G—high speed mixture, A—idle mixture, and N—idle speed. *Midland Press Corp.—Caterpillar, Inc., Licensee*

The fuel leaves the tank through a copper line that runs under the magneto bracket to the fuel pump located on the right front of the engine. The fuel passes through the fuel pump and exits through a copper line that leads between the two sets of cylinders and enters the Zenith K5A updraft carburetor. A valve is placed at the base of the gas tank and if the auxiliary tank is used, a valve is placed there as well. On some models the selector for the tanks was placed on a small console located at the front of the gas tank in the operator's compartment. This selector had three positions and could either draw fuel from the main tank or auxiliary tank or shut the fuel supply off completely.

Three styles of fuel pumps were used over the production run of these tractors. The first was a brass assembly with a glass sediment bowl that used two coil elements to filter the gasoline as it entered the bowl. The second was also a brass assembly but used an oval screen to filter the fuel as it entered the bowl. Both of these fuel pumps were made by the AC Company. A Stewart Warner fuel pump was used on many of the early tractors but seldom is mentioned in the parts catalog. Some tractors have surfaced with a more modern fuel pump that did not use a sediment bowl and had an aluminum or white metal housing. This style of fuel pump could have been a later aftermarket style.

The carburetor used was a cast-iron Zenith K5A updraft that bolted to the bottom of the intake manifold. It was equipped with a choke assembly and a fuel drain that were located on the air intake portion of the carburetor. Some of the early Model 22 tractors may have been equipped with the Ensign AeLC carburetor, but it is not clear how many or if it was standard.

The starting setting for the Zenith carburetor is to turn the high-speed screw located on the left side of the carburetor one turn. The

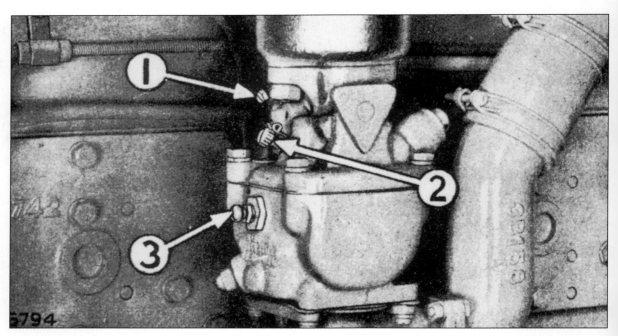

Zenith K5A updraft carburetor used on Model 22 tractor with three external adjustments: 1—idle speed screw, 2—idle adjust screw, and 3—high-speed mixture screw. *Midland Press Corp.—Caterpillar, Inc., Licensee*

idle adjust screw located just above it should be set one-quarter of a turn from close. After the engine has warmed up, you can turn the high-speed screw out to make richer and in to make leaner. The idle screw can be turned in to make richer and out to make leaner. The idle screw is located behind the carburetor.

Model 30 PS Series

The Model 30 was the smaller tractor with the barrel fuel tank located on the left fender. Due to the location of the fuel tank, it was often damaged with regular use. Many are found to be patched or dented beyond adequate repair.

The fuel flows directly from the fuel tank to the inlet of the carburetor. There were several styles of the carburetor over its long production run. The first was a brass Stromberg that had a round float chamber with a primer button and no choke. The next type, the Ensign 1 1/2-inch AE, was used in tractor num-

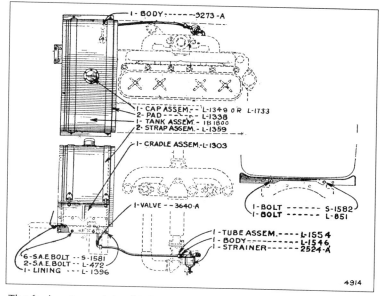

The fuel system of the "5E" R-2 is very similar to that of the Model 22. *Midland Press Corp.—Caterpillar, Inc., Licensee*

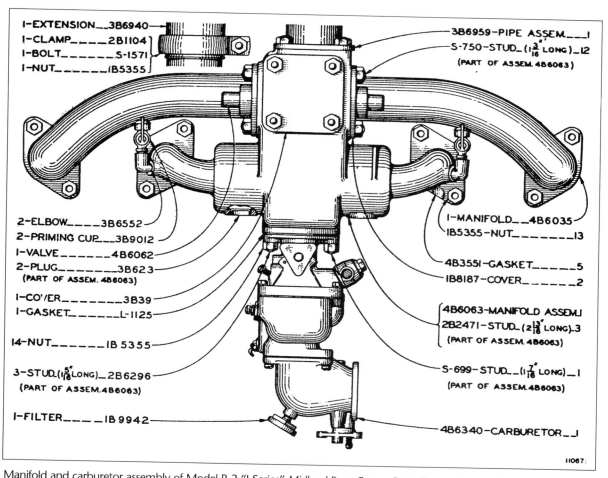

Manifold and carburetor assembly of Model R-2 "J Series" *Midland Press Corp.—Caterpillar, Inc., Form P-1190*

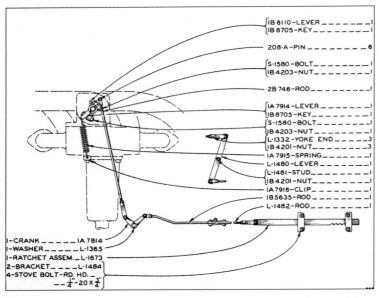

IB 6110 - LEVER _ _ _ _ _ _ _ _ 1
IB 8705 - KEY _ _ _ _ _ _ _ _ _ 1
208-A - PIN _ _ _ _ _ _ _ 6
S-1580 - BOLT _ _ _ _ _ _ 1
IB 4203 - NUT _ _ _ _ _ _ _ 1
2B 746 - ROD _ _ _ _ _ _ _ 1
IA 7914 - LEVER _ _ _ _ _ _ 1
IB 8705 - KEY _ _ _ _ _ _ _ 1
S-1580 - BOLT _ _ _ _ _ _ 1
IB 4203 - NUT _ _ _ _ _ _ _ 1
L-1332 - YOKE END _ _ _ _ _ 3
IB 4201 - NUT _ _ _ _ _ _ _ 3
IA 7915 - SPRING _ _ _ _ _ _ 1
L-1480 - LEVER _ _ _ _ _ _ _ 1
L-1481 - STUD _ _ _ _ _ _ _ 1
IB 4201 - NUT _ _ _ _ _ _ _ 1
IA 7916 - CLIP _ _ _ _ _ _ _ 1
IB 5635 - ROD _ _ _ _ _ _ _ 1
L-1482 - ROD _ _ _ _ _ _ _ 1

1 - CRANK _ _ _ _ _ IA 7814
1 - WASHER _ _ _ _ _ L-1365
1 - RATCHET ASSEM. _ L-1673
2 - BRACKET _ _ _ _ L-1484
4 - STOVE BOLT - RD. HD. _
_ _ $\frac{1}{4}$" - 20 X $\frac{1}{2}$"

The manifold heat exchanger linkage on the Model R-3 tractor. *Midland Press Corp.—Caterpillar, Inc., Licensee*

ber PS2369 and from S4683 to S6368, with the tube type manifold. The AE had the air intake coming in at a 90-degree angle to the carburetor with the air cleaner mounted at the left side

of the radiator. This system also used the S1138 air heater assembly.

The same carburetor was used from tractor PS2370 to PS3582 and S6369 to S6837. The air heater assembly was replaced with a plain pipe and the tube manifold was discontinued. The air intake was still at a 90-degree angle to the rest of the body and the fuel entered through a brass banjo fitting. At tractor number S6848 and PS3583, the air intake was placed in a straight line with the air cleaner, although the remainder of the carburetor body stayed the same. The air cleaner was still located at the left side of the radiator with a pipe connecting the two components.

The location of the air cleaner was changed to a location near the left corner of the cylinder head at machine S8843 and PS8122. Through this change the manifold and carburetor stayed the same, but the pipe was removed and a small cast elbow was installed. This combination, with minor changes, continued until the end of production of both series.

When cleaning this carburetor, first remove the screens from the fuel strainer and banjo fitting fuel inlet. Remember to take care

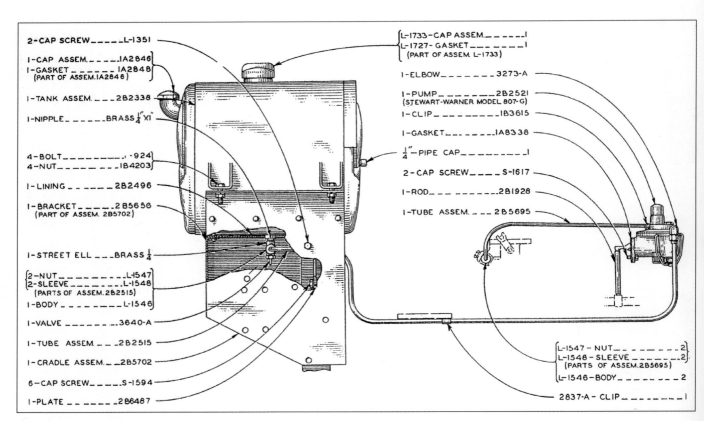

2 - CAP SCREW _ _ _ _ _ L-1351
1 - CAP ASSEM. _ _ _ _ _ IA2846
1 - GASKET _ _ _ _ _ _ IA2848
(PART OF ASSEM. IA2846)
1 - TANK ASSEM. _ _ _ 2B2338
1 - NIPPLE _ _ _ _ _ BRASS $\frac{1}{4}$" X1"
4 - BOLT _ _ _ _ _ _ _ 1 -924
4 - NUT _ _ _ _ _ _ IB4203
1 - LINING _ _ _ _ _ 2B2496
1 - BRACKET _ _ _ _ 2B5656
(PART OF ASSEM. 2B5702)
1 - STREET ELL _ _ _ BRASS $\frac{1}{4}$
2 - NUT _ _ _ _ _ _ _ L-1547
2 - SLEEVE _ _ _ _ _ _ L-1548
(PARTS OF ASSEM. 2B2515)
1 - BODY _ _ _ _ _ _ L-1546
1 - VALVE _ _ _ _ _ 3640-A
1 - TUBE ASSEM. _ _ 2B2515
1 - CRADLE ASSEM. _ _ 2B5702
6 - CAP SCREW _ _ _ _ S-1594
1 - PLATE _ _ _ _ _ 2B6487

L-1733 - CAP ASSEM. _ _ _ _ _ 1
L-1727 - GASKET _ _ _ _ _ _ 1
(PART OF ASSEM. L-1733)
1 - ELBOW _ _ _ _ _ _ 3273-A
1 - PUMP _ _ _ _ _ 2B2521
(STEWART-WARNER MODEL 807-G)
1 - CLIP _ _ _ _ _ _ IB3615
1 - GASKET _ _ _ _ _ IA8338
$\frac{1}{4}$" PIPE CAP _ _ _ _ _ _ 1
2 - CAP SCREW _ _ _ _ S-1617
1 - ROD _ _ _ _ _ _ 2B1928
1 - TUBE ASSEM. _ _ 2B5695

L-1547 - NUT _ _ _ _ _ _ 2
L-1548 - SLEEVE _ _ _ _ _ 2
(PARTS OF ASSEM. 2B5695)
L-1546 - BODY _ _ _ _ _ 2
2837-A - CLIP _ _ _ _ _ _ 1

Fuel tank and valve assembly for PL Model 20 tractor. *Midland Press Corp.—Caterpillar, Inc., Licensee*

when moving the acorn nut, which holds the inlet fitting to the rear portion of the carburetor. Do not overtighten. The exterior carburetor adjustments are in the same location as on others of this style and are adjusted in the same manner.

Models 30 6G and R-4

These tractors have a fuel system similar to the Model 22 and R-2 tractors but on a larger scale. The gas tank of these two machines forms the division between the engine and operator's compartment and is the place where the throttle lever and gauge panel are mounted. This tank was dual-chambered with the smaller of the two tanks used for starting fuel.

Like other models being produced in this time period, these machines were equipped with a fuel pump. Two styles of pump were used over the production run. The first, which is most common to the Model 30, was virtually the same as the early style pump used on the 22. It was brass, had a glass sediment bowl, and used two coil strainers to deliver the fuel to the bowl. This fuel pump was not adjustable.

The second type was most common to Model R-4 and was adjustable. It too was equipped with a sediment bowl with the adjusting screw located on top of the pump assembly. The glass sediment bowl was larger than previous models and was fed by one coil type strainer rather than one. Both pumps were manufactured by either the AC Company or Stewart Warner.

There were three carburetors available for these tractors. All styles are an updraft, cast-iron Zenith carburetor. Internally, the carburetors have different components for burning gasoline, alcohol, and tractor fuel or distillate. It is important to identify which carburetor your tractor is equipped with.

The tractor fuel carburetor is jetted with a number 20 and number 25 jet, while the alcohol carburetor uses a number 12 and number 50 jet. These numbers may be legibly stamped on the jets.

The gasoline carburetor uses a number 12 and number 32 jet. By identifying these you can determine the type of fuel used on your tractor.

The exterior adjustments of this carburetor are the same as those used with the Model 22 updraft Zenith carburetor. This style of fuel system is similar in components to the R-2 J Series tractors.

Model 35, 40, 50, and R-5

With the exception of the fuel tank, the fuel system used on the above tractors is similar to the system used on the later Model

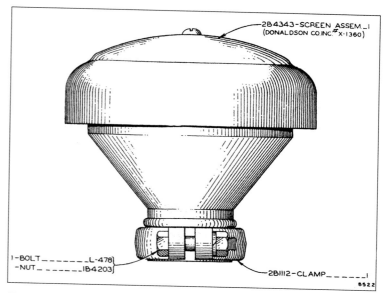

Typical pre-cleaner used on air intake pipe. *Midland Press Corp.—Caterpillar, Inc., Licensee*

30 PS Series tractors. The fuel tank is located in front of the operator and separates this compartment from the engine. The throttle lever and instrument panel are also attached to the front face of the tank. The early Model 50s had the fuel tank in front of the operator, while machines after 5A757 had it behind the seat.

As the fuel leaves the tank, it passes through the valve located at the base of the tank and enters a copper fuel line. This line leads to the AC fuel pump which is bolted to the side of the crankcase. This is the same fuel pump style as was used on many other of the gas tractors of this period.

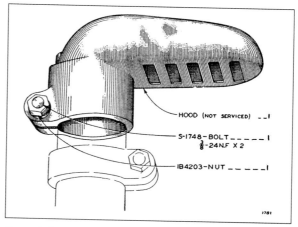

Duck bill style air pre-cleaner used often on orchard tractors. *Midland Press Corp.—Caterpillar, Inc., Licensee*

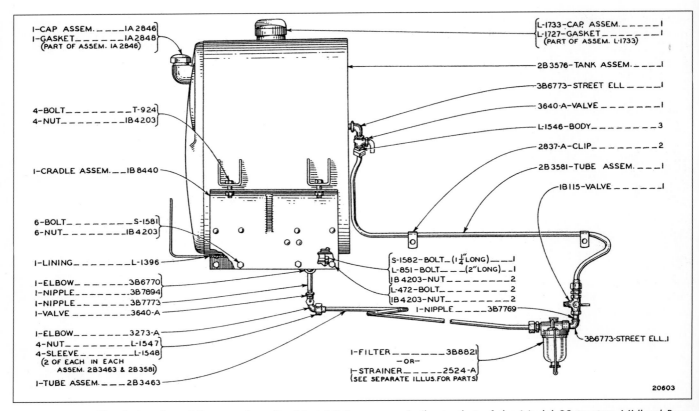

The fuel tank and lines used on the Model R-3 are very similar to that of the Model 28 tractor. *Midland Press Corp.—Caterpillar, Inc., Licensee*

The fuel then enters the Ensign AeLC carburetor through a brass banjo fitting located on the pot metal float chamber of the carburetor. The air intake portion of the carburetor is brass and is attached to the air cleaner by a cast elbow. The three exterior adjustments for high speed and load mixture, idle mixture, and idle speed are the same as with the other Ensign updraft carburetors of this style.

Models 60, 65, and 70

Models 60 and 65 were the two larger gas tractors to be equipped with the large 70-gallon barrel gas tank. The Model 60 used a Stewart Warner vacuum pump to aid fuel in its flow to the carburetor. The Model 65 tractor used an AC fuel pump similar to the one used on other tractors of this era.

The original carburetor used on the Model 60 was the Ensign Model GT-e two-inch fuel carburetor, but was replaced by a Stromberg MT 4, 1 3/4-inch at about tractor number 1700A. The MT 4 was used to tractor numbers 3192A and PA384, when it was replaced with the Ensign Model AA-e carburetor, which was also an updraft style. Model 65 used the Ensign Model Keb 1 3/4-inch carburetor. The external adjustments of these

two carburetors [WT.] are the same as those found on the other Ensign models used at this time.

The 70 also used the Ensign Keb carburetor but was jetted differently from the one used on Model 65. Two different fuel pumps were used on the 70 tractor. Both were brass and made by the AC Company, but there was with a minor difference in the fuel inlet to the sediment bowl. One style used a flat screen to filter the fuel, while the other used a round coil strainer.

The fuel tank of the Model 70 was located behind the seat rather than the old location on the left fender that was common on the earlier large tractors. This new location eventually became standard and is found on most models of tractors produced in the years that followed. A combustion chamber was also used on these machines. The 65 had two chamber sizes available. The standard size chamber was most generally used, but an optional chamber for 6,000-foot altitude was also available. The 70 had three sizes available: the standard, the 6,000-foot altitude, and 12,000-foot altitude. The size of the chamber became smaller as the altitude became larger. This was to give higher compression at these increased altitudes.

Machines such as the Model 22 were equipped with a three-position valve. This valve allowed the operator to switch to the main or auxiliary tank and shut the fuel off from the seat. *Midland Press Corp.—Caterpillar, Inc., Licensee*

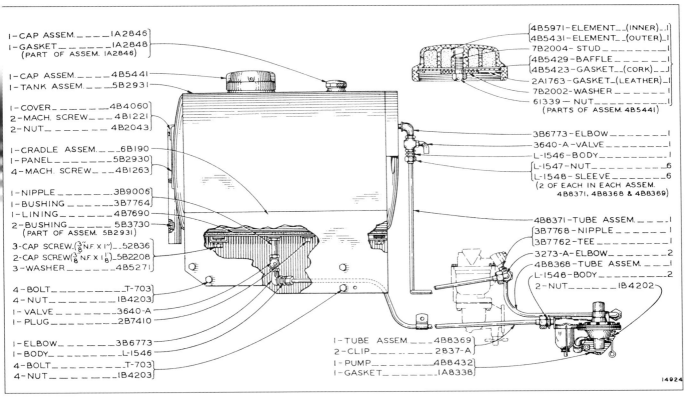

1-CAP ASSEM._ _ _ _ _ IA2846
1-GASKET_ _ _ _ _ _ _ IA2848
(PART OF ASSEM. IA2846)

1-CAP ASSEM._ _ _ _ 4B5441
1-TANK ASSEM._ _ _ 5B2931

1-COVER_ _ _ _ _ _ 4B4060
2-MACH. SCREW_ _ _ 4B1221
2-NUT_ _ _ _ _ _ _ 4B2043

1-CRADLE ASSEM._ _ _ 6B190
1-PANEL_ _ _ _ _ _ _ 5B2930
4-MACH. SCREW_ _ _ 4B1263

1-NIPPLE _ _ _ _ _ _ 3B9006
1-BUSHING _ _ _ _ _ 3B7764
1-LINING _ _ _ _ _ 4B7690
2-BUSHING _ _ _ _ _ 5B3730
(PART OF ASSEM. 5B2931)

3-CAP SCREW.($\frac{3}{8}$N.F. X 1")_ 52836
2-CAP SCREW($\frac{3}{8}$ N.F X 1$\frac{1}{8}$)_5B2208
3-WASHER_ _ _ _ _ _ 4B5271

4-BOLT_ _ _ _ _ _ _ _T-703
4-NUT_ _ _ _ _ _ _ IB4203
1-VALVE _ _ _ _ _ _ 3640-A
1-PLUG _ _ _ _ _ _ 2B7410

1-ELBOW_ _ _ _ _ _ 3B6773
1-BODY_ _ _ _ _ _ _ L-1546
4-BOLT_ _ _ _ _ _ _ _ T-703
4-NUT _ _ _ _ _ _ IB4203

4B5971-ELEMENT_ _(INNER)_ I
4B5431-ELEMENT_ _(OUTER)_ I
7B2004-STUD _ _ _ _ _ _ _ I
4B5429-BAFFLE _ _ _ _ _ _ I
4B5423-GASKET_(CORK)_ _ I
2AI763-GASKET (LEATHER)-I
7B2002-WASHER _ _ _ _ _ _ I
61339 — NUT_ _ _ _ _ _ _ I
(PARTS OF ASSEM. 4B5441)

3B6773-ELBOW_ _ _ _ _ _ _I
3640-A-VALVE _ _ _ _ _ _ _I
L-1546-BODY_ _ _ _ _ _ _ _I
L-1547-NUT_ _ _ _ _ _ _ _6
L-1548-SLEEVE _ _ _ _ _ _6
(2 OF EACH IN EACH ASSEM.
4B8371, 4B8368 & 4B8369)

4B8371-TUBE ASSEM._ _ _ _I
3B7768-NIPPLE _ _ _ _ _ _I
3B7762-TEE _ _ _ _ _ _ _ _I
3273-A-ELBOW _ _ _ _ _ _2
4B8368-TUBE ASSEM._ _ _ I
L-1546-BODY _ _ _ _ _ _ _2
2-NUT_ _ _ _ _ IB4202

1-TUBE ASSEM._ _ _4B8369
2-CLIP_ _ _ _ _ _ _2837-A
1-PUMP_ _ _ _ _ _ _4B8432
1-GASKET_ _ _ _ _ _IA8338

14924

This is the fuel tank and fuel pump combination found on the "J" series R-2 tractors. *Midland Press Corp.—Caterpillar, Inc., Licensee*

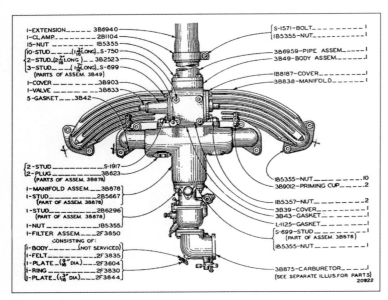

Intake and exhaust manifold assembly used with the Model R-4 tractor. *Midland Press Corp.—Caterpillar, Inc., Licensee*

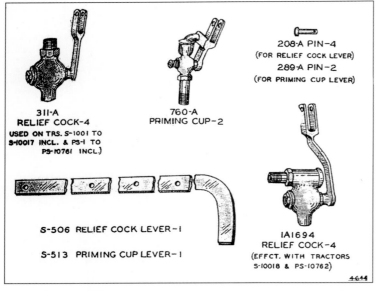

Compression relief and priming cup assembly for PS series 30 tractor. *Midland Press Corp.—Caterpillar, Inc., Licensee*

The manifold and carburetor used on the Caterpillar Model 28. *Clark and Sons*

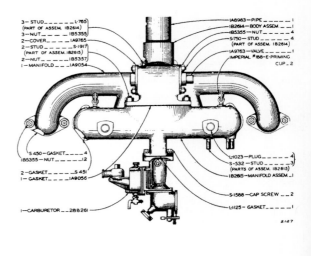

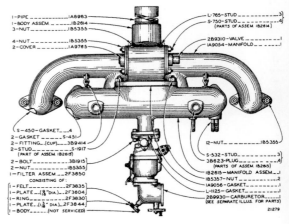

Manifold and Zenith carburetor combination used on the Model 40 tractor. *Midland Press Corp.—Caterpillar, Inc., Licensee*

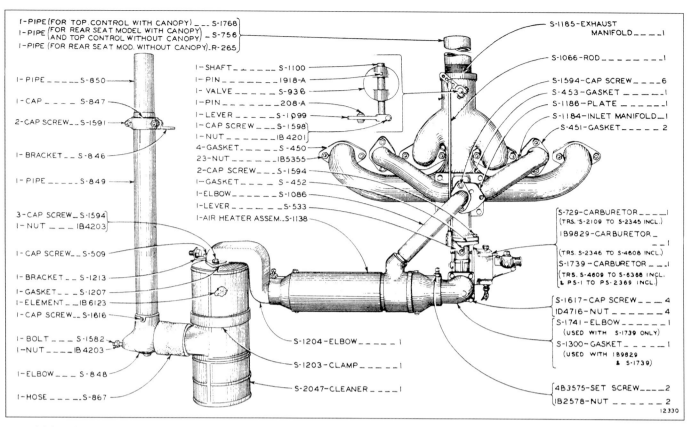

Manifold and air cleaner system of early Model 30 tractor. Note the pre-heater tube.

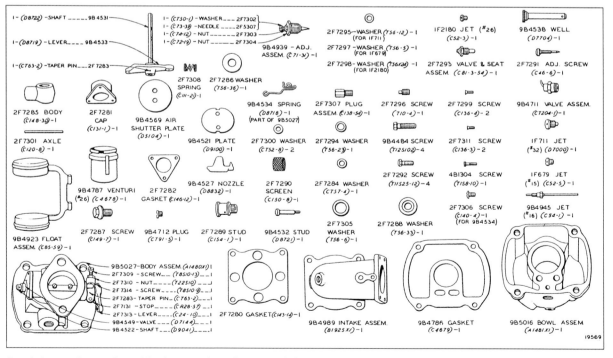

Breakdown of parts found in the Zenith carburetor of the Model R-5 tractor. *Midland Press Corp.—Caterpillar, Inc., Licensee*

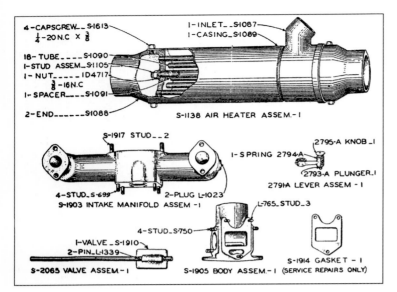

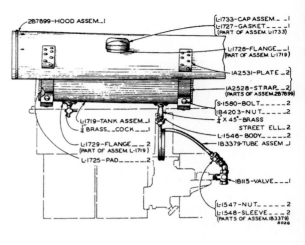

Air pre-heater tube for PS series Model 30. *Midland Press Corp.—Caterpillar, Inc., Licensee*

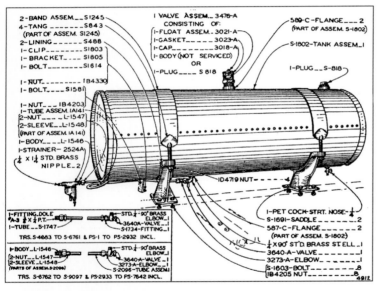

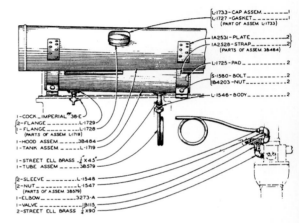

Fuel tank and pump used on the Model 40. This combination was also used on the R-5 and 35. *Midland Press Corp.—Caterpillar, Inc., Licensee*

Round barrel type fuel tank used on Model 30. This gave the tractor a look similar to the larger 60. *Midland Press Corp.—Caterpillar, Inc., Licensee*

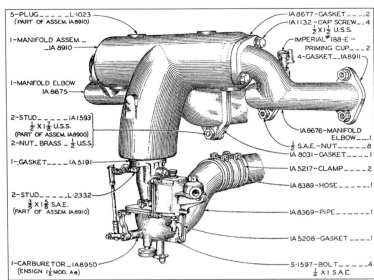

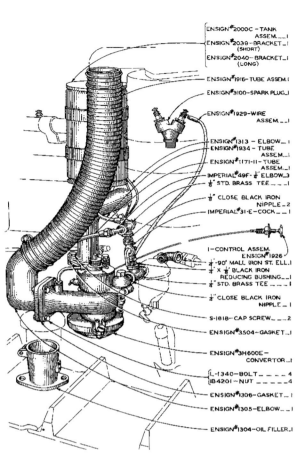

ENSIGN #2000C - TANK
ASSEM.__I
ENSIGN #2039 - BRACKET_I
(SHORT)
ENSIGN #2040 - BRACKET_I
(LONG)

ENSIGN #1916 - TUBE ASSEM._I

ENSIGN #3100 - SPARK PLUG_I

ENSIGN #1929 - WIRE
ASSEM._I

ENSIGN #1313 - ELBOW _ I
ENSIGN #1934 - TUBE
ASSEM._I
ENSIGN #1171-11 - TUBE
ASSEM._I
IMPERIAL #49F - ½ ELBOW_3
½ STD. BRASS TEE _ _ I
½" CLOSE BLACK IRON
NIPPLE_2
IMPERIAL #31-E-COCK _ _ I

I - CONTROL ASSEM.
ENSIGN #1926
½ - 90° MALL IRON ST. ELL. I
½ X ¼ BLACK IRON
REDUCING BUSHING_I
¼ STD. BRASS TEE _ _ I

¼" CLOSE BLACK IRON
NIPPLE _ I

S-1818 - CAP SCREW _ _ 2

ENSIGN #3504 - GASKET _ I

ENSIGN #3H600E -
CONVERTOR _ I

L-1340 - BOLT _ _ _ _ 4
IB4201 - NUT _ _ _ _ _ 4
ENSIGN #1306 - GASKET _ I

ENSIGN #1305 - ELBOW _ _ I

ENSIGN #1304 - OIL FILLER_I

Kerosene conversion carburetor for 8c series Model 20 tractor.

5 - PLUG _ _ _ _ L-1023
(PART OF ASSEM. IA8910)
I - MANIFOLD ASSEM. _
_ IA 8910

I - MANIFOLD ELBOW
IA 8675

2 - STUD _ _ _ _ IA 1593
½ X 1⅞ U.S.S.
(PART OF ASSEM. IA8900)
2 - NUT _ BRASS _ ½ U.S.S

I - GASKET _ _ _ _ IA 5191

2 - STUD _ _ _ _ L-2332
⅜ X 1⅝ S.A.E.
(PART OF ASSEM. IA8910)

I - CARBURETOR _ IA 8950
(ENSIGN 1½ MOD. Ae)

IA 8677 - GASKET _ _ _ _ 2
IA 1132 - CAP SCREW _ _ 4
½ X 1½ U.S.S.
IMPERIAL #188-E -
PRIMING CUP _ _ _ 2
4 - GASKET _ _ IA 8911

IA 8676 - MANIFOLD
ELBOW _ _ I
½ S.A.E. - NUT _ _ _ _ 8
IA 8031 - GASKET _ _ _ _ I

IA 5217 - CLAMP _ _ _ _ 2

IA 8389 - HOSE _ _ _ _ _ I

IA 8369 - PIPE _ _ _ _ _ I

IA 5208 - GASKET _ _ _ _ I

S-1597 - BOLT _ _ _ _ _ 4
¼ X 1 S.A.E.

Intake manifold and carburetor of Model 50. The engine of the 50 is a cross flow design. *Midland Press Corp.—Caterpillar, Inc., Licensee*

Carburetor Interchange

Caterpillar Model Part	Ten	Fifteen 7C	Fifteen PV	Twenty PL	Twenty 8C	Twenty Two	Twenty Five	Twenty Eight	Thirty PS	Thirty 6G	R2-5E	Thirty Five	Forty	Sixty	Sixty Five	Seventy
Ensign BeT - 1"	X	X	X		X											
Ensign AeL - 1 1/4"				X												
Ensign AeLC - 1 1/4"							X	X				X	X			
Zenith K5A						X					X					
Ensign AE - 1 1/2"									X	X						
Ensign GTe - 2"														X		
Ensign Keb - 1 3/4"															X	X

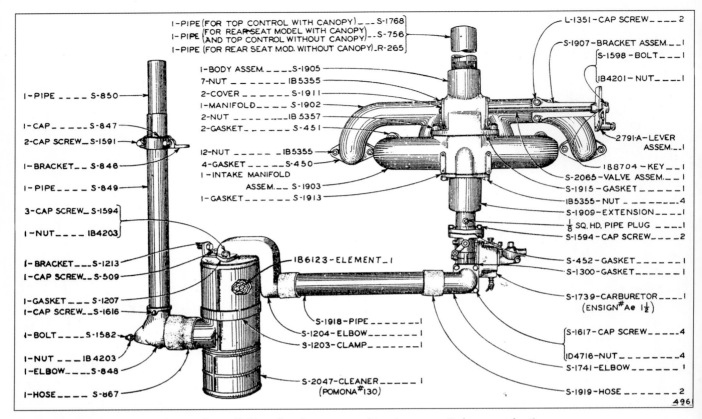

The Model 30 PS series used several manifold and carburetor combinations over its long production run.

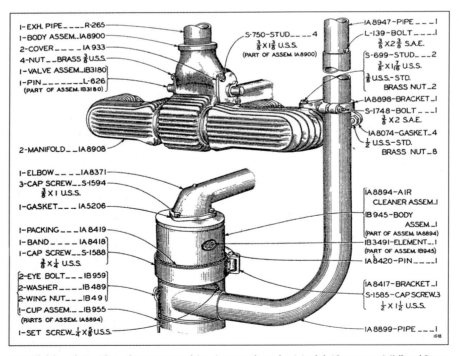

Manifold and Zenith carburetor combination used on the Model 40 tractor. *Midland Press Corp.—Caterpillar, Inc., Licensee*

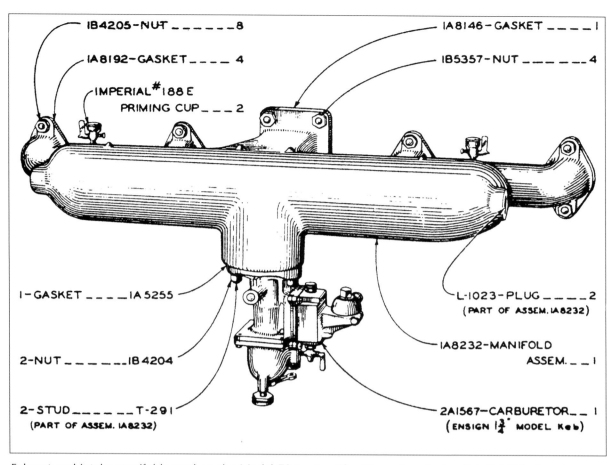

IB4205-NUT _ _ _ _ _ _8

IA8192-GASKET _ _ _ _ 4

IMPERIAL#188E
PRIMING CUP _ _ _ 2

IA8146-GASKET _ _ _ _ I

IB5357-NUT _ _ _ _ _4

I-GASKET _ _ _ _IA5255

2-NUT _ _ _ _ _ _IB4204

2-STUD _ _ _ _ _ _T-291
(PART OF ASSEM. IA8232)

L-1023-PLUG _ _ _ _2
(PART OF ASSEM. IA8232)

IA8232-MANIFOLD
                ASSEM. _ _ I

2A1567-CARBURETOR _ _ I
(ENSIGN 1¾" MODEL Keb)

Exhaust and intake manifolds used on the Model 70 tractor. The 70 used an Ensign Keb 1 3/4-inch carburetor. *Midland Press Corp.—Caterpillar, Inc., Licensee*

Exhaust manifold of the Model 70 tractor. The intake manifold is found on the opposite side.

COOLING SYSTEMS

The cooling systems used on most Caterpillar tractors are all similar. Some early models such as Models 30 and 60 used a tube radiator that was replaced with a core radiator. These radiators generally give you little problem. Usually if the radiator core is in poor condition you will have to remove it and have it redone by a repair shop or have it recored. It is recommended to first thoroughly flush and back flush the cooling system to remove as much debris as possible before starting the tractor. You may find it necessary to remove the water manifold

The Model 10 has a modest four-gallon cooling system capacity.

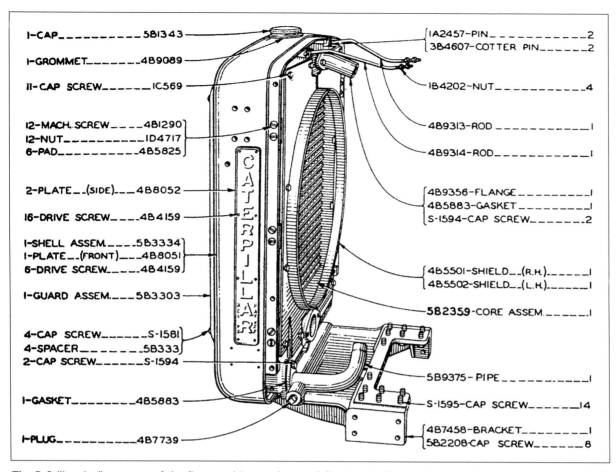

1-CAP _____ 5B1343	1A2457-PIN _____ 2
1-GROMMET _____ 4B9089	3B4607-COTTER PIN _____ 2
11-CAP SCREW _____ 1C569	1B4202-NUT _____ 4
12-MACH. SCREW _____ 4B1290	4B9313-ROD _____ 1
12-NUT _____ 1D4717	4B9314-ROD _____ 1
6-PAD _____ 4B5825	
2-PLATE __(SIDE)___4B8052	4B9356-FLANGE _____ 1
16-DRIVE SCREW ____ 4B4159	4B5883-GASKET _____ 1
	S-1594-CAP SCREW _____ 2
1-SHELL ASSEM ____ 5B3334	
1-PLATE __(FRONT)___4B8051	4B5501-SHIELD __(R.H.) _____ 1
6-DRIVE SCREW _____ 4B4159	4B5502-SHIELD __(L.H.) _____ 1
1-GUARD ASSEM ____ 5B3303	5B2359-CORE ASSEM _____ 1
4-CAP SCREW _____ S-1581	
4-SPACER _____ 5B333	
2-CAP SCREW _____ S-1594	5B9375 - PIPE _____ 1
1-GASKET _____ 4B5883	S-1595-CAP SCREW _____ 14
1-PLUG _____ 4B7739	4B7458-BRACKET _____ 1
	5B2208-CAP SCREW _____ 8

The R-2 "J series" was one of the first machines to have a full outer shell around the radiator tanks and core. *Midland Press Corp.—Caterpillar, Inc., Form P-1190*

pipes and top and bottom radiator tanks. At this time, you can also check for play in the water pump assembly, and if there is, remove and replace the bearings and packing. Many collectors have found that the packing nuts on the water pumps of their tractors leak when started. It is common that the packing may dry up if the machine has sat for a long time. After starting the tractor and letting the cooling systems thoroughly circulate, tighten the packing nut until the leak stops.

When in good condition, the cooling system of the Caterpillar tractor is able to cool the engine up to about 110 degrees under full load at normal speed. This is more than adequate for the conditions most collectors will be running their machines at. Some tractors, such as Models 22 and 30 6G Series, were equipped with thermostats that open at 180 degrees. Not all tractors were equipped with thermostats, but this is the opening temperature for the ones that were.

In years past, alcohol and methanol were the two most widely used antifreeze mixtures. The problem with these substances was that the boiling point of alcohol is 172 degrees and 150 degrees for methanol. Operators found that some of their cooling system capacity was being lost due to the low boiling point. The glycerin-based antifreeze solutions used today were at first discouraged because the solution was found to loosen rust and scale from the water passages. As time went on, the ethylene glycol solution became the most widely used.

The levels of protection of antifreeze are given in a percentage. For example, on the Caterpillar 28 with a cooling system capacity of 24 quarts, to arrive at a solution of 37 1/2 percent, you have to add three parts antifreeze to five parts water. This totals 9 quarts of antifreeze and 15 quarts of water to arrive at a 37 1/2 percent solution. If you have a copy of the manufacturer's recommendation for the solution needed, follow those guidelines for the proper protection.

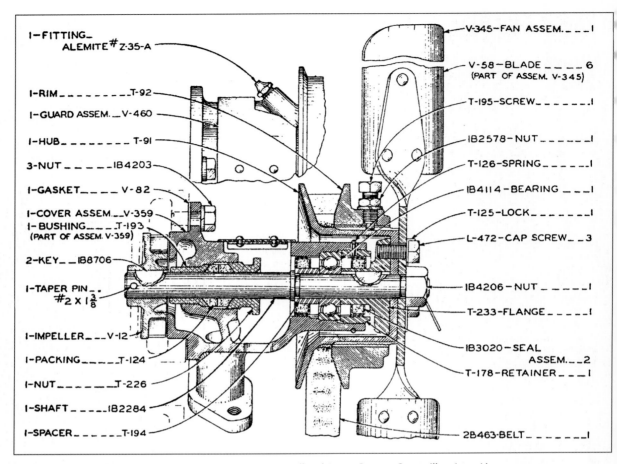

I—FITTING_
ALEMITE # Z-35-A

I—RIM_ _ _ _ _ _ _ _ T-92
I—GUARD ASSEM._ V-460
I—HUB_ _ _ _ _ _ _ T-91
3—NUT _ _ _ _ _ IB4203
I—GASKET_ _ _ _ V-82
I—COVER ASSEM._ _V-359
I—BUSHING_ _ _ T-193
(PART OF ASSEM. V-359)
2—KEY_ _ IB8706
I—TAPER PIN _ .
#2 x 1¾
I—IMPELLER_ _ _ V-12
I—PACKING_ _ _ _ _ T-124
I—NUT_ _ _ _ _ _ T-226
I—SHAFT _ _ _ _ IB2284
I—SPACER _ _ _ _ _ T-194

V-345—FAN ASSEM._ _ _ _ I
V-58—BLADE _ _ _ _ 6
(PART OF ASSEM. V-345)
T-195—SCREW _ _ _ _ _ _ I
IB2578—NUT _ _ _ _ _ I
T-126—SPRING _ _ _ _ _ I
IB4114—BEARING _ _ _ I
T-125—LOCK _ _ _ _ _ _ I
L-472—CAP SCREW_ _ 3
IB4206—NUT _ _ _ _ _ I
T-233—FLANGE _ _ _ _ I
IB3020—SEAL
ASSEM._ _ 2
T-178—RETAINER _ _ _ I
2B463—BELT _ _ _ _ _ _ I

Water pump cross section of PV series 15 tractor. *Midland Press Corp.—Caterpillar, Inc., Licensee*

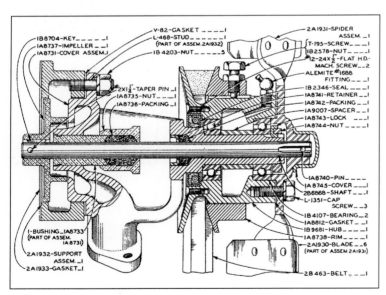

IB8704—KEY_ _ _ _ _ I
IA8737—IMPELLER _ _ I
IA8731—COVER ASSEM._

V-82—GASKET _ _ _ _ I
L-468—STUD _ _ _ _ _ I
(PART OF ASSEM. 2A1932)
IB 4203—NUT _ _ _ _ _ 5

2A1931—SPIDER
ASSEM._
T-195—SCREW _ _ I
IB2578—NUT _ _ _ I
12-24x½—FLAT HD.
MACH. SCREW_ _ 2
ALEMITE #1688
FITTING _ _ I

2x1¼—TAPER PIN _ _ I
IA8735—NUT _ _ _ _ I
IA8736—PACKING_ _ I

IB 2346—SEAL _ _ _ I
IA8741—RETAINER _ _ I
IA8742—PACKING _ _ I
IA9007—SPACER _ _ _ I
IA8743—LOCK _ _ _ I
IA8744—NUT _ _ _ _ I

IA8740—PIN _ _ _ _
IA 8745—COVER _ _ I
2B6868—SHAFT _ _ I
L-1351—CAP
SCREW_ _ 3
IB4107—BEARING _ 2
IA8812—GASKET _ _ I
IB 9681—HUB _ _ _ _ I
IA8738—RIM _ _ _ _ I
2A1930—BLADE _ _ 6
(PART OF ASSEM 2A1931)

2B 463—BELT _ _ _ I

I—BUSHING _IA8733_
(PART OF ASSEM.
IA8731)
2A1932—SUPPORT
ASSEM._ _ I
2A1933—GASKET_ I

Fan and water pump cross section of Model 22. *Midland Press Corp.—Caterpillar, Inc., Licensee*

The cooling system capacity of the Model 10 and 15 7C Series is 4 gallons. The Model 15 PV and 20 8C Series have a cooling system capacity of 4 3/4 gallons. The Model 22 and R-2 5E Series have a total capacity of 5 gallons for their cooling system. Model 20 and 25 both have a capacity of 5 1/2 gallons. Model 28 and R-3 have a capacity of 6 gallons, and S and PS Model 30 have a capacity of 9 3/4 gallons. Models 35 and 40 both require a 9 1/4-gallon capacity, while Model 50 contains 11 1/2 gallons. Finally, the Model 60 tractor uses a 18 3/4-gallon system, while the slightly larger Model 65 uses 29 gallons. The last big tractor of this period, the Model 70, used a staggering 36 gallons.

On tractors using a belt-driven water pump, adjustment is important. Proper adjustment for this belt should be 1 inch of slack when the belt is pushed inward from the centerline of two pulleys. This will ensure that the

The Model 28 cooling system contains eight gallons.

water pump is turning properly and cooling the engine like it should. The tension adjustment is made at the adjustable pulley on the fan shaft. If you find that the outer rims of the pulley are too far apart, the belt will be loose and slip. The belt should not bottom in the pulley or ride in the rims. Keep the belt clean and free of any oil or any other petroleum products.

If you live or store your tractor in an area with temperatures that drop below zero for any long period of time, it is important to test your antifreeze periodically to ensure it is giving the proper protection. If you use water in the cooling system, make sure it is properly drained prior to cold weather.

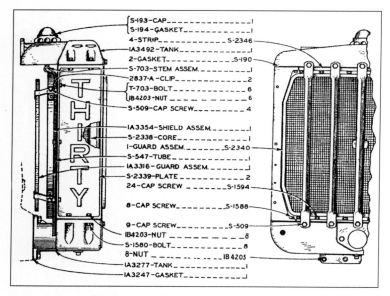

Radiator of PS series Model 30 tractor. *Midland Press Corp.—Caterpillar, Inc., Licensee*

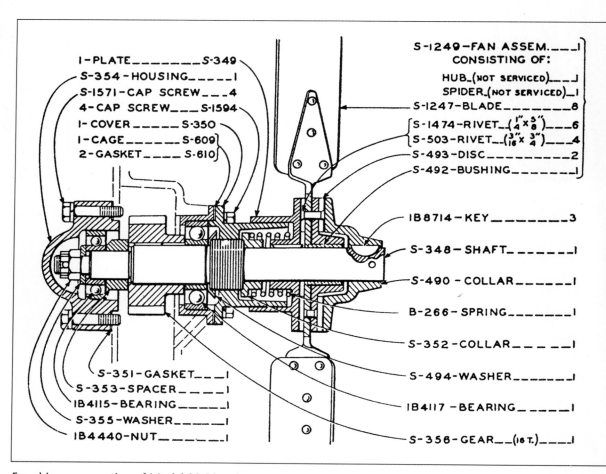

Fan drive cross section of Model 30 PS series. *Midland Press Corp.—Caterpillar, Inc., Licensee*

The large Model 65 tractor has a 29 gallon cooling system capacity.

CHAPTER SEVEN

UNDERCARRIAGE AND DRIVETRAIN

The undercarriage and drivetrain components of the yearly Caterpillar tractors are all similar in design and principle. The undercarriage of the tractor is the portion that the machine travels on. It is made up of several components that are essentially made to undergo wear. These components can be replaced individually, depending on the conditions in which the tractor was operated.

The track shoes bolted to the track rail are commonly called grousers. The grousers are the portion of the track that directly contacts the ground. Many styles were made available for the application in which the tractor was used. Standard track pads are generally flat and contain only a single bar for gripping the terrain and a combination of bolt holes to attach the pad to the rail. Street pads are completely flat and are usually notched on the outside edge to accept a bolt-on dirt or ice stud. A track pad used for snow and ice conditions is often found with a single hole cut in the center of the pad. This hole allows snow and ice to pass from the inner area of the track assembly to the outside, where it will fall from the pad. In areas where operations were conducted on ice, a skeleton ice

The method for adjusting tracks is to uniformly tighten the adjusting bolts on each side of the front idler wheel.

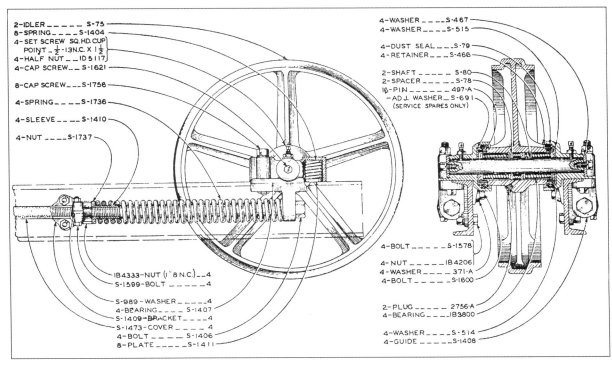

2-IDLER _ _ _ _ S-75
8-SPRING _ _ _ S-1404
4-SET SCREW SQ.HD.CUP
POINT $\frac{1}{2}$-13N.C. X $1\frac{1}{2}$
4-HALF NUT _ _ ID 5117
4-CAP SCREW _ _ S-1621

8-CAP SCREW _ _ _ S-1756

4-SPRING _ _ _ _ S-1736

4-SLEEVE _ _ _ _ S-1410

4-NUT _ _ _ _ S-1737

IB4333-NUT (1" 8 N.C.) _ _ 4
S-1599-BOLT _ _ _ _ _ 4

S-989-WASHER _ _ _ _ _ 4
4-BEARING _ _ _ _ S-1407
S-1409-BRACKET _ _ _ _ 4
S-1473-COVER _ _ _ _ 4
4-BOLT _ _ _ _ S-1406
8-PLATE _ _ _ _ S-1411

4-WASHER _ _ _ S-467
4-WASHER _ _ _ _ S-515

4-DUST SEAL _ _ _ S-79
4-RETAINER _ _ _ S-466

2-SHAFT _ _ _ _ _ S-80
2-SPACER _ _ _ _ S-78
16-PIN _ _ _ _ _ 497-A
-ADJ. WASHER_ S-691
(SERVICE SPARES ONLY)

4-BOLT _ _ _ _ S-1578

4- NUT _ _ _ _ IB 4206
4-WASHER _ _ _ 371-A
4-BOLT _ _ _ _ S-1600

2-PLUG _ _ _ _ 2756-A
4-BEARING _ _ _ IB3800

4-WASHER _ _ _ _ S-514
4-GUIDE _ _ _ _ S-1408

Front idler wheel and truck adjust springs of Model 30 tractor. *Midland Press Corp.—Caterpillar, Inc., Licensee*

An offset track pad was sometimes used to give lower ground pressure on a narrow gauge tractor.

IB 91 7" GROUSER SHOE
IB1969 7" GROUSER SHOE
(HEAT TREATED)

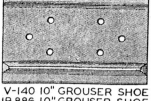

V-140 10" GROUSER SHOE
IB 886 10" GROUSER SHOE
(HEAT TREATED)

IA360 13" GROUSER SHOE
IB1970 13" GROUSER SHOE
(HEAT TREATED)

IA359 16" GROUSER SHOE
IB1971 16" GROUSER SHOE
(HEAT TREATED)

IB 57 20" GROUSER SHOE
IB 2469 20" GROUSER SHOE
(HEAT TREATED)

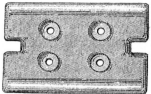

V-803 10" FLAT
UNIVERSAL SHOE

V-559 20" ANGLE SHOE

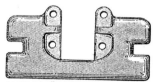

V-802 10" SKELETON SHOE

V-805 DIRT GROUSER R.H.
V-806 DIRT GROUSER L.H.
(USED WITH FLAT SHOE)

V-801 ICE & DIRT
GROUSER
(USED WITH GROUSER SHOE)

V-807 ICE GROUSER R.H.
V-808 ICE GROUSER L.H.
(USED WITH FLAT OR
SKELETON SHOE)

V-520 RUBBER
FACED SHOE

V-519 BASE PLATE
FOR V-520

V-819 BOLT $\frac{5}{8}$ X 2$\frac{1}{2}$ U.S.S.
(USED WITH: V-805, V-806, V-807, V-808)

T-490 BOLT $\frac{7}{16}$ X 1$\frac{1}{2}$ S.A.E.
(USED WITH V-801)

T-244 BOLT $\frac{7}{16}$ X 1$\frac{1}{4}$ S.A.E.
(USED WITH T-332)

T-921 BOLT $\frac{7}{16}$ X 1$\frac{5}{16}$ S.A.E.
(USED WITH: IB1969, IB886, V-803, V-802,
IB1970 IB1971 IB2469 V-559 V-519 V-520)

T-332 STREET
PLATE

T-1215 WASHER
(USED WITH: V-805,
V-806, V-807, V-808)

On some of the larger machines, a spacer was placed between the rear end housing and final drive of the tractor. This gave the machine its wide gauge.

shoe was available to permit slippage and provide better traction. The grousers, or track pads, are generally connected to the rail with a higher grade bolt, such as a grade eight.

The portion of the track that runs over the front idler wheel and sprocket is known as the rail. The parts of the rail that are in direct contact with the sprocket teeth and other areas are known as the bushings. The bushings cover the track pin, which is pressed in to hold the links of the track together. As the bushings wear, the tracks need to be adjusted periodically. Most track adjustment on these early machines is performed by turning one or two threaded bolts that run through the center of a spring to arrive at the proper adjustment.

If the pins and bushings of the tractor wear to the point that they are relatively unserviceable, the pins can be turned 180 degrees so the other half of the pin will wear. The rails can also be repinned and bushed by either an equipment dealership at their facility or by a portable track press. It may be difficult to find the correct pins and bushings for one of these older tractors, so it is important to carefully evaluate the condition of these areas when purchasing the tractor.

The front idler wheel is also commonly called a blank sprocket. This idler wheel is the non-driven portion of the track system that the rail runs on. The front idler wheels of the early small tractors are a simple spoked design with brass inner bearing and steel thrush washers with a central axle shaft. You will find that many of the tractors you will restore will have much wear in the axle and bearing areas. Often it is possible to make an axle shaft slightly oversized or place a brass bushing inside the bearing housing to take up the wear. The weight and strain put on the front idler is the source of much of this damage, and later an upper track carrier roller was added as a helper. On some of the larger tractors, such as Models 40 and 50, the front idler wheels were made in two halves with a hollow center. This design eventually gave way to the spoked wheel and on the more modern machines, a solid front idler.

The rear-drive sprocket is the main driving component of the tractor. The sprocket has teeth on it to grab the track pins and move the tractor along. On tractors such as the 10 and 15, the rear sprocket is convex to give the machine its narrow-gauge. The opposite is true on a

A Caterpillar front idler wheel. Note that the grousers are also clearly shown. *Clark and Sons*

A close look at the drive sprocket and rail. *Clark and Sons*

wide-gauge where the sprocket is concave, putting the outer ring of the sprocket further away from the body of the tractor. Generally, wide-gauge tractors are more rare than narrow-gauge, but this also causes difficulty because the wide-gauge sprockets are more difficult to find. The high-clearance model machines have sprockets specific to each machines and can be hard to find. Unlike the standard- or wide-gauge models, the high-clearance versions have a sprocket that is straight rather than convex or concave. The gauge of the high-clearance tractors is the same as the wide-gauge version, but the sprockets are not the same.

Sprocket wear is usually detected by either a pointing of the teeth of the sprocket or a rounding off of the sprocket teeth once the tip of the tooth has become brittle. The track of the machine must be removed to replace the rear drive sprocket, and a puller is generally needed to remove the sprocket from the axle shaft. In removing the sprocket, you may find a bellows seal around the inner axle shaft. These seals can be difficult to locate for the early machines, so use extreme care when removing them. You may find that the spokes of the rear drive sprocket

A Caterpillar rear drive sprocket and rail. *Clark and Sons*

A dirt or swamp pad used on a wide gauge tractor.

have been cut and a new outer ring welded to them. This may be due to the fact that the replacement sprocket was not available or the individual could not or did not remove the sprocket from the axle shaft. You may find yourself doing the same thing if you are unable to find the correct sprocket for the machine you are restoring. This is most common in a machine that had the same sprocket pitch as another but a center hub that was different. An example is a Model 22, the early models used a key way to hold the sprocket on the axle shaft, while some of the later models used a splined shaft.

On the larger tractors, regardless of whether or not the machine was wide-gauge or narrow-gauge, the sprockets stayed relatively the same. The gauge width was increased or decreased with the use of a spacer between the body of the tractor and the final drive housing. This also holds true for the Model 2-Ton, which uses the same sprocket on the narrow-gauge version and the wide and rare Swamp Special. The width is increased by a large final drive housing and does not affect the style of the sprocket.

The main drive components of the final drive are the pinion gear and ring, or bull gear. The pinion gear is generally a heavy gear formed to a shaft. The pinion is the smaller of the gears of the final drive and is usually driven through a key way. Both of these gears are subjected to a large amount of torque; therefore, it is important that these gears stay properly lubricated and maintained. On some

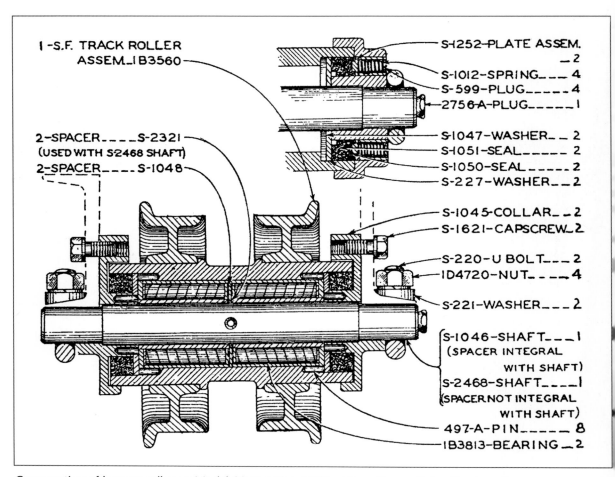

Cross section of bottom roller on Model 20 PL series. *Midland Press Corp.—Caterpillar, Inc., Licensee*

machines, such as the 20 PL Series and 30 PS Series, these gears have had many problems. Whether it be a crack in the pinion shaft from severe stress from the area of the key way or a broken tooth of a gear, these parts for the above models are difficult to locate. It is therefore important to adequately assess the condition of these gears when purchasing the above machines. I am often skeptical when purchasing these models of tractors, unless I can drive the machine myself.

The method of steering these machines is through a combination of clutch disks and plates combined with an outer drum and brake band. The lining of the brake band and steering clutch plates are often the areas that give the most trouble. If condensation or moisture finds its way into the area of the plates or break drum, these surfaces can become rusted and will not perform their required duties. To give you an idea of the number of surfaces in each steering clutch, read the following.

Model 35, R-2 J Series and 30 6G Series have 16 plates; Models 40, R-5, and 50, have 20 plates; and Model 70 has 30 plates. This is a large amount of disks when both sides of the tractor are considered. If you have poor steering, first attempt to adjust the steering clutches by removing the access cover in front of the operator's seat and turning the adjusting screws inward until you have found the best steering without overadjusting. Lubricate the necessary areas as outlined in the operator's manual. The brakes can be adjusted by removing the small access cover from the top portion of the steering clutch housing. This will allow you to tighten up the adjusting nut on the brake band when the lining becomes worn. By following the simple adjustment and lubricating instructions found in your operating manual, you will find that the steering components will give you excellent service for their age.

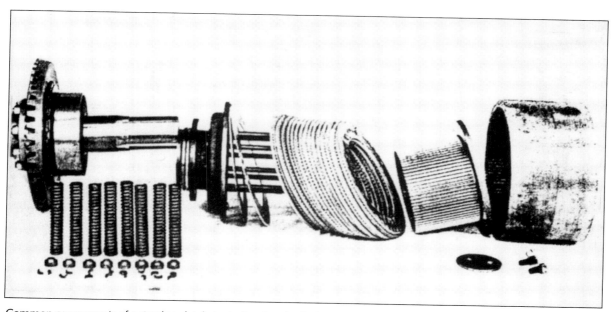

Common components of a steering clutch, including the clutch discs and drum. *Midland Press Corp.—Caterpillar, Inc., Licensee*

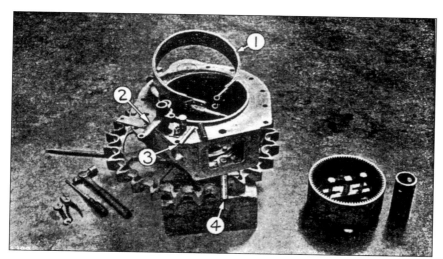

Components found in the steering brake of a Model 20 PL series. The band wraps around the outside of the drum which slides over the splined steering clutch pack. *Midland Press Corp.—Caterpillar, Inc., Licensee*

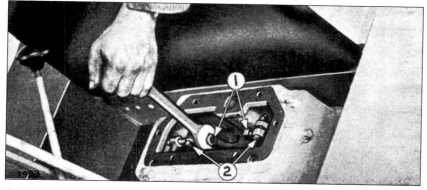

Steering clutch adjustment location on early smaller models. *Midland Press Corp.—Caterpillar, Inc., Licensee*

Cross section of transmission commonly used on most early tractors. *Midland Press Corp.—Caterpillar, Inc., Licensee*

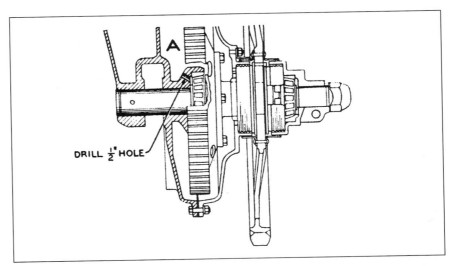

Service bulletin issued March 2, 1934. *Midland Press Corp.—Caterpillar, Inc., Licensee*

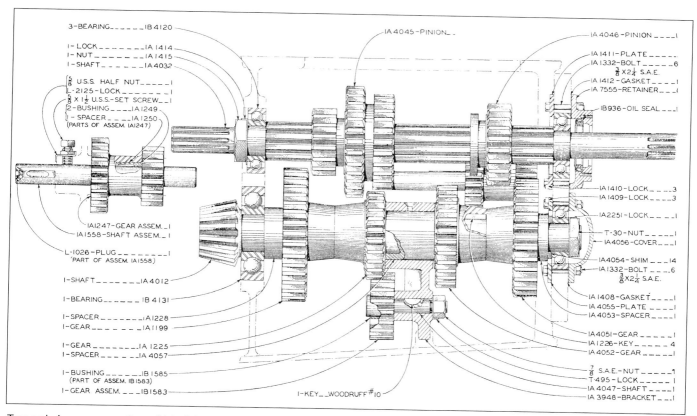

3-BEARING_____IB4120
I-LOCK_____IA1414
I-NUT_____IA1415
I-SHAFT_____IA4032
$\frac{5}{8}$ U.S.S. HALF NUT_____I
L-2125-LOCK_____I
$\frac{3}{8}$ X 1$\frac{1}{2}$ U.S.S.-SET SCREW__I
2-BUSHING____IA1249
I-SPACER____IA1250
(PARTS OF ASSEM. IA1247)

IA1247-GEAR ASSEM._I
IA1558-SHAFT ASSEM._I
L-1026-PLUG_____I
(PART OF ASSEM. IA1558)
I-SHAFT_____IA4012
I-BEARING_____IB4131
I-SPACER_____IA1228
I-GEAR_____IA1199
I-GEAR_____IA1225
I-SPACER____IA4057
I-BUSHING____IB1585
(PART OF ASSEM. IB1583)
I-GEAR ASSEM.___IB1583

IA4045-PINION_

I-KEY__WOODRUFF #10

IA4046-PINION___I
IA1411-PLATE_____
IA1332-BOLT_____6
$\frac{3}{8}$X2$\frac{1}{4}$ S.A.E.
IA1412-GASKET___I
IA7555-RETAINER___I
IB936-OIL SEAL___I

IA1410-LOCK___3
IA1409-LOCK____3
IA2251-LOCK____I
T-30-NUT____I
IA4056-COVER___I
IA4054-SHIM___14
IA1332-BOLT___6
$\frac{3}{8}$X2$\frac{1}{4}$ S.A.E.
IA1408-GASKET__I
IA4055-PLATE____I
IA4053-SPACER____I
IA4051-GEAR_____I
IA1226-KEY___4
IA4052-GEAR____I
$\frac{7}{8}$ S.A.E.-NUT_____1
T-495-LOCK_____I
IA4047-SHAFT____I
IA3948-BRACKET__I

Transmission cross section of Model 50. *Midland Press Corp.—Caterpillar, Inc., Licensee*

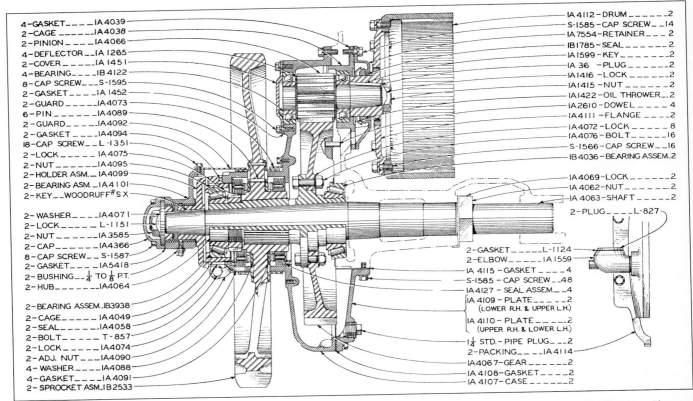

4—GASKET____IA 4039
2—CAGE_____IA 4038
2—PINION____IA 4066
4—DEFLECTOR__IA 1265
2—COVER____IA 1451
4—BEARING___IB 4122
8—CAP SCREW___S-1595
2—GASKET___IA 1452
2—GUARD____IA 4073
6—PIN_____IA 4089
2—GUARD____IA 4092
2—GASKET___IA 4094
18—CAP SCREW__L-1351
2—LOCK____IA 4075
2—NUT_____IA 4095
2—HOLDER ASM._IA 4099
2—BEARING ASM._IA 4101
2—KEY__WOODRUFF #S X

2—WASHER____IA 4071
2—LOCK_____L-1151
2—NUT____IA 3585
2—CAP____IA 4366
8—CAP SCREW__S-1587
2—GASKET___IA 5418
2—BUSHING__¼ TO ⅛ P.T.
2—HUB_____IA 4064

2—BEARING ASSEM._IB 3938
2—CAGE_____IA 4049
2—SEAL_____IA 4058
2—BOLT_____T-857
2—LOCK_____IA 4074
2—ADJ. NUT___IA 4090
4—WASHER____IA 4088
4—GASKET___IA 4091
2—SPROCKET ASM._IB 2533

IA 4112—DRUM_____2
S-1585—CAP SCREW__14
IA 7554—RETAINER__2
IB 1785—SEAL_____2
IA 1599—KEY_____2
IA 36—PLUG_____2
IA 1416—LOCK_____2
IA 1415—NUT_____2
IA 1422—OIL THROWER_2
IA 2610—DOWEL____4
IA 4111—FLANGE___2
IA 4072—LOCK_____8
IA 4076—BOLT_____16
S-1566—CAP SCREW__16
IB 4036—BEARING ASSEM.2

IA 4069—LOCK_____2
IA 4062—NUT_____2
IA 4063—SHAFT____2

2—PLUG___L-827

2—GASKET____L-1124
2—ELBOW____IA 1559
IA 4115—GASKET___4
S-1585—CAP SCREW__48
IA 4127—SEAL ASSEM._4
IA 4109—PLATE____2
(LOWER R.H. & UPPER L.H.)
IA 4110—PLATE____2
(UPPER R.H. & LOWER L.H.)
1¼ STD. PIPE PLUG__2
2—PACKING__IA 4114
IA 4067—GEAR_____2
IA 4108—GASKET___2
IA 4107—CASE_____2

Final drive cross section of Model 50 tractor including brake drum. *Midland Press Corp.—Caterpillar, Inc., Licensee*

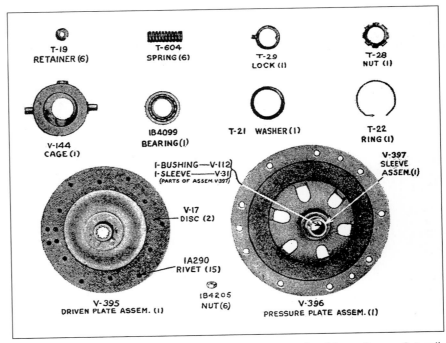

T-19
RETAINER (6)

T-604
SPRING (6)

T-29
LOCK (1)

T-28
NUT (1)

V-144
CAGE (1)

IB4099
BEARING(1)

T-21 WASHER (1)

T-22
RING (1)

I-BUSHING—V-112
I-SLEEVE___V-31
(PARTS OF ASSEM. V-397)

V-397
SLEEVE
ASSEM.(1)

V-17
DISC (2)

IA290
RIVET (15)

IB4205
NUT (6)

V-395
DRIVEN PLATE ASSEM. (1)

V-396
PRESSURE PLATE ASSEM.(1)

Master clutch components of PV series Model 15. *Midland Press Corp.—Caterpillar, Inc., Licensee*

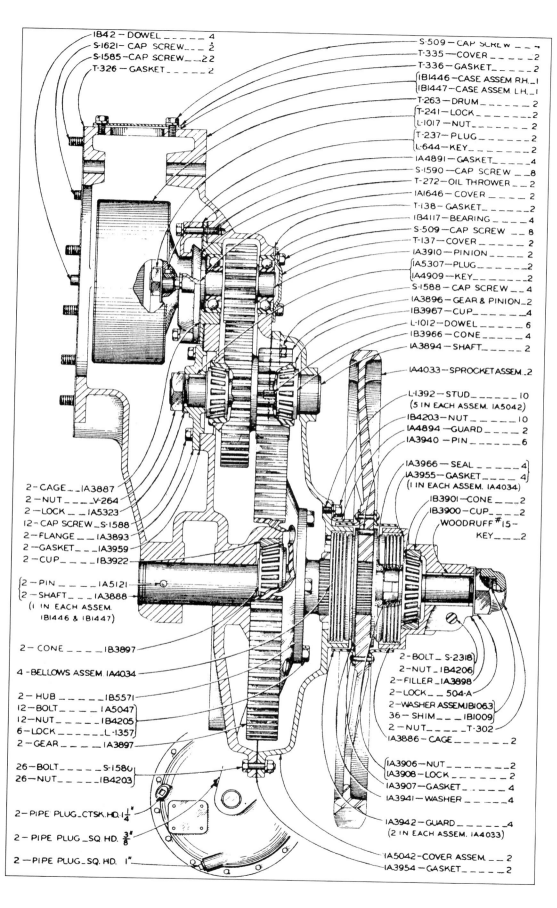

1B42 – DOWEL _ _ _ _ _ 4
S-1621 – CAP SCREW_ _ _ 2
S-1585 – CAP SCREW_ _ 22
T-326 – GASKET _ _ _ _ _ 2

S-509 – CAP SCREW _ _ _ 4
T-335 – COVER _ _ _ _ _ 2
T-336 – GASKET_ _ _ _ _ 2
1B1446 – CASE ASSEM R.H._ 1
1B1447 – CASE ASSEM L.H._ 1
T-263 – DRUM _ _ _ _ _ _ 2
T-241 – LOCK _ _ _ _ _ _ 2
L-1017 – NUT _ _ _ _ _ _ 2
T-237 – PLUG _ _ _ _ _ _ 2
L-644 – KEY _ _ _ _ _ _ 2
1A4891 – GASKET _ _ _ _ _ 4
S-1590 – CAP SCREW _ _ 8
T-272 – OIL THROWER _ _ 2
1A1646 – COVER _ _ _ _ 2
T-138 – GASKET_ _ _ _ _ 2
1B4117 – BEARING _ _ _ _ 4
S-509 – CAP SCREW _ _ 8
T-137 – COVER _ _ _ _ _ 2
1A3910 – PINION _ _ _ _ 2
1A5307 – PLUG_ _ _ _ _ 2
1A4909 – KEY_ _ _ _ _ _ 2
S-1588 – CAP SCREW _ _ 4
1A3896 – GEAR & PINION_ 2
1B3967 – CUP _ _ _ _ _ 4
L-1012 – DOWEL _ _ _ _ _ 6
1B3966 – CONE _ _ _ _ _ 4
1A3894 – SHAFT _ _ _ _ _ 2

1A4033 – SPROCKET ASSEM._ 2

L-1392 – STUD_ _ _ _ _ _ 10
(5 IN EACH ASSEM. 1A5042)
1B4203 – NUT _ _ _ _ _ _ 10
1A4894 – GUARD _ _ _ _ 2
1A3940 – PIN _ _ _ _ _ _ 6

1A3966 – SEAL _ _ _ _ _ 4
1A3955 – GASKET _ _ _ _ 4
(1 IN EACH ASSEM. 1A4034)

1B3901 – CONE _ _ 2
1B3900 – CUP _ _ _ 2
WOODRUFF #15 –
KEY _ _ _ 2

2 – CAGE _ _ 1A3887
2 – NUT _ _ _ V-264
2 – LOCK _ _ 1A5323
12 – CAP SCREW _ S-1588
2 – FLANGE _ _ 1A3893
2 – GASKET_ _ _ 1A3959
2 – CUP _ _ _ _ 1B3922

2 – PIN _ _ _ _ 1A5121
2 – SHAFT _ _ _ 1A3888
(1 IN EACH ASSEM.
1B1446 & 1B1447)

2 – CONE _ _ _ _ 1B3897

4 – BELLOWS ASSEM. 1A4034

2 – HUB _ _ _ _ _ 1B5571
12 – BOLT _ _ _ _ 1A5047
12 – NUT_ _ _ _ _ 1B4205
6 – LOCK _ _ _ _ _ L-1357
2 – GEAR _ _ _ _ 1A3897

26 – BOLT _ _ _ _ S-1580
26 – NUT _ _ _ _ 1B4203

2 – PIPE PLUG_CTSK.HD. 1¼"

2 – PIPE PLUG _SQ.HD. ⅜"

2 – PIPE PLUG _SQ.HD. 1"

2 – BOLT _ S-2318
2 – NUT _ 1B4206
2 – FILLER _ 1A3898
2 – LOCK _ _ 504-A
2 – WASHER ASSEM.1B1063
36 – SHIM _ _ _ 1B1009
2 – NUT _ _ _ _ T-302
1A3886 – CAGE _ _ _ _ _ 2

1A3906 – NUT _ _ _ _ _ _ 2
1A3908 – LOCK _ _ _ _ _ 2
1A3907 – GASKET _ _ _ _ 4
1A3941 – WASHER _ _ _ _ 4
1A3942 – GUARD _ _ _ _ _ 4
(2 IN EACH ASSEM. 1A4033)

1A5042 – COVER ASSEM. _ _ 2
1A3954 – GASKET _ _ _ _ _ 2

Final drive cross section of high-clearance 10 tractor. *Midland Press Corp.— Caterpillar, Inc., Licensee*

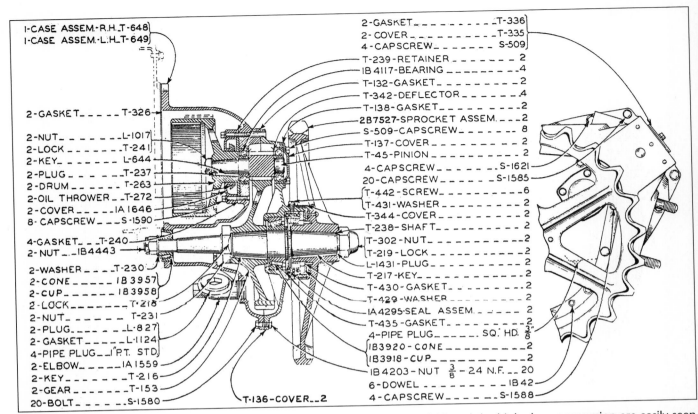

The differences between the final drive of the standard Model 10 and the high-clearance version are easily seen when compared. The cross section of the standard Model 10 final drive shown is also common to the 7C 15.

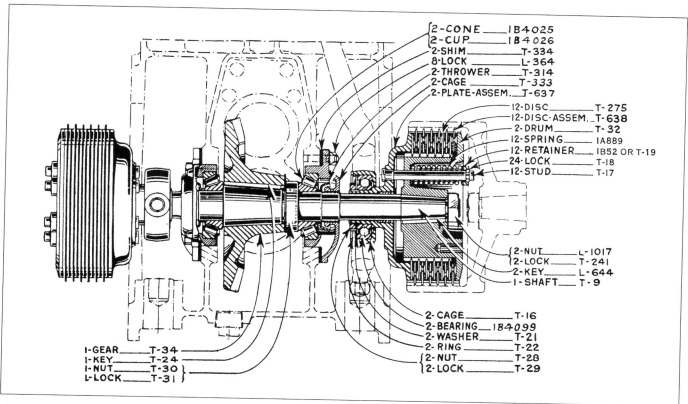

2-CONE____1B4025
2-CUP____1B4026
2-SHIM____T-334
8-LOCK____L-364
2-THROWER____T-314
2-CAGE____T-333
2-PLATE-ASSEM.__T-637

12-DISC____T-275
12-DISC-ASSEM.__T-638
2-DRUM____T-32
12-SPRING____1A889
12-RETAINER____1B52 OR T-19
24-LOCK____T-18
12-STUD____T-17

2-NUT____L-1017
2-LOCK____T-241
2-KEY____L-644
1-SHAFT____T-9

2-CAGE____T-16
2-BEARING__1B4099
2-WASHER____T-21
2-RING____T-22
2-NUT____T-28
2-LOCK____T-29

1-GEAR____T-34
1-KEY____T-24
1-NUT____T-30
L-LOCK____T-31

Steering clutch assembly of Model 10 tractor and 7C 15.

The wide gauge 10 is far more rare than the standard model. Wide gauge refers to the stance of the tractor. It is different from wide track or wide pad.

Street pad or flat pad that would accept bolt-on dirt grouser or ice shoe.

The wide gauge 10 uses a concave rear sprocket to help give it its wider stance.

Common type of steering clutch and brake arrangement. *Midland Press Corp.—Caterpillar, Inc., Licensee*

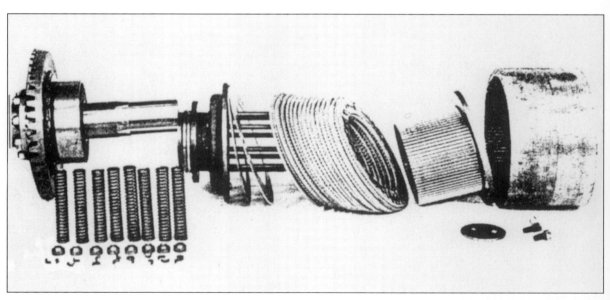

Disassembled steering clutch pack and brake drum. The inside of the brake drum is splined to accept the clutch discs. *Midland Press Corp.—Caterpillar, Inc., Licensee*

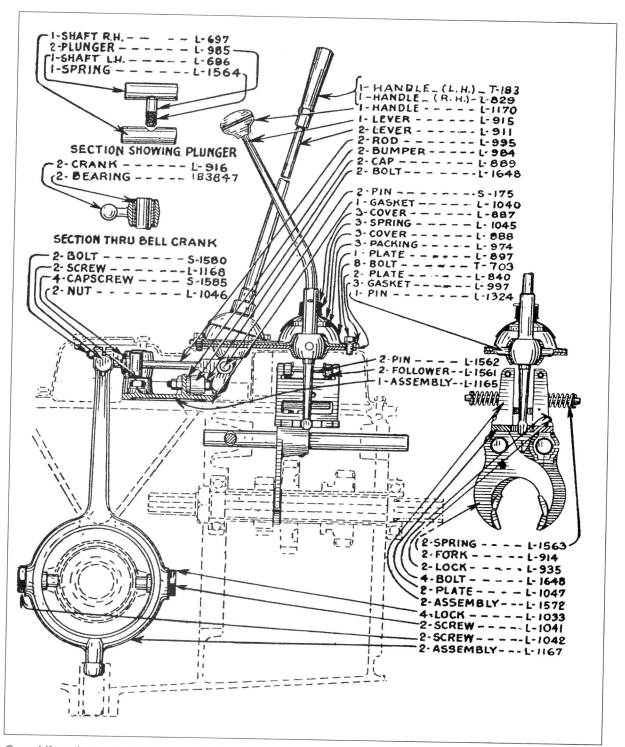

Gear shift and steering clutch control of L and PL Model 20. *Midland Press Corp.—Caterpillar, Inc., Licensee*

The labels in the figure read:

SECTION SHOWING PLUNGER

1-SHAFT R.H. — — — — L-697
2-PLUNGER — — — — — L-985
1-SHAFT L.H. — — — — L-696
1-SPRING — — — — — L-1564

2-CRANK — — — — — L-916
2-BEARING — — — — 1B3847

SECTION THRU BELL CRANK

2-BOLT — — — — — S-1580
2-SCREW — — — — — L-1168
4-CAPSCREW — — — S-1585
2-NUT — — — — — L-1046

1-HANDLE (L.H.) — T-183
1-HANDLE (R.H.) — L-829
1-HANDLE — — — — L-1170
1-LEVER — — — — L-915
2-LEVER — — — — L-911
2-ROD — — — — — L-995
2-BUMPER — — — — L-984
2-CAP — — — — — L-889
2-BOLT — — — — — L-1648

2-PIN — — — — — S-175
1-GASKET — — — — L-1040
3-COVER — — — — L-887
3-SPRING — — — — L-1045
3-COVER — — — — L-888
3-PACKING — — — L-974
1-PLATE — — — — L-897
8-BOLT — — — — T-703
2-PLATE — — — — L-840
3-GASKET — — — — L-997
1-PIN — — — — — L-1324

2-PIN — — — L-1562
2-FOLLOWER — L-1561
1-ASSEMBLY — L-1165

2-SPRING — — — L-1563
2-FORK — — — — L-914
2-LOCK — — — — L-935
4-BOLT — — — — L-1648
2-PLATE — — — L-1047
2-ASSEMBLY — — L-1572
4-LOCK — — — — L-1033
2-SCREW — — — L-1041
2-SCREW — — — L-1042
2-ASSEMBLY — — L-1167

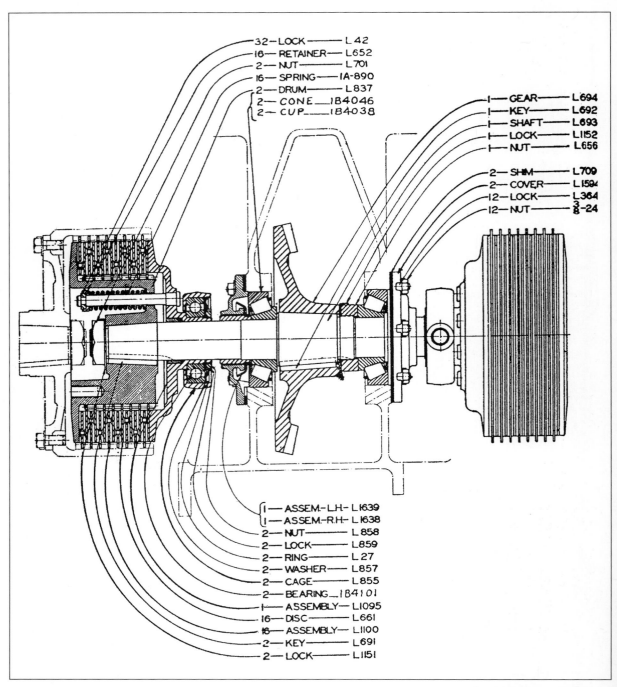

32—LOCK———— L 42
16— RETAINER— L 652
2— NUT———— L 701
16— SPRING—— IA-890
2—DRUM——— L 837
2— CONE___IB4046
2— CUP___IB4038

I— GEAR——— L 694
I— KEY——— L 692
I— SHAFT—— L 693
I— LOCK——— L II52
I— NUT——— L 656

2— SHIM—— L 709
2— COVER— L I594
12— LOCK— L 364
12— NUT—— $\frac{3}{8}$-24

I— ASSEM-LH— L I639
I— ASSEM-RH— L I638
2— NUT——— L 858
2— LOCK——— L 859
2— RING——— L 27
2— WASHER—— L 857
2— CAGE——— L 855
2— BEARING__IB4I0I
I— ASSEMBLY— L I095
16— DISC——— L 66I
16— ASSEMBLY— L II00
2— KEY——— L 69I
2— LOCK——— L II5I

Steering clutch and rear drive axleshaft assembly of Model 20 *Midland Press Corp.—Caterpillar, Inc., Licensee*

132

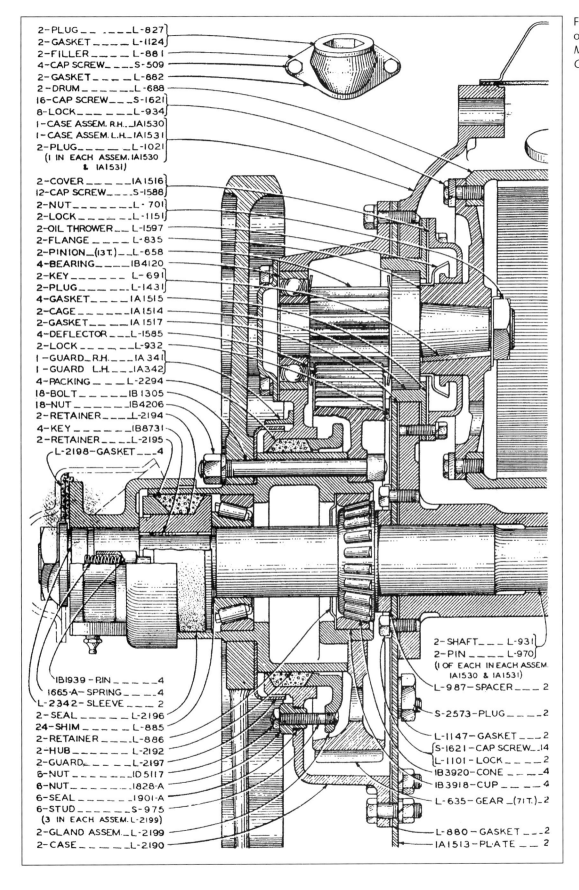

2-PLUG_ _ _ _ _ _ _L-827
2-GASKET_ _ _ _ _L-1124
2-FILLER_ _ _ _ _L-881
4-CAP SCREW_ _ _ _S-509
2-GASKET_ _ _ _L-882
2-DRUM_ _ _ _ _ _L-688
16-CAP SCREW_ _ _S-1621
8-LOCK_ _ _ _ _ _L-934
1-CASE ASSEM. R.H._IA1530
1-CASE ASSEM. L.H. IA1531
2-PLUG_ _ _ _ _L-1021
(1 IN EACH ASSEM. IA1530
& IA1531)
2-COVER_ _ _ _ _IA1516
12-CAP SCREW_ _ _ _S-1588
2-NUT_ _ _ _ _ _L-701
2-LOCK_ _ _ _ _ _L-1151
2-OIL THROWER_ _ L-1597
2-FLANGE_ _ _ _ _L-835
2-PINION_(13 T.)_ _L-658
4-BEARING_ _ _ _IB4120
2-KEY_ _ _ _ _ _L-691
2-PLUG_ _ _ _ _L-1431
4-GASKET_ _ _ _ _IA1515
2-CAGE_ _ _ _ _ _IA1514
2-GASKET_ _ _ _IA1517
4-DEFLECTOR_ _ _L-1585
2-LOCK_ _ _ _ _ _L-932
1-GUARD_R.H._ _ _IA341
1-GUARD_L.H._ _ _IA342
4-PACKING_ _ _ _L-2294
18-BOLT_ _ _ _ _IB1305
18-NUT_ _ _ _ _ _IB4206
2-RETAINER_ _ _ _L-2194
4-KEY_ _ _ _ _ _IB8731
2-RETAINER_ _ _ _L-2195
L-2198-GASKET_ _ _ 4
IB1939-PIN_ _ _ _ _4
1665-A-SPRING_ _ _4
L-2342-SLEEVE_ _ _2
2-SEAL_ _ _ _ _ _L-2196
24-SHIM_ _ _ _ _L-885
2-RETAINER_ _ _ _L-886
2-HUB_ _ _ _ _ _L-2192
2-GUARD_ _ _ _ _L-2197
6-NUT_ _ _ _ _ _ID5117
8-NUT_ _ _ _ _ _1828-A
6-SEAL_ _ _ _ _ _1901-A
6-STUD_ _ _ _ _ _S-975
(3 IN EACH ASSEM. L-2199)
2-GLAND ASSEM._L-2199
2-CASE_ _ _ _ _L-2190

2-SHAFT_ _ _ L-931
2-PIN_ _ _ _ L-970
(1 OF EACH IN EACH ASSEM.
IA1530 & IA1531)
L-987-SPACER_ _ _ 2
S-2573-PLUG_ _ _ _2
L-1147-GASKET_ _ _2
S-1621-CAP SCREW_ _14
L-1101-LOCK_ _ _ _2
IB3920-CONE_ _ _ _4
IB3918-CUP_ _ _ _ 4
L-635-GEAR_(71 T.)_2
L-880-GASKET_ _ _2
IA1513-PLATE_ _ 2

Final drive cross section
of PL series 20 tractor.
*Midland Press Corp.—
Caterpillar, Inc., Licensee*

Bevel gear, steering clutch, and final drive.

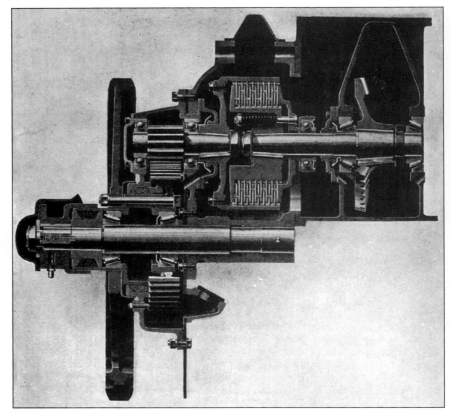

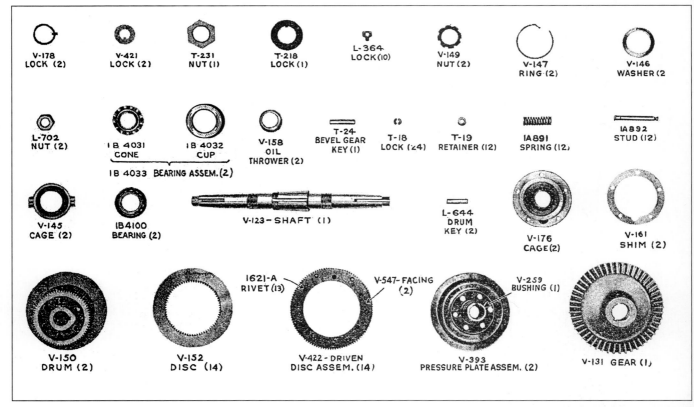

Break down of steering clutch parts for PL series 20 tractor. *Midland Press Corp.—Caterpillar, Inc., Licensee*

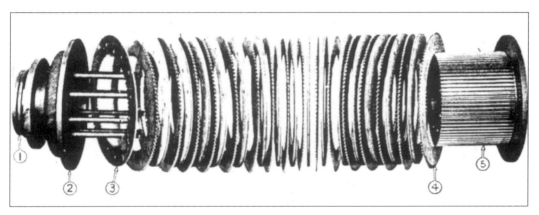

A clutch basket assembly.

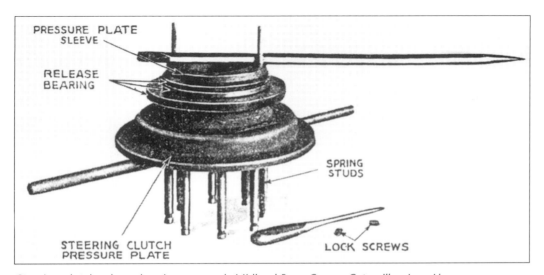

Steering clutch release bearing removal. *Midland Press Corp.—Caterpillar, Inc., Licensee*

Final drive of high-clearance Model 10 tractor.

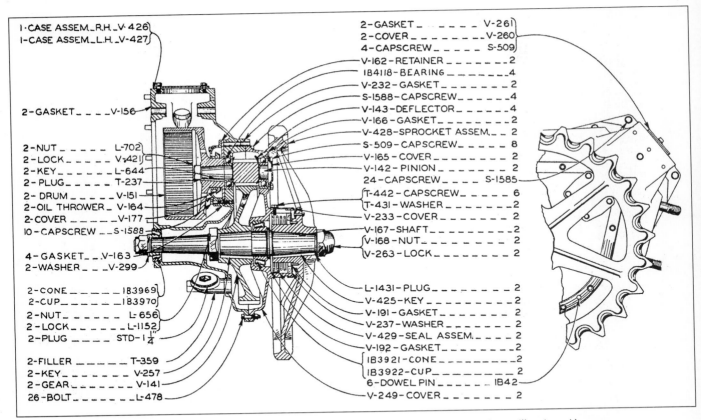

Left column labels:
- 1-CASE ASSEM._R.H._V-426
- 1-CASE ASSEM._L.H._V-427
- 2-GASKET _ _ _ _V-156
- 2-NUT _ _ _ _ _ L-702
- 2-LOCK _ _ _ _ _ V-421
- 2-KEY _ _ _ _ _ L-644
- 2-PLUG _ _ _ _ T-237
- 2-DRUM _ _ _ _ V-151
- 2-OIL THROWER _ V-164
- 2-COVER _ _ _ _ _V-177
- 10-CAPSCREW _ _ S-1588
- 4-GASKET _ _V-163
- 2-WASHER _ _ _V-299
- 2-CONE _ _ _ _ _ 1B3969
- 2-CUP _ _ _ _ _ 1B3970
- 2-NUT _ _ _ _ _ L-656
- 2-LOCK _ _ _ _ _ L-1152
- 2-PLUG _ _ _ _ STD-1¼"
- 2-FILLER _ _ _ _ _ T-359
- 2-KEY _ _ _ _ _ _ V-257
- 2-GEAR _ _ _ _ _ _ V-141
- 26-BOLT _ _ _ _ _ L-478

Right column labels:
- 2-GASKET _ _ _ _ _ _ V-261
- 2-COVER _ _ _ _ _ _ _ V-260
- 4-CAPSCREW _ _ _ _ _ S-509
- V-162 - RETAINER _ _ _ _ _ _ 2
- 1B4118 - BEARING _ _ _ _ _ _ _4
- V-232 - GASKET_ _ _ _ _ _ _ 2
- S-1588 - CAPSCREW _ _ _ _ _ 4
- V-143 - DEFLECTOR _ _ _ _ _ _4
- V-166 - GASKET _ _ _ _ _ _ _ 2
- V-428 - SPROCKET ASSEM._ _ 2
- S-509 - CAPSCREW _ _ _ _ 8
- V-165 - COVER _ _ _ _ _ _ _ 2
- V-142 - PINION _ _ _ _ _ _ _ 2
- 24-CAPSCREW _ _ _ _ S-1585
- T-442 - CAPSCREW _ _ _ _ _ 6
- T-431 - WASHER _ _ _ _ _ _ 2
- V-233 - COVER _ _ _ _ _ _ _ 2
- V-167 - SHAFT _ _ _ _ _ _ _ 2
- V-168 - NUT _ _ _ _ _ _ _ 2
- V-263 - LOCK _ _ _ _ _ _ _ 2
- L-1431 - PLUG _ _ _ _ _ _ _ 2
- V-425 - KEY _ _ _ _ _ _ _ _ 2
- V-191 - GASKET _ _ _ _ _ _ 2
- V-237 - WASHER _ _ _ _ _ _ 2
- V-429 - SEAL ASSEM. _ _ _ _ 2
- V-192 - GASKET _ _ _ _ _ _ _2
- 1B3921 - CONE _ _ _ _ _ _ _ _2
- 1B3922 - CUP _ _ _ _ _ _ _ _ 2
- 6-DOWEL PIN _ _ _ _ _ 1B42
- V-249 - COVER _ _ _ _ _ _ 2

Cross section of final drive for PV series Model 15. *Midland Press Corp.—Caterpillar, Inc., Licensee*

Right
Bull and pinion gear mechanism of Model 20 PL series. *Midland Press Corp.—Caterpillar, Inc., Licensee*

Using a puller to remove outer axle bearing. *Midland Press Corp.—Caterpillar, Inc., Licensee*

Sprocket and outer final drive housing removal on Model 10 high-clearance. *Midland Press Corp.—Caterpillar, Inc., Licensee*

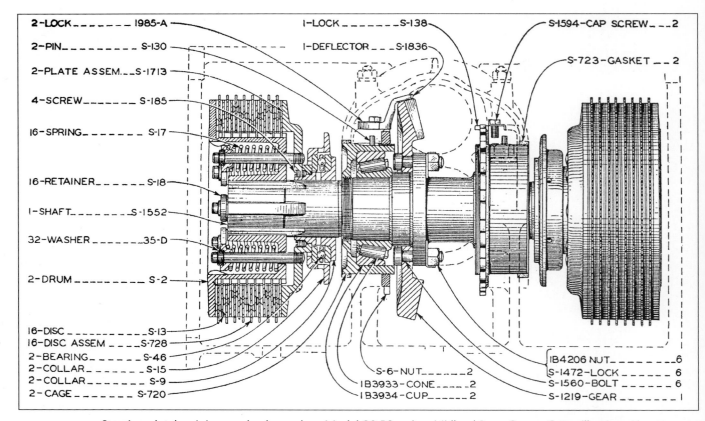

2-LOCK _ _ _ _ _ _ 1985-A —   I-LOCK _ _ _ _ _ _ S-138   S-1594-CAP SCREW _ _ 2

2-PIN _ _ _ _ _ _ _ _ S-130   I-DEFLECTOR _ _ _ _ S-1836   S-723-GASKET _ _ 2

2-PLATE ASSEM _ _ _ S-1713

4-SCREW _ _ _ _ _ _ S-185

16-SPRING _ _ _ _ _ _ S-17

16-RETAINER _ _ _ _ _ S-18

I-SHAFT _ _ _ _ _ _ S-1552

32-WASHER _ _ _ _ _ _ 35-D

2-DRUM _ _ _ _ _ _ _ S-2

16-DISC _ _ _ _ _ _ _ S-13
16-DISC ASSEM _ _ _ _ S-728
2-BEARING _ _ _ _ _ _ S-46   IB4206 NUT _ _ _ _ _ _ 6
2-COLLAR _ _ _ _ _ _ S-15   S-1472-LOCK _ _ _ _ _ 6
2-COLLAR _ _ _ _ _ _ S-9   S-6-NUT _ _ _ _ _ 2   S-1560-BOLT _ _ _ _ _ _ 6
2-CAGE _ _ _ _ _ _ S-720   IB3933-CONE _ _ _ _ 2   S-1219-GEAR _ _ _ _ _ _ I
    IB3934-CUP _ _ _ _ _ 2

Steering clutch, pinion, and axle used on Model 30 PS series. *Midland Press Corp.—Caterpillar, Inc., Licensee*

Using a spanner wrench to remove drive sprocket nut. *Midland Press Corp.—Caterpillar, Inc., Licensee*

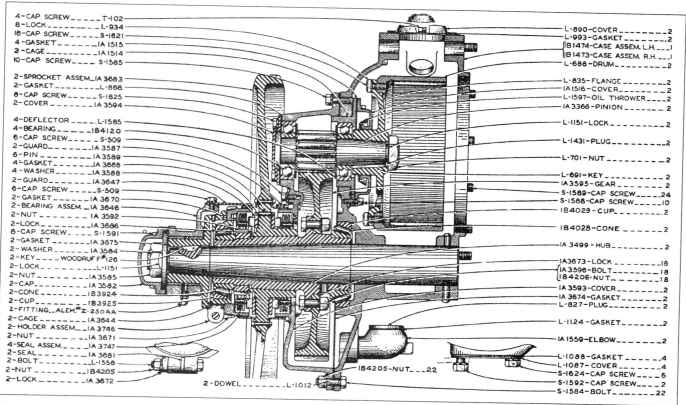

```
4-CAP SCREW _____ T-102                                              L-890-COVER _____ 2
8-LOCK _____ L-934                                              L-993-GASKET _____ 2
16-CAP SCREW _____ S-1621                                            {IB1474-CASE ASSEM. L.H. ___ 1
4-GASKET _____ IA 1515                                            {IB1473-CASE ASSEM. R.H. ___ 1
2-CAGE _____ IA 1514                                             L-688-DRUM _____ 2
10-CAP SCREW ____ S-1585

2-SPROCKET ASSEM._ IA 3683                                           L-835-FLANGE _____ 2
2-GASKET _____ L-868                                              IA1516-COVER _____ 2
8-CAP SCREW _____ S-1825                                             L-1597-OIL THROWER ___ 2
2-COVER _____ IA 3594                                             IA 3368-PINION _____ 2

4-DEFLECTOR ____ L-1585                                              L-1151-LOCK _____ 2
4-BEARING _____ IB4120                                             L-1431-PLUG _____ 2
8-CAP SCREW ____ S-509
2-GUARD _____ IA 3587                                             L-701-NUT _____ 2
6-PIN _____ IA 3589
4-GASKET _____ IA 3688                                             L-691-KEY _____ 2
4-WASHER _____ IA 3588                                             IA3595-GEAR _____ 2
2-GUARD _____ IA3647                                              S-1589-CAP SCREW ____ 24
8-CAP SCREW ____ S-509                                              S-1588-CAP SCREW ____ 10
2-GASKET _____ IA 3670                                             IB4029-CUP _____ 2
2-BEARING ASSEM._ IA 3646
2-NUT _____ IA 3592                                              IB4028-CONE _____ 2
2-LOCK _____ IA 3686
8-CAP SCREW. ___ S-1591                                             IA 3499-HUB _____ 2
2-GASKET _____ IA 3675
2-WASHER _____ IA 3584                                              IA3673-LOCK _____ 18
2-KEY ___ WOODRUFF #126                                            {IA 3596-BOLT _____ 18
2-LOCK _____ L-1151                                              {IB4206-NUT _____ 18
2-NUT _____ IA3585                                               IA 3593-COVER _____ 2
2-CAP _____ IA 3582                                              IA 3674-GASKET _____ 2
2-CONE _____ IB3924                                               L-827-PLUG _____ 2
2-CUP _____ IB3925
2-FITTING._ALEM.#Z-250AA                                           L-1124-GASKET _____ 2
2-CAGE _____ IA 3644
2-HOLDER ASSEM.__ IA 3746                                          IA1559-ELBOW _____ 2
2-NUT _____ IA 3671
4-SEAL ASSEM. ___ IA 3747                                          L-1088-GASKET _____ 4
2-SEAL _____ IA 3681                                              L-1087-COVER _____ 4
2-BOLT _____ L-1558                                              S-1624-CAP SCREW ___ 6
2-NUT _____ IB4205               IB4205-NUT ___ 22               S-1592-CAP SCREW ___ 2
2-LOCK _____ IA 3672        2-DOWEL _____ L-1012                  S-1584-BOLT _____ 22
```

Updated final drive used on Model 25 tractor. *Midland Press Corp.—Caterpillar, Inc., Licensee*

Using a puller to remove rear drive sprocket on Model 20 Pl series. *Midland Press Corp.—Caterpillar, Inc., Licensee*

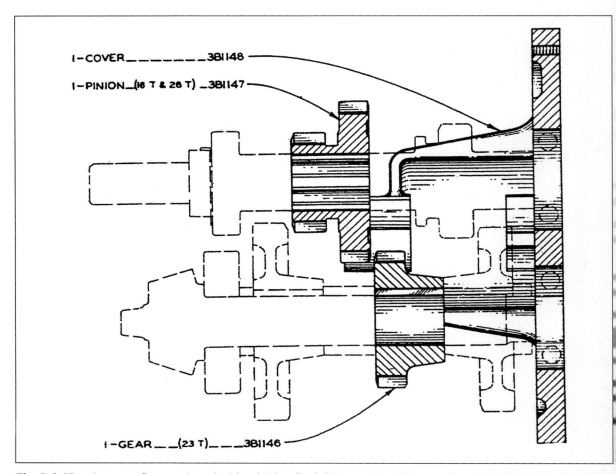

1-COVER_____381148

1-PINION_(16 T & 28 T)_381147

1-GEAR___(23 T)___381146

The R-2 5E series was often equipped with a higher final drive gearing. This may have been for use in forest fire fighting. *Midland Press Corp.—Caterpillar, Inc., Licensee*

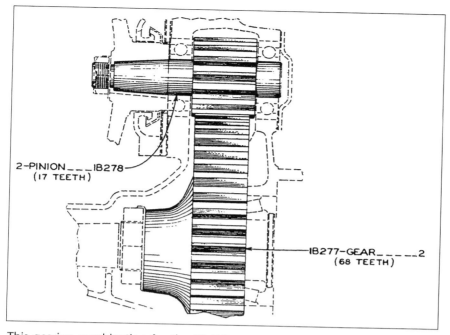

2-PINION____1B278
(17 TEETH)

1B277-GEAR____2
(68 TEETH)

This gearing combination for the 5E R-2 was used with standard transmission gears but increased speed by 38 percent. This may also have been available for the 22. *Midland Press Corp.—Caterpillar, Inc., Licensee*

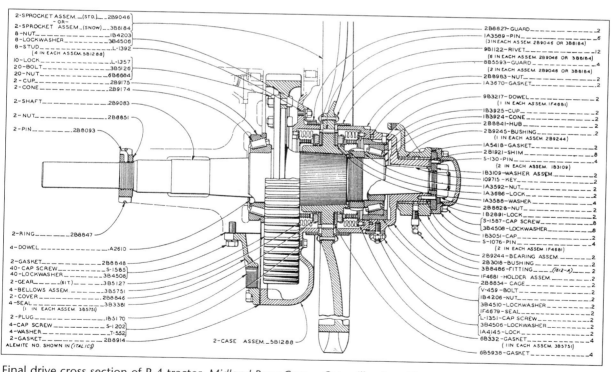

2-SPROCKET ASSEM.__(STD.)__2B9046	2B8827-GUARD_____2
—OR—	1A3589-PIN_____6
2-SPROCKET ASSEM._(SNOW)__3B8184	(3 IN EACH ASSEM 2B9046 OR 3B8184)
8-NUT_____1B4203	9B1122-RIVET_____12
8-LOCKWASHER_____3B4506	(6 IN EACH ASSEM 2B9046 OR 3B8184)
8-STUD_____L-1392	8B5593-GUARD_____4
(4 IN EACH ASSEM.5B1288)	(2 IN EACH ASSEM 2B9046 OR 3B8184)
10-LOCK_____L-1357	2B8983-NUT_____2
20-BOLT_____3B5526	1A3670-GASKET_____2
20-NUT_____6B6684	
2-CUP_____2B9175	9B3217-DOWEL_____2
2-CONE_____2B9174	(1 IN EACH ASSEM.1F4681)
	1B3925-CUP_____2
2-SHAFT_____2B9083	1B3924-CONE_____2
	2B8841-HUB_____2
2-NUT_____2B8851	2B9245-BUSHING_____2
	(1 IN EACH ASSEM.2B9244)
2-PIN_____2B8093	1A5418-GASKET_____2
	2B1921-SHIM_____8
	S-130-PIN_____4
	(2 IN EACH ASSEM. 1B3109)
	1B3109-WASHER ASSEM.____2
	10971S-KEY_____2
	1A3592-NUT_____2
	1A3686-LOCK_____2
	1A3588-WASHER_____4
	2B8828-NUT_____2
	1B2891-LOCK_____2
	S-1587-CAP SCREW_____8
	3B4508-LOCKWASHER_____8
2-RING_____2B8847	1B3051-CAP_____2
	S-1076-PIN_____4
4-DOWEL_____A2610	(2 IN EACH ASSEM.1F4681)
	2B9244-BEARING ASSEM.___2
2-GASKET_____2B8848	2B3018-BUSHING_____2
40-CAP SCREW_____S-1585	3B8486-FITTING___(1812-A)_2
40-LOCKWASHER_____3B4508	1F4681-HOLDER ASSEM.____2
2-GEAR_____(61 T.)____3B5127	2B8854-CAGE_____2
4-BELLOWS ASSEM._____3B5751	V-459-BOLT_____2
2-COVER_____2B8846	1B4206-NUT_____2
4-SEAL_____3B3381	3B4510-LOCKWASHER_____2
(1 IN EACH ASSEM 3B5751)	1F4679-SEAL_____2
2-PLUG_____1B5170	L-1351-CAP SCREW_____2
4-CAP SCREW_____S-1202	3B4506-LOCKWASHER_____2
4-WASHER_____T-552	1A4145-LOCK_____2
2-GASKET_____2B8914	6B332-GASKET_____4
ALEMITE NO. SHOWN IN (ITALICS)	(1 IN EACH ASSEM 3B5751)
2-CASE ASSEM._5B1288	6B5938-GASKET_____4

Final drive cross section of R-4 tractor. *Midland Press Corp.—Caterpillar, Inc., Licensee*

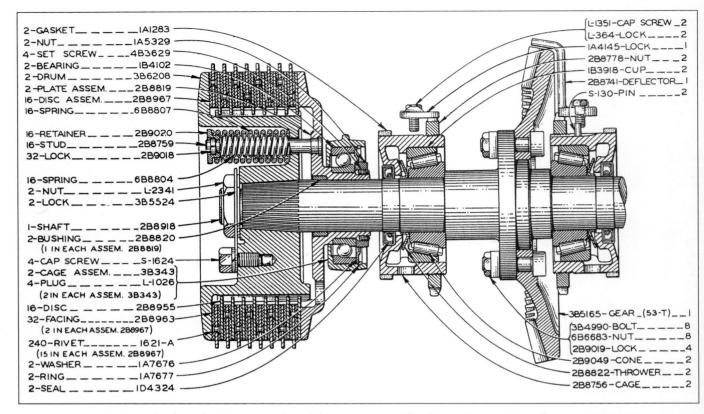

2-GASKET _ _ _ _ _1A1283
2-NUT _ _ _ _ _ _ _1A5329
4-SET SCREW _ _ _ _4B3629
2-BEARING _ _ _ _ _1B4102
2-DRUM _ _ _ _ _ _3B6208
2-PLATE ASSEM. _ _ _ _2B8819
16-DISC ASSEM. _ _ _2B8967
16-SPRING _ _ _ _ _6B8807

16-RETAINER _ _ _ _2B9020
16-STUD _ _ _ _ _ _2B8759
32-LOCK _ _ _ _ _ _2B9018

16-SPRING _ _ _ _ _6B8804
2-NUT _ _ _ _ _ _L-2341
2-LOCK _ _ _ _ _3B5524

1-SHAFT _ _ _ _ _2B8918
2-BUSHING _ _ _ _2B8820
   (1 IN EACH ASSEM. 2B8819)
4-CAP SCREW _ _ _ _S-1624
2-CAGE ASSEM. _ _ _3B343
4-PLUG _ _ _ _ _L-1026
   (2 IN EACH ASSEM. 3B343)
16-DISC _ _ _ _ _2B8955
32-FACING _ _ _ _ _2B8963
   (2 IN EACH ASSEM. 2B8967)
240-RIVET _ _ _ _ _1621-A
   (15 IN EACH ASSEM. 2B8967)
2-WASHER _ _ _ _ _1A7676
2-RING _ _ _ _ _1A7677
2-SEAL _ _ _ _ _1D4324

L-1351-CAP SCREW _2
L-364-LOCK _ _ _ _2
1A4145-LOCK _ _ _ _1
2B8778-NUT _ _ _2
1B3918-CUP _ _ _2
2B8741-DEFLECTOR _1
S-130-PIN _ _ _ _ _2

3B5165-GEAR _(53-T) _ _1
3B4990-BOLT _ _ _ _ _8
6B6683-NUT _ _ _ _ _8
2B9019-LOCK _ _ _ _ _4
2B9049-CONE _ _ _ _2
2B8822-THROWER _ _ 2
2B8756-CAGE _ _ _ _2

Steering clutch and pinion gear of Model R-4 tractor. *Midland Press Corp.—Caterpillar, Inc., Licensee*

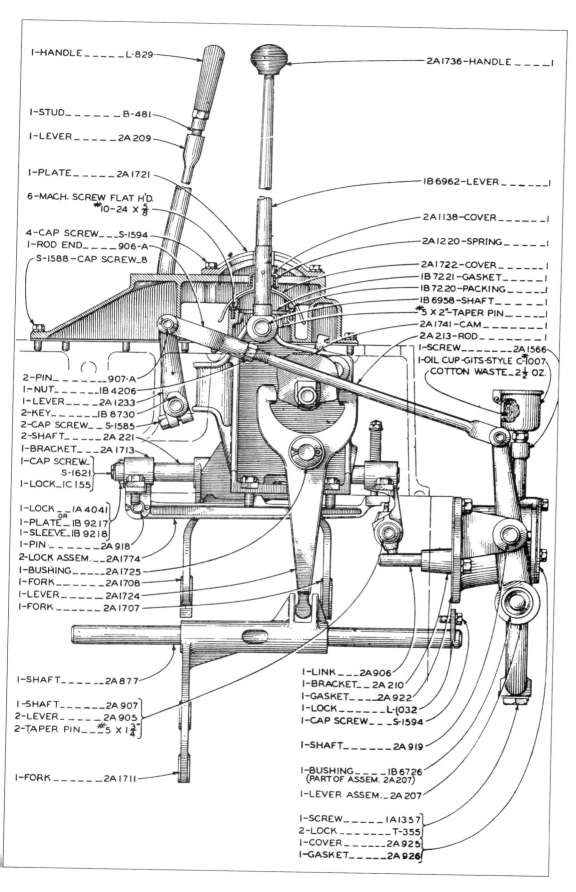

1-HANDLE _ _ _ _ _ L-829

1-STUD _ _ _ _ _ B-481
1-LEVER _ _ _ _ 2A 209

1-PLATE _ _ _ _ 2A 1721
6-MACH. SCREW FLAT H'D.
  #10-24 X $\frac{5}{8}$

4-CAP SCREW _ _ _ S-1594
1-ROD END _ _ _ 906-A
  S-1588 - CAP SCREW _ 8

2-PIN _ _ _ _ _ _ 907-A
1-NUT _ _ _ _ _ IB 4206
1-LEVER _ _ _ 2A 1233
2-KEY _ _ _ _ _ IB 8730
2-CAP SCREW _ _ S-1585
2-SHAFT _ _ _ _ 2A 221
1-BRACKET _ _ _ 2A 1713
1-CAP SCREW
  S-1621
1-LOCK _ IC 155

1-LOCK _ _ IA 4041
  or
1-PLATE _ IB 9217
1-SLEEVE _ IB 9218
1-PIN _ _ _ _ _ _ 2A 918
2-LOCK ASSEM. _ _ 2A1774
1-BUSHING _ _ _ _ _ 2A1725
1-FORK _ _ _ _ _ 2A1708
1-LEVER _ _ _ _ 2A1724
1-FORK _ _ _ _ _ 2A1707

1-SHAFT _ _ _ _ _ 2A 877

1-SHAFT _ _ _ _ _ 2A 907
2-LEVER _ _ _ _ 2A 905
2-TAPER PIN _ _ #5 X 1$\frac{3}{4}$"

1-FORK _ _ _ _ _ _ 2A1711

2A1736 - HANDLE _ _ _ _ I

IB 6962 - LEVER _ _ _ _ _ I

2A 1138 - COVER _ _ _ _ _ I

2A 1220 - SPRING _ _ _ _ I

2A 1722 - COVER _ _ _ _ _ I
IB 7221 - GASKET _ _ _ _ I
IB 7220 - PACKING _ _ _ _ I
IB 6958 - SHAFT _ _ _ _ _ I
#5 X 2" - TAPER PIN _ _ _ _ I
2A1741 - CAM _ _ _ _ _ _ _ I
2A 213 - ROD _ _ _ _ _ _ I
1-SCREW _ _ _ _ _ _ 2A 1566
1-OIL CUP-GITS-STYLE C-1007
  COTTON WASTE-2$\frac{1}{2}$ OZ.

1-LINK _ _ _ 2A906
1-BRACKET _ _ 2A 210
1-GASKET _ _ _ 2A 922
1-LOCK _ _ _ _ _ _ L-1032
1-CAP SCREW _ _ _ S-1594

1-SHAFT _ _ _ _ _ _ 2A 919

1-BUSHING _ _ _ IB 6726
  (PART OF ASSEM. 2A 207)
1-LEVER ASSEM. _ 2A 207

1-SCREW _ _ _ _ _ IA1357
2-LOCK _ _ _ _ _ _ _ T-355
1-COVER _ _ _ _ _ _ 2A 925
1-GASKET _ _ _ _ _ 2A 926

Transmission cross section of Model 70. *Midland Press Corp.—Caterpillar, Inc., Licensee*

CHAPTER EIGHT

SHEET METAL REPAIR AND REFINISHING

Most of the sheet metal used on the various models covered in this book have the same basic design and composition. The panels are generally made of a heavy-gauge steel with the lightest of the pieces being the hood and side curtains. The steps used in refinishing these components are all basically the same.

First, you must evaluate the overall condition of the steel. If the tractor spent most of its life near the ocean or in humid climates, you may find it in very poor condition. Tractors that were subjected to a wide variety of climites such as snow, rain, and heat may also be beyond repair. Generally, the machines that are found in the warm, dry areas and machines that were usually kept inside are in far better condition.

Upon your initial evaluation, keep in mind the cost and work required in replacing or completely manufacturing new components. Many of these pieces can be purchased from individuals who are reproducing the more commonly needed pieces. You may find these reproduced parts quite costly, but they are of good quality and similar to the originals.

If the sheet metal of your tractor is restorable, you will first want to completely dismantle the pieces and properly clean them. Sandblasting is by far the best method of removing heavy layers of rust and paint. Make sure you properly cover all entrances to

the engine and other moving parts when sandblasting around them. I tend not to blast around the undercarriage. Some collectors prefer to use chemical strippers such as aircraft finish remover or other acidic paint removers. These work well when used outdoors and in combination with a high-pressure washer. When using these chemicals, adequate ventilation and proper protective clothing are needed.

To remove the heavier deposits of rust and paint, it is sometimes beneficial to use an abrasive wheel on an electric or air tool. A knotted wire brush or 2 1/2-inch cup brush can remove quite a substantial amount of corrosion in a small amount of time. Another tool is called a paint-buster wheel and is made by 3M. It attaches to a drill and does an excellent job of removing layers of paint and thick grease.

If you have decided to make new sheet metal pieces for your tractor, you can use the old pieces for templates. Most of the pieces, once they are dismantled, are fairly easy to make and can be cut out with a torch and touched up with a grinder. A plasma cutter works the best for cutting the thin

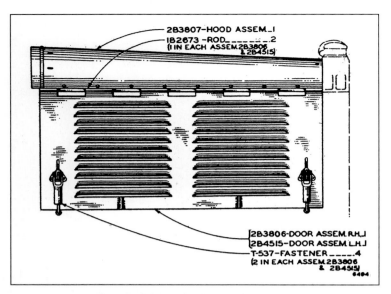

The Model R-2 "5E" series has horizontal louvers on the side curtains like its cousin the 22. *Midland Press Corp.—Caterpillar, Inc., Licensee*

sheet steel, but if you are careful and use a straight edge, a common cutting torch will work fine. Many of the pieces are riveted together. These rivets can be removed with a cold chisel and a hammer. After the new components are made, you can replace the rivets with ones that are the same size.

Next, the new pieces you have built will have to be prepared for painting. I begin by using a metal conditioner to clean any film off

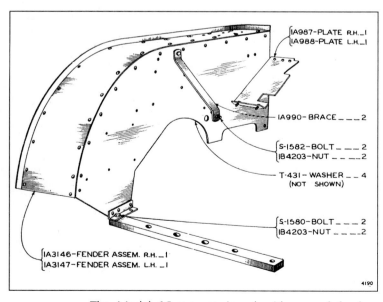

The Model 15 was equipped with curved fenders when used in orchard work. *Midland Press Corp.— Caterpillar, Inc., Licensee*

the new steel. Use some fine steel wool and gently rub the metal conditioner around the panel; rinse off with clean water or an enamel reducer. The DuPont Kwik-Prep, number 244S, is an adequate metal cleaner. After you have thoroughly cleaned these pieces, you will next want to prepare them for painting. DuPont number 5717S metal conditioner is an excellent choice.

Try to hang the panels from a wire so you can get to both sides easily with the paint gun. You will first want to use a self-etching primer such as DuPont Vari-Prime number 615S and converter 620S. Mix the primer and converter as directed, and spray the piece you are working on. You do not want the piece to sit long after priming before applying the paint coat. Usually 24 hours is about the limit between priming and painting when using a self-etching

The Caterpillar logo used on the Model 60.

primer. If you go beyond this time frame, lightly sand the primed panel to renew its adhesive properties. If you are preparing an original panel for the final finish, you may want to use a sand-and-fill primer, such as DuPont number 131S, to fill any pits or imperfections. You will have to wet-sand the panel after each coat and repeat until you have found the proper finish.

For your final paint coat, you may choose to use one of the many automotive finishes available. The Highway Yellow paint is still available through your local Caterpillar dealer in several sizes of containers. I have used this paint many times and am very satisfied with it. The paint is also available through many of the auto parts stores in either DuPont or PPG. They

Side curtains add a special look to a restored tractor. Although they are now being reproduced, it is ideal to find an original set.

usually mix it at the store from a formula provided by the paint manufacturer. I always ask to see a paint chip before I have them mix it so you know you are getting the right color.

The gray paint formula is not known at the present time. I have been using a PPG Delstar DTR 600 paint. The code is DAR 32170. This color is close to the original, but we all have our own preference. Everybody sees a different shade in the gray. Use your judgment, and remember, you only have to please yourself. Once you have placed all of the finished panels back on the tractor, you will want give the whole machine a final coat of paint. Generally, I do not paint magnetos, generators, starters, or carburetors. I do my best to clean them up and detail them to their original appearance.

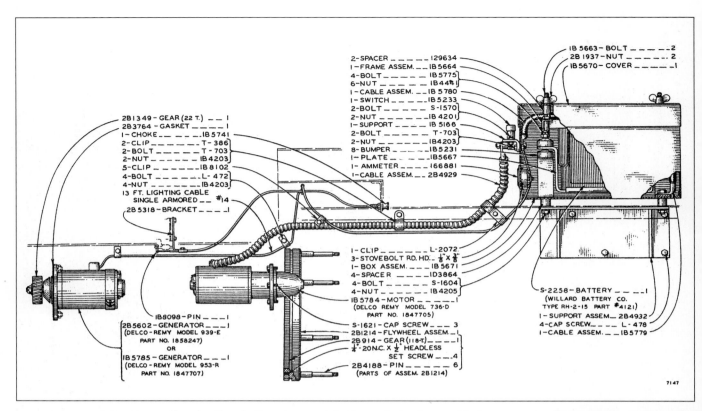

2B1349 - GEAR (22 T.) __ __1
2B3764 - GASKET ____ __1
1 - CHOKE __ __ __ 1B 5741
2 - CLIP ____ __ __ T- 386
2 - BOLT ____ __ __T - 703
2 - NUT __ ____ 1B 4203
5 - CLIP __ ____ 1B 8102
4 - BOLT __ __ __ L- 472
4 - NUT __ ____ 1B 4203
13 FT. LIGHTING CABLE
 SINGLE ARMORED __ #14
2B 5318 - BRACKET ___ __1

2 - SPACER __ __ __ 129634
1 - FRAME ASSEM. __ 1B 5664
4 - BOLT __ __ __ 1B 5775
6 - NUT __ __ __ __ 1B 44½1
1 - CABLE ASSEM. __ 1B 5780
1 - SWITCH __ __ __ 1B 5233
2 - BOLT __ __ __ __ S-1570
2 - NUT __ __ __ __ 1B 4201
1 - SUPPORT __ __ __ 1B 5166
2 - BOLT __ __ __ __ T-703
2 - NUT __ __ __ __ 1B4203
8 - BUMPER __ __ __ 1B 5231
1 - PLATE __ . __ __ 1B5667
1 - AMMETER __ __ __ 166881
1 - CABLE ASSEM. __ 2B4929

1B 5663 - BOLT __ __ __2
2B 1937 - NUT __ __ __ __ 2
1B 5670 - COVER __ __ __1

1 - CLIP __ __ __ __ L-2072
3 - STOVEBOLT RD. HD. __ ⅛" X ⅜"
1 - BOX ASSEM. __ __ 1B 5671
4 - SPACER __ __ __ 1D3864
4 - BOLT __ __ __ __ S-1604
4 - NUT __ __ __ __ 1B 4205
1B 5784 - MOTOR __ __ __1
(DELCO REMY MODEL 736-D
 PART NO. 1847705)
S-1621 - CAP SCREW __ __ 3
2B1214 - FLYWHEEL ASSEM. __1
2B914 - GEAR (118-T.) __ __1
¼"-20 N.C. X ½" HEADLESS
 SET SCREW __ __ 4
2B4188 - PIN __ __ __ __ 6
(PARTS OF ASSEM. 2B1214)

1B8098 - PIN __ __ __1
2B5602 - GENERATOR __ __1
(DELCO - REMY MODEL 939-E
 PART NO. 1858247)
 OR
1B 5785 - GENERATOR __ __1
(DELCO - REMY MODEL 953-R
 PART NO. 1847707)

S-2258 - BATTERY __ __ __1
(WILLARD BATTERY CO.
 TYPE RH-2-15 PART #4121)
1 - SUPPORT ASSEM. 2B4932
4 - CAP SCREW __ __ __ L- 478
1 - CABLE ASSEM. __ 1B5779

7147

A tractor equipped with a battery box and lights or starter have added appearance. The addition of these rare options give them a more modern look.

Serial number tags such as these found on a Model 30 are often damaged or missing. These tags are a nice addition to a restored tractor and contain good information on lubrication and adjustments.

This D-2 is equipped with orchard fenders but is a top seat model. The fenders and toolbox are in excellent condition, making the restoration less difficult.

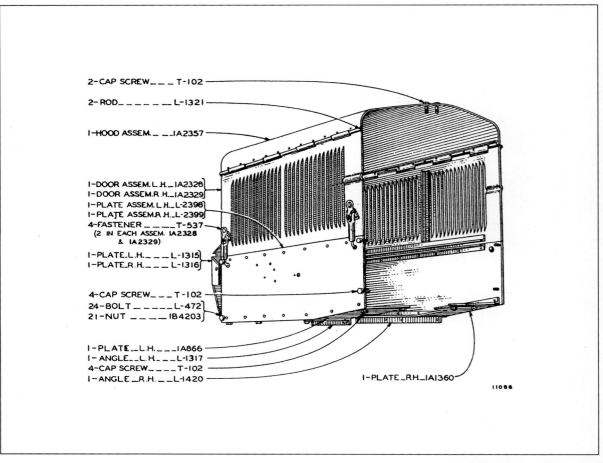

2-CAP SCREW_ _ _ _ T-102
2-ROD_ _ _ _ _ _ L-1321
1-HOOD ASSEM._ _ _IA2357
1-DOOR ASSEM.L.H._IA2328
1-DOOR ASSEM.R.H._IA2329
1-PLATE ASSEM.L.H._L-2398
1-PLATE ASSEM.R.H._L-2399
4-FASTENER _ _ _ _T-537
(2 IN EACH ASSEM. IA2328 & IA2329)
1-PLATE.L.H._ _ _ _ L-1315
1-PLATE.R.H._ _ _ _ L-1316
4-CAP SCREW_ _ _ T-102
24-BOLT _ _ _ _ _ L-472
21-NUT _ _ _ _ IB4203
1-PLATE_ _L.H._ _ _IA866
1-ANGLE_ _L.H._ _ L-1317
4-CAP SCREW_ _ _ _T-102
1-ANGLE _R.H._ _ L-1420
1-PLATE _RH_IA1360
11086

The hood and side curtains of the PL series Model 20. The louvers were changed to horizontal on the 8C series small 20. *Midland Press Corp.—Caterpillar, Inc., Licensee*

PAINT COLOR BY MODEL

Old Gray with wavy logo decals	Highway Yellow with block print decals
Ten PT	Fifteen 7C
Fifteen PV	Fifteen High Clearance 1D
Twenty L & PL	Twenty 8C
Thirty S & PS	Twenty-Two 2F & 1J
Sixty PA	Twenty-Five 3C
	Twenty-Eight 4F
	Thirty 6G
	R-4 6G
	Thirty-Five 5C
	Forty 5G
	Fifty 5A
	Sixty-Five 1D
	Seventy 8D
	R-2 5E
	R-2 J
	R-3 5E
	R-5 5E, 4H & 3R

Machines produced during the December 7, 1931 color change, may have models painted either color.

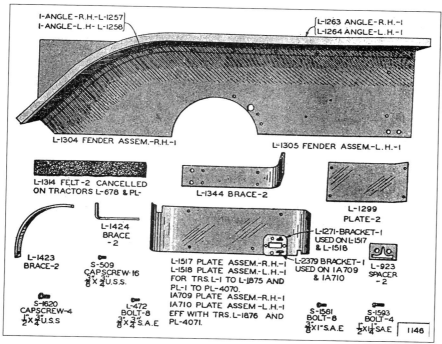

The curved rear fenders of the big 20 are often found to be damaged or cut. This design was abandoned when the 20 became the 25. *Midland Press Corp.—Caterpillar, Inc., Licensee*

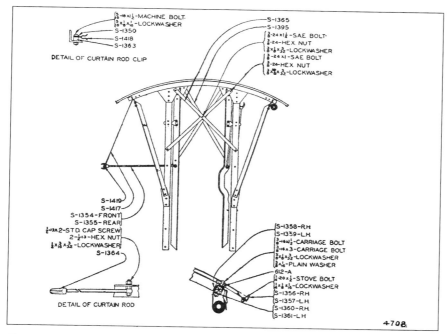

Canopy top installed on Model 30 Orchard version. *Midland Press Corp.—Caterpillar, Inc., Licensee*

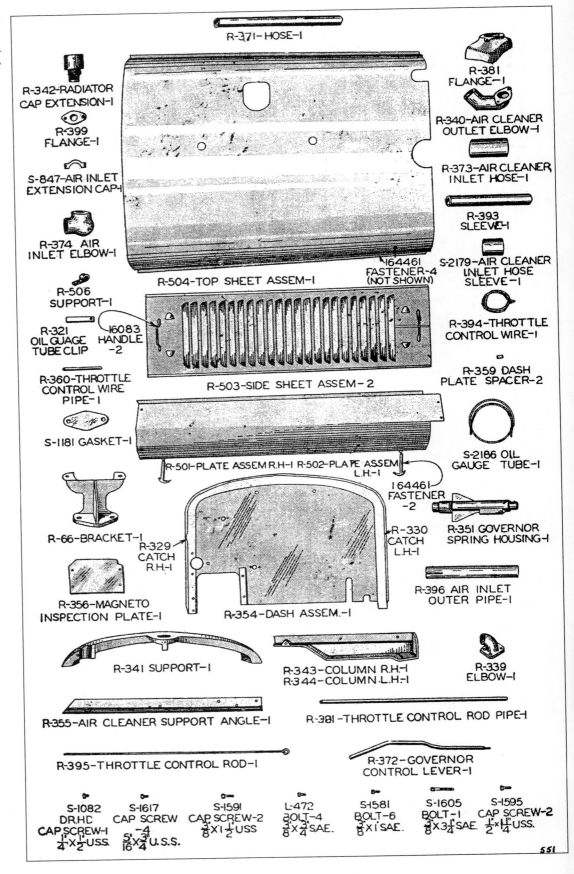

Cold weather package for PS series 30 tractor. *Midland Press Corp.— Caterpillar, Inc., Licensee*

R-371-HOSE-1

R-342-RADIATOR CAP EXTENSION-1

R-399 FLANGE-1

S-847-AIR INLET EXTENSION CAP-1

R-374 AIR INLET ELBOW-1

R-506 SUPPORT-1

R-321 OIL GUAGE TUBE CLIP

16083 HANDLE -2

R-360-THROTTLE CONTROL WIRE PIPE-1

S-1181 GASKET-1

R-66-BRACKET-1

R-356-MAGNETO INSPECTION PLATE-1

R-504-TOP SHEET ASSEM-1

164461 FASTENER-4 (NOT SHOWN)

R-381 FLANGE-1

R-340-AIR CLEANER OUTLET ELBOW-1

R-373-AIR CLEANER INLET HOSE-1

R-393 SLEEVE-1

S-2179-AIR CLEANER INLET HOSE SLEEVE-1

R-394-THROTTLE CONTROL WIRE-1

R-359 DASH PLATE SPACER-2

R-503-SIDE SHEET ASSEM-2

S-2186 OIL GAUGE TUBE-1

R-501-PLATE ASSEM R.H-1 R-502-PLATE ASSEM L.H-1

164461 FASTENER -2

R-351 GOVERNOR SPRING HOUSING-1

R-329 CATCH R.H-1

R-330 CATCH L.H-1

R-354-DASH ASSEM.-1

R-396 AIR INLET OUTER PIPE-1

R-341 SUPPORT-1

R-343-COLUMN R.H-1
R-344-COLUMN L.H-1

R-339 ELBOW-1

R-355-AIR CLEANER SUPPORT ANGLE-1

R-381-THROTTLE CONTROL ROD PIPE-1

R-395-THROTTLE CONTROL ROD-1

R-372-GOVERNOR CONTROL LEVER-1

S-1082 DR.HD CAP SCREW-1 $\frac{1}{4}$ x $\frac{1}{2}$ USS.

S-1617 CAP SCREW -4 $\frac{5}{16}$ x $\frac{3}{4}$ U.S.S.

S-1591 CAP SCREW-2 $\frac{3}{8}$ x 1 $\frac{1}{2}$ USS

L-472 BOLT-4 $\frac{3}{8}$ x $\frac{3}{4}$ SAE.

S-1581 BOLT-6 $\frac{3}{8}$ x 1 SAE.

S-1605 BOLT-1 $\frac{3}{8}$ x 3 $\frac{1}{4}$ SAE.

S-1595 CAP SCREW-2 $\frac{1}{2}$ x 1 $\frac{1}{4}$ USS.

551

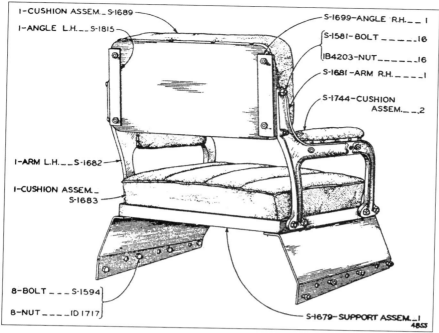

I-CUSHION ASSEM.__S-1689
I-ANGLE L.H.___S-1815
I-ARM L.H.___S-1682
I-CUSHION ASSEM._ S-1683

S-1699-ANGLE R.H.__ I
S-1581-BOLT _ _ _ _ _16
IB4203-NUT_ _ _ _ _16
S-1681-ARM R.H._ _ _ _I
S-1744-CUSHION ASSEM.__2

8-BOLT _ _ _ S-1594
8-NUT _ _ _ _ID 1717

S-1679-SUPPORT ASSEM.__I
4855

Seat assembly with cast-iron arm rests for Model 30. The arm rests are often damaged or missing. *Midland Press Corp.—Caterpillar, Inc., Licensee*

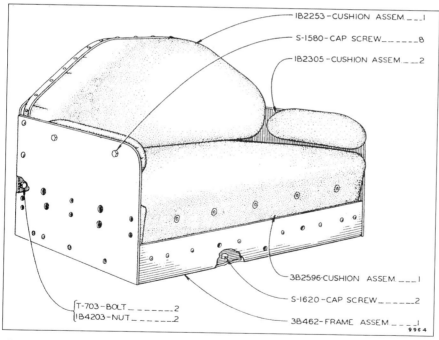

IB2253-CUSHION ASSEM.__ _I
S-1580-CAP SCREW_ _ _ _ _ _8
IB2305-CUSHION ASSEM.__ _2

T-703-BOLT_ _ _ _ _ _2
IB4203-NUT_ _ _ _ _ _2

3B2596-CUSHION ASSEM.__ _I
S-1620-CAP SCREW_ _ _ _ _ _2
3B462-FRAME ASSEM_ _ _ _I
9964

Seat and cushion assembly used on Model 22. *Midland Press Corp.—Caterpillar, Inc., Licensee*

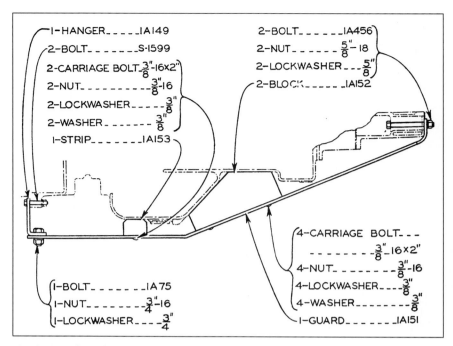

I-HANGER _ _ _ _ _ IA149
2-BOLT _ _ _ _ _ _ _ S-1599
2-CARRIAGE BOLT _ $\frac{3}{8}$"-16x2"
2-NUT _ _ _ _ _ _ _ _ _ $\frac{3}{8}$"-16
2-LOCKWASHER _ _ _ _ _ $\frac{3}{8}$"
2-WASHER _ _ _ _ _ _ $\frac{3}{8}$"
I-STRIP _ _ _ _ _ _ IA153

2-BOLT _ _ _ _ _ _ IA456
2-NUT _ _ _ _ _ _ $\frac{5}{8}$"-18
2-LOCKWASHER _ _ _ $\frac{5}{8}$"
2-BLOCK _ _ _ _ _ IA152

4-CARRIAGE BOLT _ _ _
_ _ _ _ _ _ $\frac{3}{8}$"-16x2"
4-NUT _ _ _ _ _ _ $\frac{3}{8}$"-16
4-LOCKWASHER _ _ _ $\frac{3}{8}$"
4-WASHER _ _ _ _ _ _ $\frac{3}{8}$"
I-GUARD _ _ _ _ _ _ IA151

I-BOLT _ _ _ _ _ _ IA75
I-NUT _ _ _ _ _ _ $\frac{3}{4}$"-16
I-LOCKWASHER _ _ _ $\frac{3}{4}$"

Options such as the crank case guard may have helped protect your tractor over its years of use. It is also a nice option. *Midland Press Corp.—Caterpillar, Inc., Licensee*

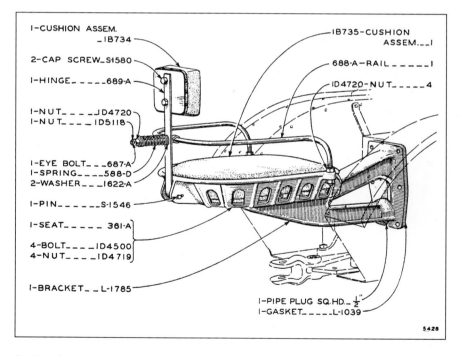

I-CUSHION ASSEM.
_ _ 1B734

2-CAP SCREW _ S-1580

I-HINGE _ _ _ _ _ 689-A

I-NUT _ _ _ _ ID4720
I-NUT _ _ _ ID5118

I-EYE BOLT _ _ 687-A
I-SPRING _ _ _ 588-D
2-WASHER _ _ 1622-A

I-PIN _ _ _ _ _ S-1546

I-SEAT _ _ _ _ _ 361-A

4-BOLT _ _ _ _ ID4500
4-NUT _ _ _ ID4719

I-BRACKET _ _ L-1785

1B735-CUSHION
ASSEM. _ _ I

688-A-RAIL _ _ _ _ _ I

ID4720-NUT _ _ _ _ _ 4

I-PIPE PLUG SQ.HD. _ $\frac{1}{2}$"
I-GASKET _ _ _ _ L-1039

5428

Seat, cushions, and mount.

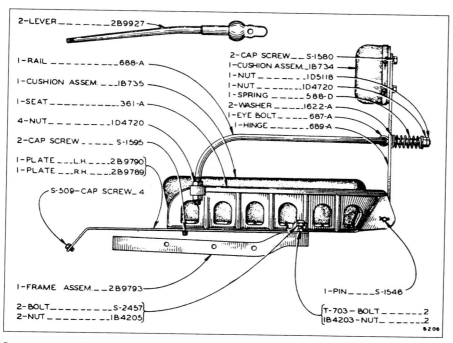

2-LEVER _ _ _ _ _ _ _2B9927 _
1-RAIL _ _ _ _ _ _ _ _688-A
1-CUSHION ASSEM. _ _ _1B735 _
1-SEAT _ _ _ _ _ _ _ _361-A
4-NUT _ _ _ _ _ _ _1D4720
2-CAP SCREW _ _ _ _ _ S-1595 _
1-PLATE _ _ _L.H. _ _ _2B9790
1-PLATE _ _ _R.H. _ _ _2B9789
S-509-CAP SCREW_ 4

2-CAP SCREW_ _ S-1580
1-CUSHION ASSEM._1B734
1-NUT _ _ _ _ _ _1D5118
1-NUT _ _ _ _ _ _1D4720
1-SPRING _ _ _ _ _588-D
2-WASHER _ _ _ _1622-A
1-EYE BOLT _ _ _ _687-A
1-HINGE _ _ _ _ _689-A

1-FRAME ASSEM._ _2B9793
2-BOLT_ _ _ _ _ _ _ _S-2457
2-NUT _ _ _ _ _ _ _ 1B4205

1-PIN _ _ _S-1546
T-703 – BOLT _ _ _ _ _ _2
1B4203 – NUT _ _ _ _ _ _2

B206

Rear seat or tailseat used for orchard work. *Midland Press Corp.—Caterpillar, Inc., Licensee*

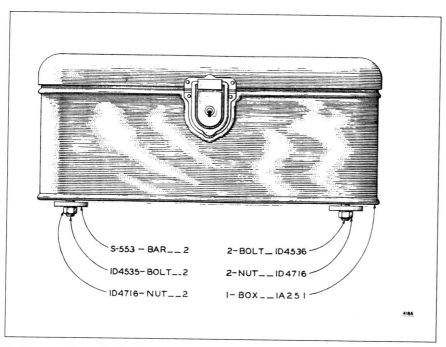

S-553 – BAR _ _ 2
1D4535-BOLT_ _2
1D4716-NUT_ _2

2-BOLT_ 1D4536
2-NUT_ _1D4716
1-BOX_ _1A251

4186

Factory tool box. *Midland Press Corp.—Caterpillar, Inc., Licensee*

Tractor Attachments

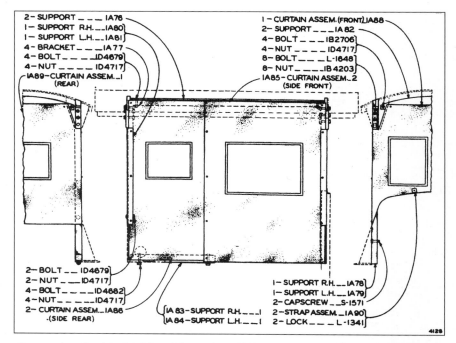

2 – SUPPORT _ _ _ IA76
1 – SUPPORT R.H. _ _IA80
1 – SUPPORT L.H. _ _IA81
4 – BRACKET _ _ _ IA77
4 – BOLT _ _ _ _ID4679
4 – NUT _ _ _ _ ID4717
IA89 – CURTAIN ASSEM. _ I
(REAR)

1 – CURTAIN ASSEM. (FRONT) IA88
2 – SUPPORT _ _ _ IA 82
4 – BOLT _ _ _ IB2706
4 – NUT _ _ _ _ ID4717
8 – BOLT _ _ _ L-1648
8 – NUT _ _ _ _ IB 4203
IA85 – CURTAIN ASSEM. _ 2
(SIDE FRONT)

2 – BOLT _ _ ID4679
2 – NUT _ _ _ID4717
4 – BOLT _ _ _ _ID4682
4 – NUT _ _ _ _ _ID4717
2 – CURTAIN ASSEM. _IA86
-(SIDE REAR)

IA 83 – SUPPORT R.H. _ _ I
IA 84 – SUPPORT L.H. _ _ I

1 – SUPPORT R.H. _ _IA78
1 – SUPPORT L.H. _ _ IA79
2 – CAPSCREW _ _S-1571
2 – STRAP ASSEM. _IA90
2 – LOCK _ _ _ _ L -1341

4128

Canopy top for Model 15 serial numbers PV1 to PV7559. *Midland Press Corp.—Caterpillar Inc. Licensee*

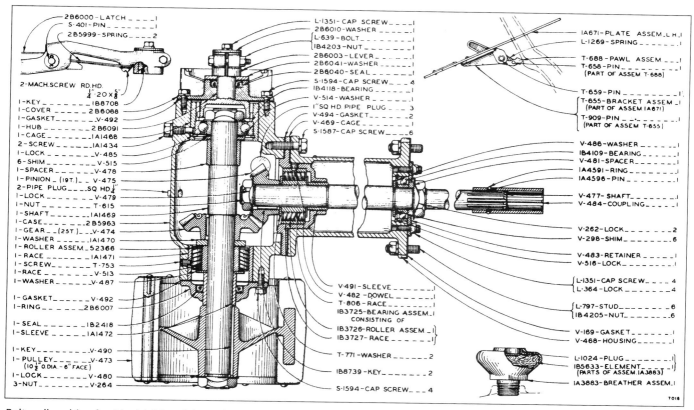

Belt pulley drive for Model 15 serial numbers PV5060 to PV7559, Model 20 serial numbers 8C1 to 8C652, and Model 22 serial numbers 2F1 and up. *Midland Press Corp.—Caterpillar Inc. Licensee*

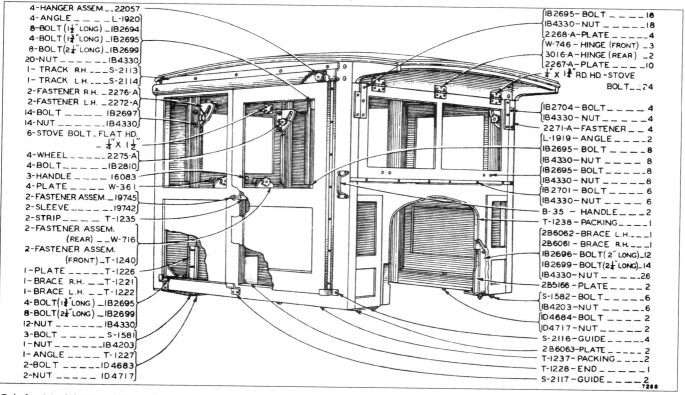

Cab for Model 22 serial numbers 2F1 and up. *Midland Press Corp.—Caterpillar Inc. Licensee*

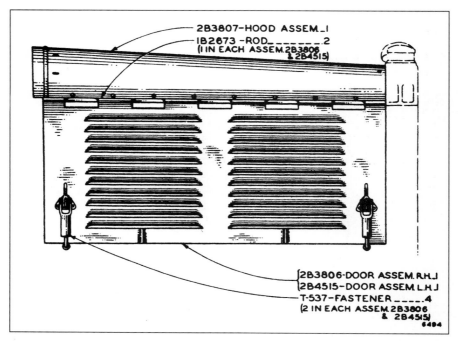

Hood door for Model 22 serial numbers 2F1 to 2F2317. *Midland Press Corp.—Caterpillar Inc. Licensee*

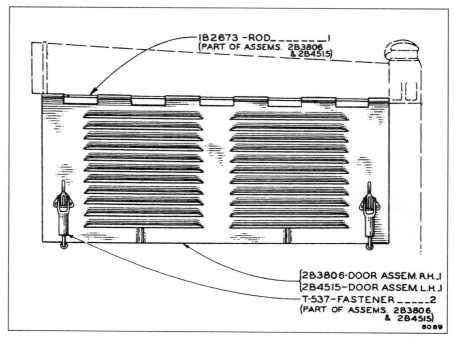

Hood door for Model 22 serial numbers 2F2318 and up. *Midland Press Corp.—Caterpillar Inc. Licensee*

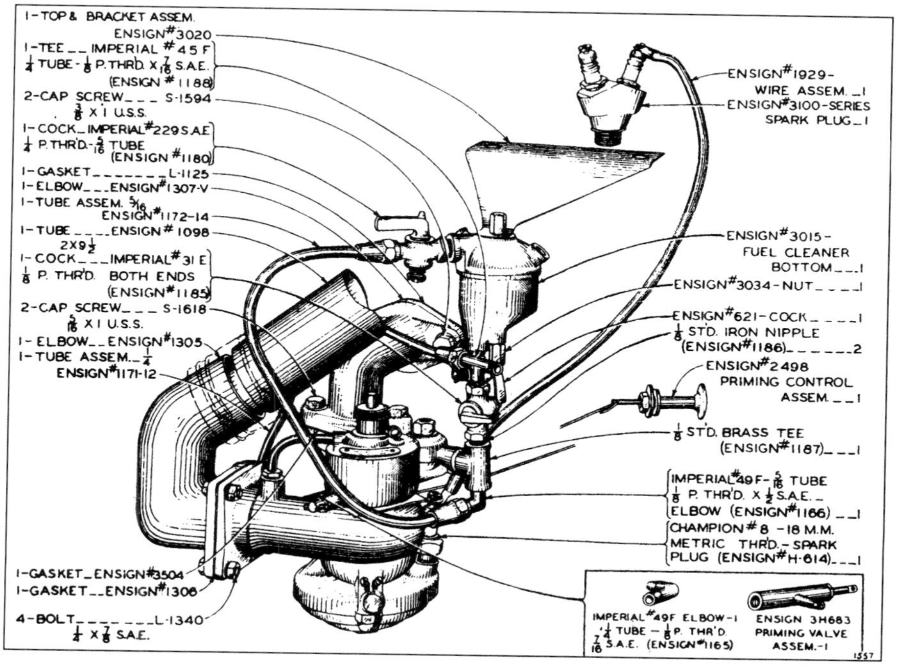
1-TOP & BRACKET ASSEM. ENSIGN#3020
1-TEE__ IMPERIAL #45 F 1/4 TUBE-1/8 P.THR'D. X 7/16 S.A.E. (ENSIGN #1188)
2-CAP SCREW___ S-1594 3/8 X 1 U.S.S.
1-COCK_IMPERIAL#229S.A.E. 1/4 P.THR'D.-5/16 TUBE (ENSIGN #1180)
1-GASKET_______L-1125
1-ELBOW___ENSIGN#1307-V
1-TUBE ASSEM. 5/16 ENSIGN#1172-14
1-TUBE____ENSIGN#1098 2X9 1/2
1-COCK___IMPERIAL#31 E 1/8 P. THR'D. BOTH ENDS (ENSIGN#1185)
2-CAP SCREW___ S-1618 5/16 X 1 U.S.S.
1-ELBOW__ENSIGN#1305
1-TUBE ASSEM.__1/4 ENSIGN#1171-12
1-GASKET_ENSIGN#3504
1-GASKET__ENSIGN#1306
4-BOLT________L-1340 1/4 X 7/8 S.A.E.
ENSIGN#1929-WIRE ASSEM._1
ENSIGN#3100-SERIES SPARK PLUG_1
ENSIGN#3015-FUEL CLEANER BOTTOM__1
ENSIGN#3034-NUT____1
ENSIGN#621-COCK____1
1/8 STD. IRON NIPPLE (ENSIGN#1186)______2
ENSIGN#2498 PRIMING CONTROL ASSEM.__1
1/8 STD. BRASS TEE (ENSIGN#1187)___1
IMPERIAL#49F-5/16 TUBE 1/8 P. THR'D. X 1/2 S.A.E._ ELBOW (ENSIGN#1166)__1
CHAMPION# 8 -18 M.M. METRIC THR'D.-SPARK PLUG (ENSIGN#H-614)___1
IMPERIAL#49F ELBOW-1 1/4 TUBE - 1/8 P. THR'D. 7/16 S.A.E. (ENSIGN#1165)
ENSIGN 3H683 PRIMING VALVE ASSEM.-1
1557

This kerosene carburetor is part of the kerosene fuel system group for Model 15 PV1 to PV7559. *Midland Press Corp.—Caterpillar Inc. Licensee*

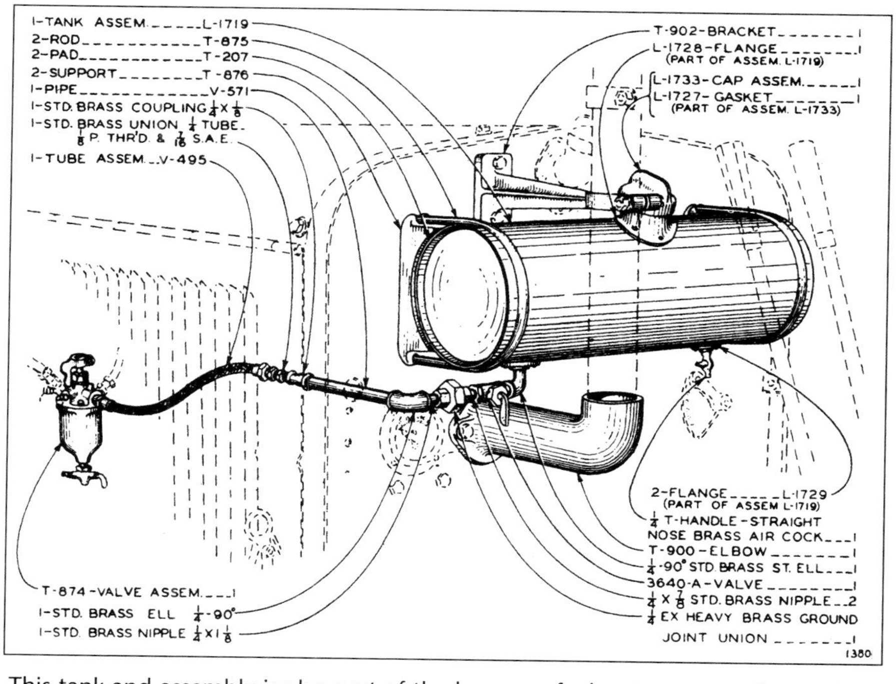
1-TANK ASSEM.______L-1719
2-ROD_____________T-875
2-PAD_____________T-207
2-SUPPORT_________T-876
1-PIPE____________V-571
1-STD. BRASS COUPLING 1/4 X 1/8
1-STD. BRASS UNION 1/4 TUBE. 1/8 P. THR'D. & 7/16 S.A.E.
1-TUBE ASSEM.__V-495
T-902-BRACKET________1
L-1728-FLANGE________1 (PART OF ASSEM. L-1719)
L-1733-CAP ASSEM.______1
L-1727-GASKET__________1 (PART OF ASSEM. L-1733)
2-FLANGE_____L-1729 (PART OF ASSEM. L-1719)
1/4 T-HANDLE-STRAIGHT NOSE BRASS AIR COCK___1
T-900-ELBOW________1
1/4-90° STD BRASS ST. ELL___1
3640-A-VALVE________1
1/4 X 7/8 STD. BRASS NIPPLE__2
1/4 EX HEAVY BRASS GROUND JOINT UNION ________1
T-874-VALVE ASSEM.___1
1-STD. BRASS ELL 1/4-90°
1-STD. BRASS NIPPLE 1/4 X 1 1/8
1380

This tank and assembly is also part of the kerosene fuel system group for Model 15 PV1 to PV7559. The third bit is a radiator curtain. *Midland Press Corp.—Caterpillar Inc. Licensee*

The kerosene fuel group for the Model 20 serial numbers 8C1 to 8C652 consists of this carburetor assembly and a radiator curtain. *Midland Press Corp.— Caterpillar Inc. Licensee*

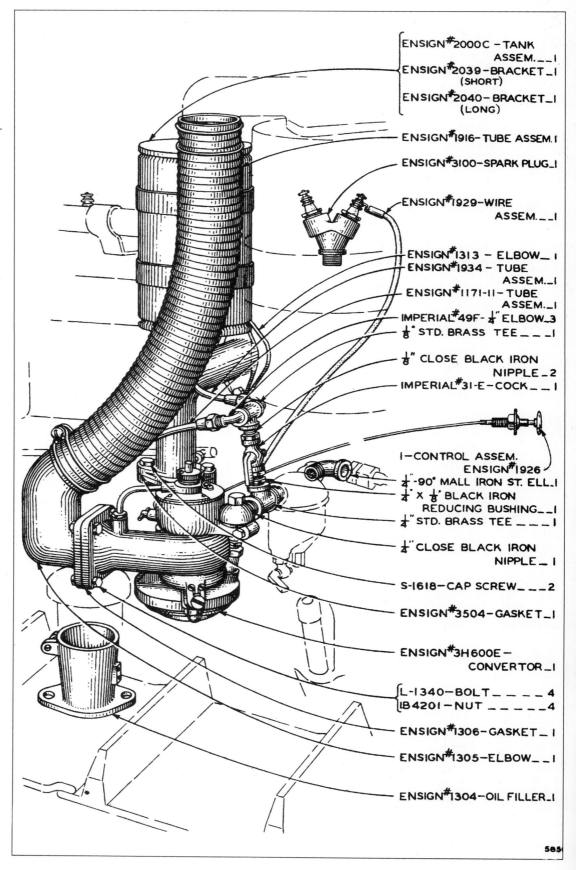

ENSIGN#2000C – TANK ASSEM.___1

ENSIGN#2039–BRACKET_1 (SHORT)

ENSIGN#2040–BRACKET_1 (LONG)

ENSIGN#1916–TUBE ASSEM. 1

ENSIGN#3100–SPARK PLUG_1

ENSIGN#1929–WIRE ASSEM.___1

ENSIGN#1313 – ELBOW_ 1

ENSIGN#1934 – TUBE ASSEM.__1

ENSIGN#1171-11 – TUBE ASSEM.__1

IMPERIAL#49F- $\frac{1}{4}$" ELBOW_3

$\frac{1}{8}$" STD. BRASS TEE ___1

$\frac{1}{8}$" CLOSE BLACK IRON NIPPLE_2

IMPERIAL#31-E–COCK___1

1–CONTROL ASSEM. ENSIGN#1926

$\frac{1}{4}$"-90° MALL IRON ST. ELL.1

$\frac{1}{4}$" X $\frac{1}{8}$" BLACK IRON REDUCING BUSHING__1

$\frac{1}{4}$" STD. BRASS TEE ___1

$\frac{1}{4}$" CLOSE BLACK IRON NIPPLE_1

S-1618–CAP SCREW___2

ENSIGN#3504–GASKET_1

ENSIGN#3H600E– CONVERTOR_1

L-1340–BOLT____4

IB4201–NUT____4

ENSIGN#1306–GASKET_ 1

ENSIGN#1305–ELBOW__1

ENSIGN#1304–OIL FILLER_1

585

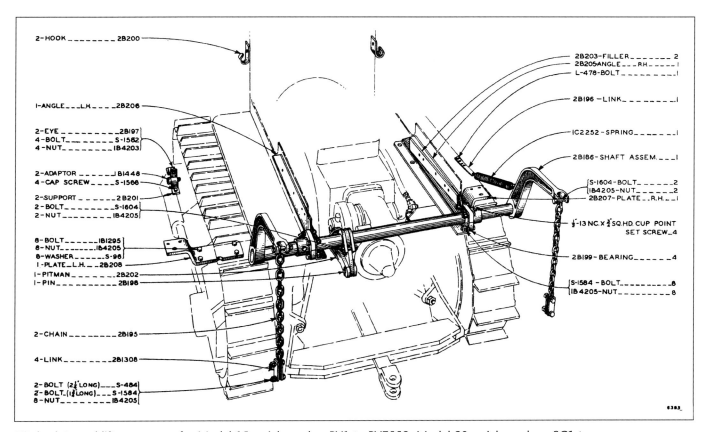

2-HOOK _____ 2B200
1-ANGLE ___ L.H. ___ 2B206
2-EYE _____ 2B197
4-BOLT _____ S-1582
4-NUT _____ 1B4203
2-ADAPTOR _____ JB1448
4-CAP SCREW ____ S-1566
2-SUPPORT _____ 2B201
2-BOLT _____ S-1604
2-NUT _____ 1B4205
8-BOLT _____ 1B1295
8-NUT _____ 1B4205
8-WASHER _____ S-96
1-PLATE L.H. __ 2B208
1-PITMAN _____ 2B202
1-PIN _____ 2B198
2-CHAIN _____ 2B195
4-LINK _____ 2B1308
2-BOLT (2¼ LONG)___ S-484
2-BOLT (1¾ LONG) __ S-1584
8-NUT _____ 1B4205

2B203-FILLER _____ 2
2B205 ANGLE ___ R.H. ___ 1
L-478-BOLT _____ 1
2B196 -LINK _____ 1
IC2252 -SPRING _____ 1
2B186-SHAFT ASSEM. ___ 1
S-1604-BOLT _____ 2
1B4205-NUT _____ 2
2B207-PLATE R.H. __ 1
½-13 N.C. X ⅞" SQ. HD. CUP POINT SET SCREW 4
2B199-BEARING _____ 4
S-1584 - BOLT _____ 8
1B4205-NUT _____ 8

Hitch plate and lift arm group for Model 15 serial number PV1 to PV7559, Model 20 serial numbers 8C1 to

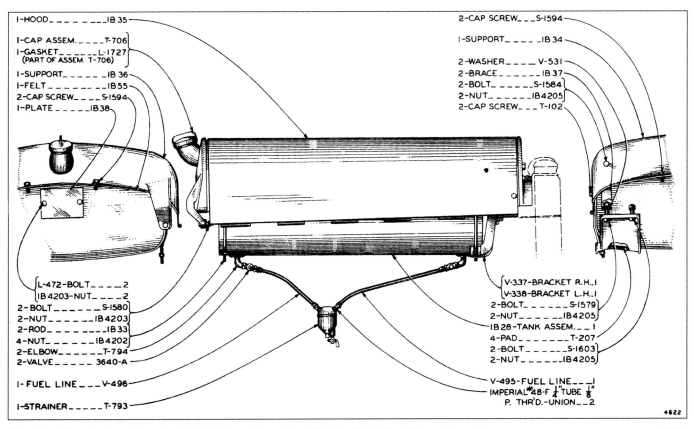

1-HOOD _____ 1B 35
1-CAP ASSEM. ____ T-706
1-GASKET _____ L-1727
(PART OF ASSEM. T-706)
1-SUPPORT _____ 1B 36
1-FELT _____ 1B55
2-CAP SCREW ___ S-1594
1-PLATE _____ 1B38

2-CAP SCREW __ S-1594
1-SUPPORT ____ 1B 34
2-WASHER ____ V-531
2-BRACE _____ 1B 37
2-BOLT _____ S-1584
2-NUT _____ 1B4205
2-CAP SCREW __ T-102

L-472-BOLT ____ 2
1B4203-NUT ___ 2
2-BOLT _____ S-1580
2-NUT _____ 1B4203
2-ROD _____ 1B 33
4-NUT _____ 1B4202
2-ELBOW _____ T-794
2-VALVE _____ 3640-A
1-FUEL LINE ___ V-496
1-STRAINER _____ T-793

V-337-BRACKET R.H. 1
V-338-BRACKET L.H. 1
2-BOLT _____ S-1579
2-NUT _____ 1B4205
1B28-TANK ASSEM. __ 1
4-PAD _____ T-207
2-BOLT _____ S-1603
2-NUT _____ 1B4205
V-495-FUEL LINE __ 1
IMPERIAL #48-F ½"TUBE ⅛"
P. THR'D.-UNION __ 2

The 40-gallon fuel tank for the Model 15 serial numbers PV1 to PV7465. *Midland Press Corp.—Caterpillar Inc. Licensee*

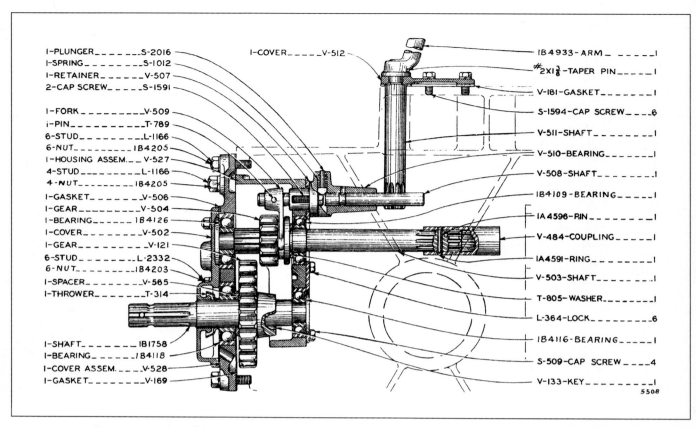

I-PLUNGER _____ S-2016
I-SPRING _____ S-1012
I-RETAINER _____ V-507
2-CAP SCREW ____ S-1591

I-FORK _____ V-509
I-PIN _____ T-789
6-STUD _____ L-1166
6-NUT _____ IB4205
I-HOUSING ASSEM.__ V-527
4-STUD _____ L-1166
4-NUT _____ IB4205
I-GASKET _____ V-506
I-GEAR _____ V-504
I-BEARING _____ IB4126
I-COVER _____ V-502
I-GEAR _____ V-121
6-STUD _____ L-2332
6-NUT _____ IB4203
I-SPACER _____ V-565
I-THROWER _____ T-314

I-SHAFT _____ IB1758
I-BEARING _____ IB4118
I-COVER ASSEM. ___ V-528
I-GASKET _____ V-169

I-COVER ____ V-512

IB4933-ARM _ _____I
#2X1⅜-TAPER PIN_____I
V-181-GASKET _____I
S-1594-CAP SCREW ___6
V-511-SHAFT _____I
V-510-BEARING _____I
V-508-SHAFT _____I
IB4109-BEARING _____I
IA4596-PIN _____I
V-484-COUPLING _____I
IA4591-RING _____I
V-503-SHAFT _____I
T-805-WASHER _____I
L-364-LOCK _____6
IB4116-BEARING _____I
S-509-CAP SCREW ____4
V-133-KEY _____I

5508

Rear power take-off for use on top seat or rear seat Model 15 serial number PV1 to PV7559, Model 20 serial numbers 8C1 to 8C652, and Model 22 serial numbers 2F1 and up. *Midland Press Corp.—Caterpillar Inc. Licensee*

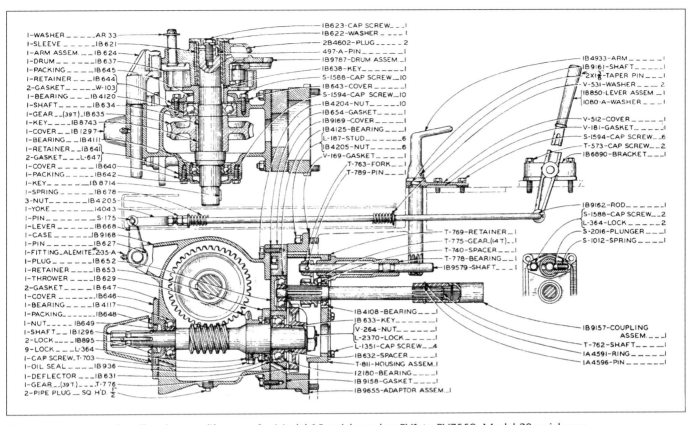

1-WASHER _ _ _ _ _ AR 33	1B623-CAP SCREW _ _ _1
1-SLEEVE _ _ _ _ 1B 621	1B622-WASHER _ _ _ _1
1-ARM ASSEM. _ _1B 624	2B4602-PLUG _ _ _ _ 2
1-DRUM _ _ _ _ _ 1B 637	497-A-PIN _ _ _ _1
1-PACKING _ _ _ 1B645	1B9787-DRUM ASSEM _1
1-RETAINER _ _ _1B644	1B638-KEY _ _ _ _ _1
2-GASKET _ _ _ _ W-103	S-1588-CAP SCREW _ _10
1-BEARING _ _ _ 1B 4120	1B643-COVER _ _ _ _1
1-SHAFT _ _ _ _1B 634	S-1594-CAP SCREW _10
1-GEAR _ (37T) 1B635	1B4204-NUT _ _ _10
1-KEY _ _ _1B8743	1B654-GASKET _ _ _1
1-COVER _ _ _1B 1297	1B9169-COVER _ _ _ _1
1-BEARING _ _ 1B4111	1B4125-BEARING _ _ _1
1-RETAINER _1B641	L-187-STUD _ _ _ _ _6
2-GASKET _ _ L-647	1B4205-NUT _ _ _ _6
1-COVER _ _ _ _1B640	V-169-GASKET _ _ _1
1-PACKING _ _1B642	T-763-FORK _ _ _1
1-KEY _ _ _ _1B 8714	T-789-PIN _ _ _ _1
1-SPRING _ _ _1B 678	
3-NUT _ _ _ _1B4205	
1-YOKE _ _ _ _14043	
1-PIN _ _ _ _ _S-175	
1-LEVER _ _ _ _1B668	T-769-RETAINER _ 1
1-CASE _ _ _ _1B 9168	T-775-GEAR (14T) _1
1-PIN _ _ _ _1B627	T-740-SPACER _ _1
1-FITTING ALEMITE _235-A	T-778-BEARING _ _1
1-PLUG _ _ _ _1B652	1B9579-SHAFT _ _ _1
1-RETAINER _1B653	
1-THROWER _ _1B629	
2-GASKET _ _ _1B647	
1-COVER _ _ _ _1B646	
1-BEARING _ _ _1B 4117	1B4108-BEARING _ _ _1
1-PACKING _ _1B648	1B 633-KEY _ _ _ _ _1
1-NUT _ _ _ 1B649	V-264-NUT _ _ _ _1
1-SHAFT _ _1B1296	L-2370-LOCK _ _ _ _1
2-LOCK _ _ _1B895	L-1351-CAP SCREW _4
9-LOCK _ _ _L-364	1B632-SPACER _ _ _1
1-CAP SCREW_T-703	T-811-HOUSING ASSEM _1
1-OIL SEAL _ _ _1B936	12180-BEARING _ _ _1
1-DEFLECTOR _ _1B631	1B 9158-GASKET _ _ _1
1-GEAR _ (39T.) _ T-776	1B9655-ADAPTOR ASSEM _1
2-PIPE PLUG _ SQ H'D. 1/2"	

1B4933-ARM _ _ _ _1
1B9161-SHAFT _ _ _ _1
2X18-TAPER PIN _ _1
V-531-WASHER _ _ _2
1B850-LEVER ASSEM _1
1080-A-WASHER _ _ _1
V-512-COVER _ _ _ _1
V-181-GASKET _ _ _ _1
S-1594-CAP SCREW _6
T-573-CAP SCREW _2
1B6890-BRACKET _ _1
1B9162-ROD _ _ _ _ _1
S-1588-CAP SCREW _2
L-364-LOCK _ _ _ _2
S-2016-PLUNGER _ _1
S-1012-SPRING _ _ _1
1B9157-COUPLING ASSEM. _ _1
T-762-SHAFT _ _ _ _1
1A4591-RING _ _ _ _1
1A4596-PIN _ _ _ _ _1

Rear double power take-off and power lift group for Model 15 serial number PV1 to PV7559, Model 20 serial numbers 8C1 to 8C652, and Model 22 serial numbers 2F1 and up. *Midland Press Corp.—Caterpillar Inc. Licensee*

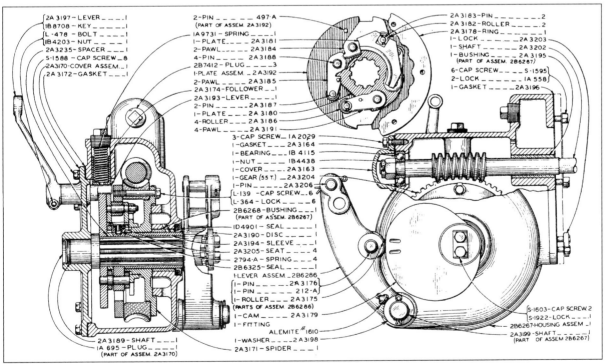

2A 3197-LEVER _ _ _1	2-PIN _ _ _ _ 497-A
1B8708-KEY _ _ _ _1	(PART OF ASSEM 2A3192)
L-478-BOLT _ _ _1	1A9731-SPRING _ _ _1
1B4203-NUT _ _ _ _1	1-PLATE _ _ _ 2A3181
2A3235-SPACER _ _ _1	2-PAWL _ _ _ 2A3184
S-1588-CAP SCREW _8	4-PIN _ _ _ 2A3188
2A3170-COVER ASSEM _1	2B7412-PLUG _ _ _3
2A 3172-GASKET _ _ _1	1-PLATE ASSEM _2A3192
	2-PAWL _ _ _ 2A3185
	2A3174-FOLLOWER _ _1
	2A3193-LEVER _ _ _1
	2-PIN _ _ _ _2A3187
	1-PLATE _ _2A 3180
	4-ROLLER _ _ _2A3186
	4-PAWL _ _ _2A3191

2A3183-PIN _ _ _ _ _2
2A3182-ROLLER _ _ _ _2
2A3178-RING _ _ _ _1
1-LOCK _ _ _ _2A3203
1-SHAFT _ _ _ _2A3202
1-BUSHING _ _ _2A3195
(PART OF ASSEM. 2B6267)
6-CAP SCREW _ _S-1595
2-LOCK _ _ _ _ _1A 558
1-GASKET _ _ _2A3196

3-CAP SCREW_1A 2029
1-GASKET _ _ _2A3164
1-BEARING _ _1B 4115
1-NUT _ _ _ _1B4438
1-COVER _ _ _2A3163
1-GEAR (55 T.) _2A3204
1-PIN _ _ _ _2A3206
L-139-CAP SCREW _6
L-364-LOCK _ _ _ _6
2B6268-BUSHING _ _ _1
(PART OF ASSEM 2B6267)
1D4901-SEAL _ _ _ _1
2A3190-DISC _ _ _ _1
2A3194-SLEEVE _ _ _1
2A3205-SEAT _ _ _ 4
2794-A-SPRING _ _ _4
2B6325-SEAL _ _ _ _1
1-LEVER ASSEM 2B6286
1-PIN _ _ _ _2A3176
1-PIN _ _ _ _212-A
1-ROLLER _ _ _2A3175
(PARTS OF ASSEM 2B6286)
1-CAM _ _ _ _2A3179
1-FITTING
ALEMITE # 1610
1-WASHER _ _ _2A3198
2A3171-SPIDER _ _ _1

S-1603-CAP SCREW 2
S-1922-LOCK _ _ _1
2B6267-HOUSING ASSEM _1
2A3199-SHAFT _ _ _ _1
(PART OF ASSEM 2B6267)

2A3189-SHAFT _ _ _1
1A 695-PLUG _ _ _1
(PART OF ASSEM. 2A3170)

Power lift group parts for Model 15 serial number PV1 to PV7559, Model 20 serial numbers 8C1 to 8C652, and Model 22 serial numbers 2F1 and up. *Midland Press Corp.—Caterpillar Inc. Licensee*

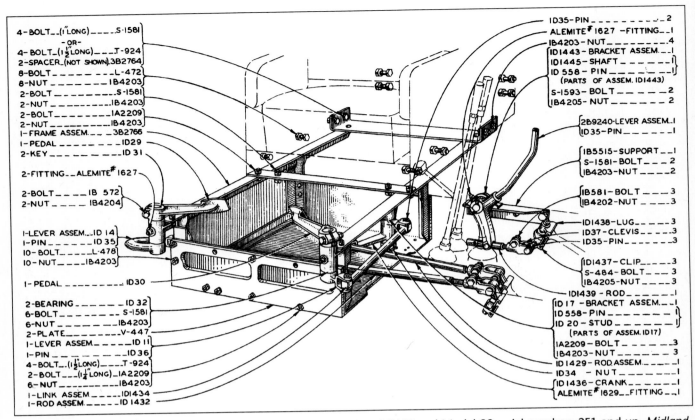

4-BOLT__(1"LONG)____S-1581
-OR-
4-BOLT_(1½LONG)___T-924
2-SPACER_(NOT SHOWN).3B2764
8-BOLT_____L-472
8-NUT_____1B4203
2-BOLT_____S-1581
2-NUT_____1B4203
2-BOLT_____1A2209
2-NUT_____1B4203
1-FRAME ASSEM___3B2766
1-PEDAL_____ID29
2-KEY_____ID31

2-FITTING_ALEMITE#1627

2-BOLT____1B572
2-NUT____1B4204

1-LEVER ASSEM...ID14
1-PIN_____ID35
10-BOLT____L-478
10-NUT____1B4203

1-PEDAL_____ID30

2-BEARING_____ID32
6-BOLT_____S-1581
6-NUT_____1B4203
2-PLATE_____V-447
1-LEVER ASSEM.____ID11
1-PIN_____ID36
4-BOLT__(1½"LONG)___T-924
2-BOLT___(1¼"LONG)_1A2209
6-NUT_____1B4203
1-LINK ASSEM____ID1434
1-ROD ASSEM____ID1432

ID35-PIN_____2
ALEMITE#1627 -FITTING__1
1B4203-NUT_____4
ID1443-BRACKET ASSEM__1
ID1445-SHAFT_____1
ID558-PIN_____1
(PARTS OF ASSEM.ID1443)
S-1593-BOLT_____2
1B4205-NUT_____2

2B9240-LEVER ASSEM_1
ID35-PIN_____1

1B5515-SUPPORT__1
S-1581-BOLT___2
1B4203-NUT____2

1B581-BOLT___3
1B4202-NUT___3

ID1438-LUG____3
ID37-CLEVIS____3
ID35-PIN_____3

ID1437-CLIP____3
S-484-BOLT___3
1B4205-NUT___3
ID1439-ROD___1
ID17-BRACKET ASSEM__1
ID558-PIN_____1
ID20-STUD_____1
(PARTS OF ASSEM.ID17)
1A2209-BOLT_____3
1B4203-NUT____3
ID1429-ROD ASSEM____1
ID34-NUT_____1
ID1436-CRANK_____1
ALEMITE#1629__FITTING__1

Side seat group for Model 20 serial numbers 8C1 to 8C652 and Model 22 serial numbers 2F1 and up. *Midland Press Corp.—Caterpillar Inc. Licensee*

164

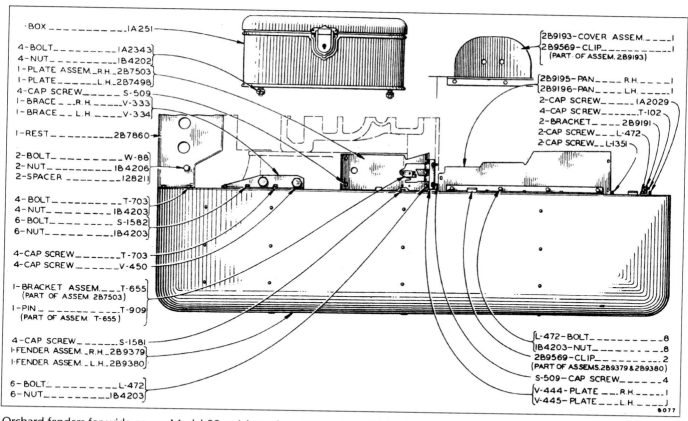

BOX _ _ _ _ _ _ _ _ _ _ IA251
4-BOLT _ _ _ _ _ _ _ _ IA2343
4-NUT _ _ _ _ _ _ _ _ _ IB4202
I-PLATE ASSEM._R.H._2B7503
I-PLATE _ _ _ _ _ L.H._2B7498
4-CAP SCREW_ _ _ _ _ S-509
I-BRACE _ _ R.H. _ _ _ _V-333
I-BRACE _ _ L.H. _ _ _ _V-334

I-REST _ _ _ _ _ _ _ _ _2B7860

2-BOLT _ _ _ _ _ _ _ _ _W-88
2-NUT _ _ _ _ _ _ _ _ _IB4206
2-SPACER _ _ _ _ _ _ _I2821I

4-BOLT _ _ _ _ _ _ _ _ T-703
4-NUT _ _ _ _ _ _ _ _ IB4203
6-BOLT _ _ _ _ _ _ _ _ S-I582
6-NUT _ _ _ _ _ _ _ _ IB4203

4-CAP SCREW _ _ _ _ _ T-703
4-CAP SCREW _ _ _ _ _ V-450

I-BRACKET ASSEM._ _ _ T-655
   (PART OF ASSEM 2B7503)
I-PIN _ _ _ _ _ _ _ _ _T-909
   (PART OF ASSEM. T-655)

4-CAP SCREW _ _ _ _ _ S-I58I
I-FENDER ASSEM._R.H._2B9379
I-FENDER ASSEM._L.H._2B9380

6-BOLT _ _ _ _ _ _ _ _ L-472
6-NUT _ _ _ _ _ _ _ _ IB4203

2B9193-COVER ASSEM._ _ _ _I
2B9569-CLIP _ _ _ _ _ _ _ _ _I
   (PART OF ASSEM. 2B9193)

2B9195-PAN _ _ _ _ R.H. _ _ _ _I
2B9196-PAN _ _ _ L.H. _ _ _ _ _I
2-CAP SCREW _ _ _ _ _ IA2029
4-CAP SCREW _ _ _ _ _ _T-102
2-BRACKET _ _ _ _ _ _ 2B9191
2-CAP SCREW _ _ _ L-472
2-CAP SCREW _ _ L-I35I

L-472-BOLT _ _ _ _ _ _ _ _ _8
IB4203-NUT _ _ _ _ _ _ _ _ _8
2B9569-CLIP _ _ _ _ _ _ _ _ _2
   (PART OF ASSEMS.2B9379 & 2B9380)
S-509-CAP SCREW _ _ _ _ _ 4
V-444-PLATE _ _ R.H. _ _ _ _I
V-445-PLATE _ _ _ L.H. _ _ _ _I

8077

Orchard fenders for wide gauge Model 22 serial numbers 2F1 and up. *Midland Press Corp.—Caterpillar Inc. Licensee*

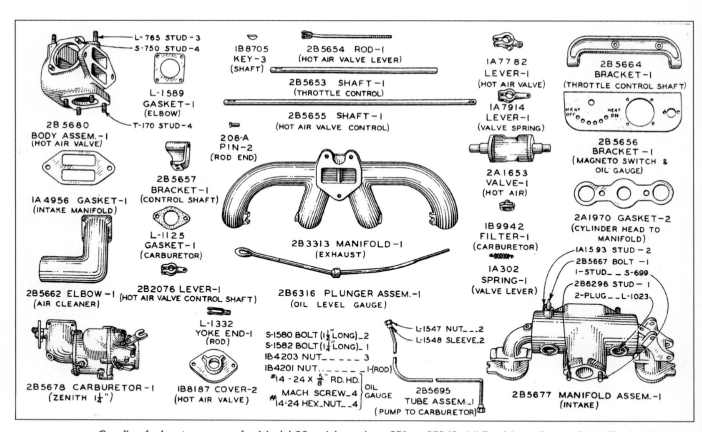

L-765 STUD-3
S-750 STUD-4

L-1589
GASKET-1
(ELBOW)

T-170 STUD-4

2B5680
BODY ASSEM.-1
(HOT AIR VALVE)

1A4956 GASKET-1
(INTAKE MANIFOLD)

2B5662 ELBOW-1
(AIR CLEANER)

2B5657
BRACKET-1
(CONTROL SHAFT)

L-1125
GASKET-1
(CARBURETOR)

2B2076 LEVER-1
(HOT AIR VALVE CONTROL SHAFT)

1B8705
KEY-3
(SHAFT)

208-A
PIN-2
(ROD END)

2B5654 ROD-1
(HOT AIR VALVE LEVER)

2B5653 SHAFT-1
(THROTTLE CONTROL)

2B5655 SHAFT-1
(HOT AIR VALVE CONTROL)

2B3313 MANIFOLD-1
(EXHAUST)

2B6316 PLUNGER ASSEM.-1
(OIL LEVEL GAUGE)

1A7782
LEVER-1
(HOT AIR VALVE)

1A7914
LEVER-1
(VALVE SPRING)

2A1653
VALVE-1
(HOT AIR)

1B9942
FILTER-1
(CARBURETOR)

1A302
SPRING-1
(VALVE LEVER)

2B5664
BRACKET-1
(THROTTLE CONTROL SHAFT)

HEAT OFF   HEAT ON

2B5656
BRACKET-1
(MAGNETO SWITCH &
OIL GAUGE)

2A1970 GASKET-2
(CYLINDER HEAD TO
MANIFOLD)

1A1593 STUD-2
2B5667 BOLT-1
1-STUD__S-699
2B6296 STUD-1
2-PLUG__L-1023

2B5678 CARBURETOR-1
(ZENITH 1¼")

L-1332
YOKE END-1
(ROD)

1B8187 COVER-2
(HOT AIR VALVE)

S-1580 BOLT (1½"LONG)_2
S-1582 BOLT (1¼"LONG)_1
1B4203 NUT_____3
1B4201 NUT_____1 (ROD)
#14-24 X ⅝" RD. HD.
MACH. SCREW_4
#14-24 HEX. NUT_4

OIL
GAUGE

L-1547 NUT__2
L-1548 SLEEVE_2

2B5695
TUBE ASSEM._1
(PUMP TO CARBURETOR)

2B5677 MANIFOLD ASSEM.-1
(INTAKE)

Gasoline fuel system group for Model 22 serial numbers 2F1 to 2F963. *Midland Press Corp.—Caterpillar Inc. Licensee*

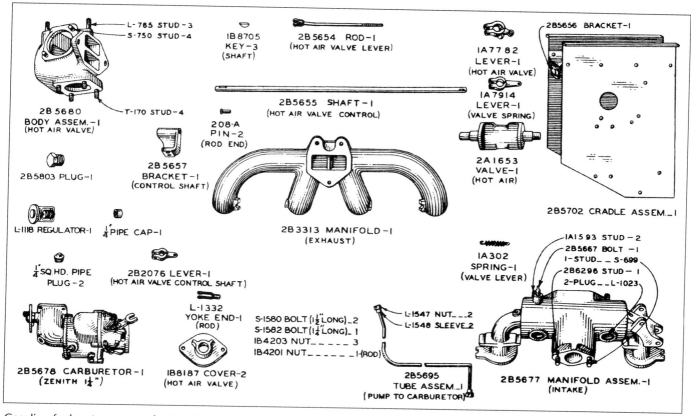

Gasoline fuel system group for Model 22 serial numbers 2F964 to 2F1350. *Midland Press Corp.—Caterpillar Inc. Licensee*

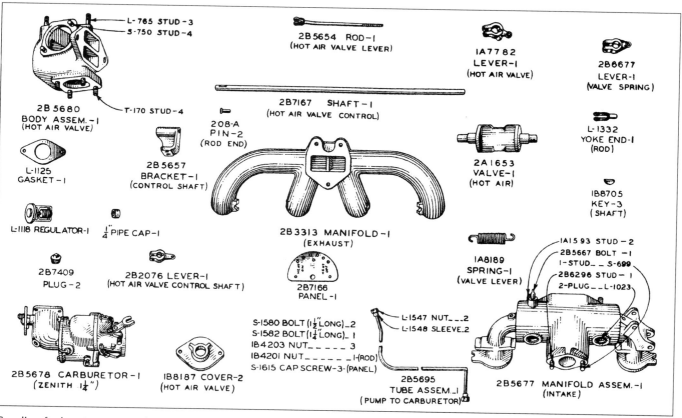

Gasoline fuel system group for Model 22 serial numbers 2F1351 and up. *Midland Press Corp.— Caterpillar Inc. Licensee*

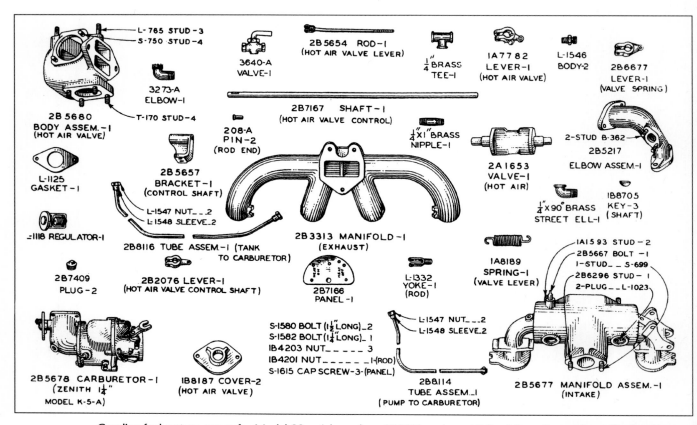

L-785 STUD-3
S-750 STUD-4

2B5680
BODY ASSEM.-1
(HOT AIR VALVE)

3273-A
ELBOW-1

T-170 STUD-4

3640-A
VALVE-1

2B5654 ROD-1
(HOT AIR VALVE LEVER)

$\frac{1}{4}''$ BRASS
TEE-1

1A7782
LEVER-1
(HOT AIR VALVE)

L-1546
BODY-2

2B6677
LEVER-1
(VALVE SPRING)

L-1125
GASKET-1

208-A
PIN-2
(ROD END)

2B7167 SHAFT-1
(HOT AIR VALVE CONTROL)

$\frac{1}{4}'' \times 1''$ BRASS
NIPPLE-1

2A1653
VALVE-1
(HOT AIR)

2-STUD B-362
2B5217
ELBOW ASSEM.-1

2B5657
BRACKET-1
(CONTROL SHAFT)

L-1547 NUT___2
L-1548 SLEEVE_2

$\frac{1}{4}'' \times 90°$ BRASS
STREET ELL-1

1B8705
KEY-3
(SHAFT)

1118 REGULATOR-1

2B8116 TUBE ASSEM.-1 (TANK
TO CARBURETOR)

2B3313 MANIFOLD-1
(EXHAUST)

1A8189
SPRING-1
(VALVE LEVER)

1A1593 STUD-2
2B5667 BOLT-1
1-STUD__ S-699
2B6296 STUD-1
2-PLUG__L-1023

2B7409
PLUG-2

2B2076 LEVER-1
(HOT AIR VALVE CONTROL SHAFT)

2B7166
PANEL-1

L-1332
YOKE-1
(ROD)

L-1547 NUT___2
L-1548 SLEEVE_2

2B5678 CARBURETOR-1
(ZENITH $1\frac{1}{4}''$
MODEL K-5-A)

1B8187 COVER-2
(HOT AIR VALVE)

S-1580 BOLT ($1\frac{1}{2}''$LONG)_2
S-1582 BOLT ($1\frac{1}{4}''$LONG)_1
1B4203 NUT_____3
1B4201 NUT_____1-(ROD)
S-1615 CAP SCREW-3-(PANEL)

2B8114
TUBE ASSEM._1
(PUMP TO CARBURETOR)

2B5677 MANIFOLD ASSEM.-1
(INTAKE)

Gasoline fuel system group for Model 22 serial numbers 2F1351 and up. *Midland Press Corp.—Caterpillar Inc. Licensee*

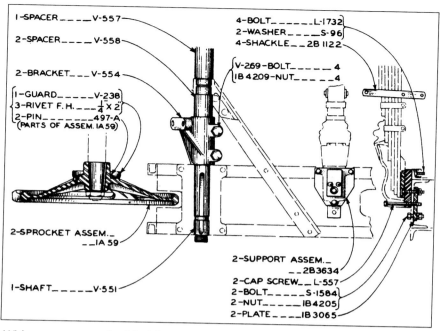

Wide gauge group for Model 22 serial numbers 2F1 and up. *Midland Press Corp.—Caterpillar Inc. Licensee*

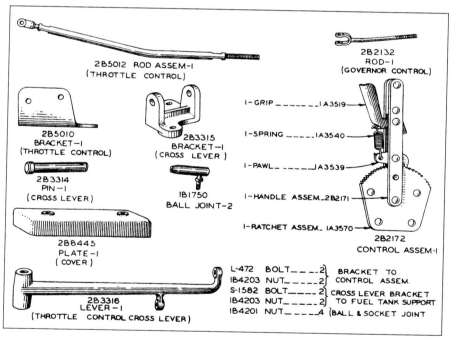

Rear seat group miscellaneous parts for Model 22 serial numbers 2F1351 and up. *Midland Press Corp.—Caterpillar Inc. Licensee*

169

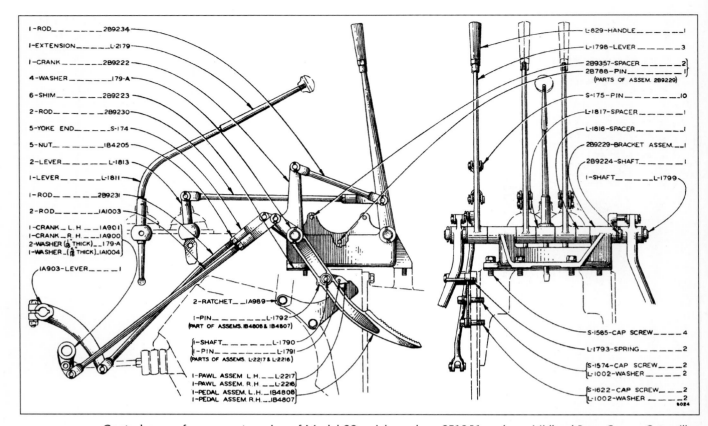

I-ROD _ _ _ _ _ _ 2B9234
I-EXTENSION _ _ _ _ _ L-2179
I-CRANK _ _ _ _ _ _ 2B9222
4-WASHER _ _ _ _ _ _ 179-A
6-SHIM _ _ _ _ _ 2B9223
2-ROD _ _ _ _ _ 2B9230
5-YOKE END _ _ _ _ _ S-174
5-NUT _ _ _ _ ASSEM. IB4205
2-LEVER _ _ _ _ _ L-1813
I-LEVER _ _ _ _ _ L-1811
I-ROD _ _ _ _ _ 2B9231
2-ROD _ _ _ _ _ IA1003
I-CRANK _ L.H. _ _ _ IA901
I-CRANK _ R.H. _ _ _ IA900
2-WASHER (⅛ THICK) _ _ 179-A
I-WASHER _(⅛ THICK) IA1004
I-IA903-LEVER _ _ _ _ I

2-RATCHET _ _ IA989
I-PIN _ _ _ _ _ _ _ L-1792
(PART OF ASSEMS. IB4808 & IB4807)
I-SHAFT _ _ _ _ _ _ L-1790
I-PIN _ _ _ _ _ _ L-1791
(PARTS OF ASSEMS. L-2217 & L-2216)
I-PAWL ASSEM L.H. _ _ _ L-2217
I-PAWL ASSEM. R.H. _ _ L-2216
I-PEDAL ASSEM. L.H. _ IB4808
I-PEDAL ASSEM. R.H. _ IB4807

L-829-HANDLE _ _ _ _ _ _ I
L-1798-LEVER _ _ _ _ _ 3
2B9357-SPACER _ _ _ _ _ 2
2B788-PIN _ _ _ _ _ _ I
(PARTS OF ASSEM. 2B9229)
S-175-PIN _ _ _ _ _ _ 10
L-1817-SPACER _ _ _ _ _ I
L-1816-SPACER _ _ _ _ _ I
2B9229-BRACKET ASSEM._ I
2B9224-SHAFT _ _ _ _ _ I
I-SHAFT _ _ _ _ _ _ L-1799

S-1585-CAP SCREW _ _ _ _ 4
L-1793-SPRING _ _ _ _ _ 2
S-1574-CAP SCREW _ _ _ 2
L-1002-WASHER _ _ _ _ 2
S-1622-CAP SCREW _ _ _ 2
L-1002-WASHER _ _ _ _ _ 2
8024

Control group for rear seat version of Model 22 serial numbers 2F1351 and up. *Midland Press Corp.—Caterpillar Inc. Licensee*

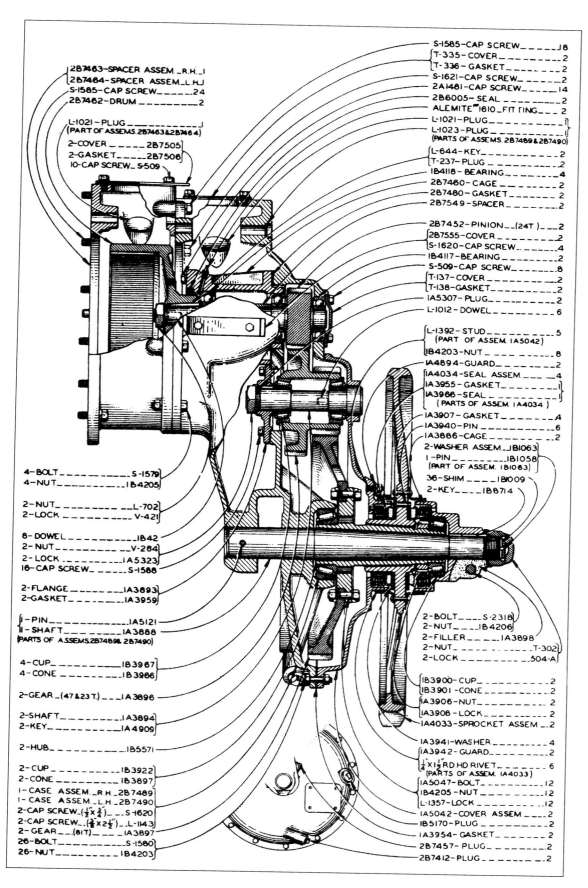

2B7463—SPACER ASSEM._R.H._I
2B7464—SPACER ASSEM._L.H._I
S-1585—CAP SCREW_____24
2B7462—DRUM _____2

L-1021—PLUG _____
(PART OF ASSEMS.2B7463&2B7464)
2—COVER _____2B7505
2—GASKET____2B7506
10—CAP SCREW_ S-509

4—BOLT _____S-1579
4—NUT_____1B4205

2—NUT _____L-702
2—LOCK _____V-421

8—DOWEL _____1B42
2—NUT _____V-264
2—LOCK _____1A5323
16—CAP SCREW _____S-1588

2—FLANGE _____1A3893
2—GASKET_____1A3959

1—PIN_____1A5121
1—SHAFT_____1A3888
(PARTS OF ASSEMS.2B7489&2B7490)

4—CUP_____1B3967
4—CONE _____1B3966

2—GEAR _(47&23 T.)___1A3896

2—SHAFT_____1A3894
2—KEY_____1A4909

2—HUB _____1B5571

2—CUP _____1B3922
2—CONE _____1B3897
1—CASE ASSEM._R.H._2B7489
1—CASE ASSEM._L.H._2B7490
2—CAP SCREW_(½"x¾")__S-1620
2—CAP SCREW__(¾"x2½")_L-1143
2—GEAR___(8T.)___1A3897
26—BOLT _____S-1580
26—NUT _____1B4203

S-1585—CAP SCREW_____18
T-335—COVER _____2
T-336—GASKET _____2
S-1621—CAP SCREW_____2
2A1481—CAP SCREW_____14
2B6005—SEAL _____2
ALEMITE 1610_FITTING___2
L-1021—PLUG _____1
L-1023—PLUG _____1
(PARTS OF ASSEMS.2B7489&2B7490)
L-644—KEY_____2
T-237—PLUG _____2
1B4118—BEARING_____4
2B7480—CAGE _____2
2B7480—GASKET _____2
2B7549—SPACER _____2

2B7452—PINION__(24T.)__2
2B7555—COVER _____2
S-1620—CAP SCREW_____4
1B4117—BEARING_____2
S-509—CAP SCREW_____8
T-137—COVER _____2
T-138—GASKET_____2
1A5307—PLUG _____2
L-1012—DOWEL _____6

L-1392—STUD_____5
(PART OF ASSEM.1A5042)
1B4203—NUT _____8
1A4894—GUARD_____2
1A4034—SEAL ASSEM.____4
1A3955—GASKET _____1
1A3966—SEAL _____1
(PARTS OF ASSEM.1A4034)
1A3907—GASKET_____4
1A3940—PIN _____6
1A3886—CAGE _____2
2—WASHER ASSEM._1B1063
1—PIN_____1B1058
(PART OF ASSEM.1B1063)
36—SHIM ____1B1009
2—KEY____1B8714

2—BOLT____S-2318
2—NUT____1B4206
2—FILLER_____1A3898
2—NUT _____T-302
2—LOCK _____504-A

1B3900—CUP _____2
1B3901—CONE _____2
1A3906—NUT _____2
1A3908—LOCK _____2
1A4033—SPROCKET ASSEM._2
1A3941—WASHER _____4
1A3942—GUARD_____2
¼"x1½"RD.HD.RIVET_____6
(PARTS OF ASSEM.1A4033)
1A5047—BOLT _____12
1B4205—NUT _____12
L-1357—LOCK _____12
1A5042—COVER ASSEM._2
1B5170—PLUG _____2
1A3954—GASKET _____2
2B7457—PLUG_____2
2B7412—PLUG _____2

High-clearance final drive group for Model 22 serial numbers 2F1 and up. *Midland Press Corp.—Caterpillar Inc. Licensee*

171

Service and Resource Directory

Engine Parts
Engine Valves
Kernan's Valves
3018 Woods Road E.
Port Orchard, WA 98366

Gaskets
Olson's Gaskets
3059 Opdal Road E.
Port Orchard, WA 98366

Piston Rings
Paul Weavers Garage
680 Sylvan Way
Bremerton, WA 98310

Manifolds
George Logue
120 South Arch Street
Montoursville, PA 17754

Complete Restoration Services

Sterling Equipment Company
Antique Restoration
11125 49th Street N.
Clearwater, FL 34622

Decals
George Logue
120 South Arch Street
Montoursville, PA 17754

Richard Gilman
East Hill Farm
Nr. Kemsing
Kent, England TN15 6YD

Antique Caterpillar Machinery Owners
Club (ACMOC)
10816 Monitor-McKee Road NE
Woodburn, OR 97071

Used Parts
Bill Mancus
(Most smaller gas models)
19210 El Cerrito Court
Watsonville, CA 95076

Bill Vassar
(D-2 and D-4, other gas models)
Route 1
Niagara, WI 54151

Sheet Metal
Side Curtains/Hoods
George Logue
120 South Arch Street
Montoursville, PA 17754

Track Shields
Steve Weaver
370 Vista Park Drive
Pittsburgh, PA 15205

Specialty Pieces
Northend Heavy Duty
Ron Yunk
Old Highway 13
Park Falls, WI 54552

Manuals and Service Magazines

Caterpillar Legendary Service Literature
Midland Press Corporation
5440 Corporate Park Drive
Davenport, IA 52807

Reproduction Tags

Sterling Equipment Company
Antique Restoration
11125 49th Street N.
Clearwater, FL 34622

Clubs

Antique Caterpillar Machinery Owners
Club (ACMOC)
10816 Monitor-McKee Road NE
Woodburn, OR 97071

Suggested Reading

Benjamin Holt: the Story of the Caterpillar Tractor. University of the Pacific, 1982.

Budy, Jerry D., and Young, James A., *Endless Tracks in the Woods*. Crestline Publications, 1989.

Leffingwell, Randy, *Caterpillar*. Motorbooks International, 1994.

Leffingwell, Randy, *The American Farm Tractor*. Motorbooks International, 1991.

Letourneau, P. A., *Caterpillar 30 and Caterpillar 60 Photo Archives*. Iconografix, 1993.

Longfoot, Peter J., *Caterpillar Tractors, 1926 to 1959*. Global Publishing, 1993.

Pripps, Robert, *Farm Crawlers*. Motorbooks International, 1994.

Rasmussen, Henry, *Caterpillar; Great American Legend*. Motorbooks International, 1986 (out of print).
The Caterpillar Story. Caterpillar, Inc.,1990.

Wik, Reynold M., *Benjamin Holt and Caterpillar Tracks and Combines*. American Society of Agricultural Engineers, 1984.

Caterpillar Gas Tractor Serial Number List

Serial Numbers

Model	Beg.	End	Prod. Span
Model 10	PT-1	PT-4929	1928-1932
Model 15	7C-1	7C-307	1932-1934
Model 15	PV-1	PV-7559	1928-1932
Model 15 High Clearance	1D-1	1D-95	1932-1934
Model 20	8C-1	8C-652	1932-1934
Model 20	L-1	L-1970	1927-1928
Model 20	PL-1	PL-6319	1928-1931
Model 22	2F-1	2F-9999	1934-1939
Model 22	1J-1	1J-5155	1938-1939
Model 25	3C-1	3C-638	1931-1933
Model 28	4F-1	4F-1171	1933-1935
Model 30	PS-1	PS-14294	1927-1932
Model 30	S-1001	S-10536	1925-1930
Model 30 R-4	6G-1	6G-5383	1935-1944

Model	Beg.	End	Prod. Span
Model 35	5C-1	5C-1728	1932-1934
Model 40	5G-1	5G-584	1934-1936
Model 50	5A-1	5A-18808	1931-1937
Model 60	PA-1	PA-13516	1925-1931
Model 65	2D-1	2D-S21	1933-1933
Model 70	8D-1	8D-266	1932-1935
Model R-2	5E-3501	5E-3583	1934-1937
Model R-2	4J-1	4J-1185	1938-1942
Model R-2 Wide Gauge	6J-1	6J-1150	1938-1942
Model R-3	5E-2501	5E-2560	1934-1935
Model R-5	5E-3001	5E-3500	1934-1936
Model R-5	4H-501	4H-1500	1934-1936
Model R-5	3R-1	3R-49	1934-1936

Index